History of the Indies

Bartolomé de las Casas

History
of the Indies

Translated and Edited by
ANDRÉE COLLARD

A TORCHBOOK LIBRARY EDITION
Harper & Row, Publishers
New York, Evanston, and London

HISTORY OF THE INDIES

First TORCHBOOK LIBRARY edition published 1971

STANDARD BOOK NUMBER: 06–131540–0

Contents

Translator's Note

In his will, Las Casas stipulated that the *History of the Indies* should be kept from publication for forty years after his death, but it is known that the manuscript circulated before that date. Although a version of the *History* was first published by the Royal Academy of Madrid in 1875, the first edition based on the original signed manuscript is the one I have used for my translation: the *Historia de las Indias* in three volumes, edited by Agustín Millares Carlo (Mexico, 1951), which also contains a long and useful preliminary study by the dean of Lascasian scholars, Lewis Hanke.

Unfortunately, the total length of the *History* has made it necessary to sacrifice narrative continuity; I have therefore tried to select those chapters most representative of the broad spectrum of Las Casas's interests. In the original text, Book I consists of an account of the colonization of the Canary Islands, as well as including the journals of Christopher Columbus. Since the history of the Canaries is not relevant to this selection, I have omitted it. As for the journals, they have been translated and edited separately by Cecil Jane (London, 1930). Thus, I have chosen entries followed by those commentaries of Las Casas that are most related to the general themes of the *History*.

I have taken into account the needs of the modern reader and have attempted to make Las Casas's diffuse style more accessible: his long periods have been shortened; his repetitions and the plethora of conjunctions they entail have been eliminated whenever possible; most of his quotations have been omitted and marked with ellipses except where they are short and especially to the point.

Lastly, I wish to thank my colleagues, Professors Denah Lida, William H. Matheson and Mordeca Jane Pollock, for their expert assistance in smoothing over the rough spots of my translation. Each has made valuable suggestions which I took into account in my Introduction.

Introduction

Roughly 500 years after the discovery of America man again accomplishes spectacular achievements in space while nations again threaten to be destroyed by their imperialistic expansion and disregard for human rights. Just as twentieth-century America has its angry voices to denounce these human failings, so Spain in the sixteenth century had Bartolomé de las Casas or Casaus (1474–1566),[1] a man whose obsession to end the Spanish tyranny in the New World evolved into a scathing attack against imperialism. Although Las Casas was among the first Europeans to understand the implications of the discovery of America and to praise Columbus for his extraordinary courage and intelligence, he saw that, on the human level, the discoverer and all who followed after him were selfish and greedy operators: their most cherished institution, the *encomienda*, destroys the humanity of the Indian when it does not destroy his life altogether, and their most cherished concept, that Indians are "tools of the devil," justifies oppression and private interests as well as betrays a blind belief in Spanish superiority.

Thus, the *History of the Indies* is an epoch-making and controversial work. Not only does it give a lengthy and well-docu-

1. Late in life, Las Casas added "or Casaus" to his name and explained it as being the spelling of his noble French ancestors in the Canaries, a claim now proven false. The obscurity that surrounds his life before reaching America has long puzzled every student of Las Casas and has led many to suspect that he came from a family of converted Jews. So far, the only clue to this problem is a document found by Claudio Guillén and reprinted in "Un padrón de conversos sevillanos (1510)," *Bulletin Hispanique*, LXV (1963), 49–98, which suggests the possibility of a family relationship between our Las Casas and several other Las Casases of Seville, converts and victims of the Inquisition.

mented account of the Spanish discovery and conquest of the New World from 1492 to 1520; it also contains the first sustained criticism of the conquest—criticism plainly verging on the polemical—and in relating historical events, it raises much larger questions: the moral issues of war, slavery, human rights and the mission of secular government.

Las Casas intended his *History* to be a work of moral enlightenment and awakening, leading to political and social change. He wanted to make the Spanish reading public aware of its collective guilt for the enslavement and massacre of the Indians; he wanted his words to influence the notables of the Spanish government and the King himself. The conquest, he argues constantly, is in point of fact a mission of evangelization that has been distorted and perverted by rapacious colonists and by a vicious system of landholding. Thus, it is up to the King to take the part of the Indians against the opportunist colonizers and to abolish the exploitative *encomienda*, giving *de facto* recognition to the hard-won legal statutes (the Laws of Burgos, 1512; the New Laws, 1542) acknowledging the freedom and human rights of the Indians. This the King must do despite the poverty of the nation and despite the landholding clerics (the president and the most important members of the council of the Indies) who influence him to maintain a sinful and unjust system. Las Casas's sense of mission, dramatically manifest in his thesis, is the outcome of what might best be called a cosmic-apocalyptic world view. The *History* is both an indictment and a prophecy: the price of Spain's moral aberration will be nothing less than the nation's political, economic and moral suicide. "Should God decide to destroy Spain," he wrote at the close of his life, "this history will make it clear that Spain deserved the punishment for the destruction we have brought to the Indies."

While the religious or political affiliations of Las Casas's interpreters have often determined their judgment of him, the very nature of the *History* also encourages a variety of explanations. For it is a hybrid work. It contains history and autobiography, fact and myth. It relates the objective truth of verifiable happenings and the subjective truth of a man who made history and at the same time weighed it against a scale of lofty values: a man intensely involved in the cause of justice, by turns resentful and compassionate, always violent, always extreme. Thus Las Casas comes to tell the story of the discovery and conquest of the New World from many points of view and to draw from many fields in order to convince his reader of the validity of his thesis. He is a political critic, the self-appointed admonisher of King Ferdinand, of the regent Cardinal Cisneros, of the Emperor Charles V and of Philip II. He is the courtier who convinced Cisneros to appoint him protector of the Indians. And he also writes as a learned jurist who is constantly pointing out the weaknesses of the existing codes on the Indies and suggesting remedies to strengthen them. But the politician is a visionary, too: he has a grand scheme of evangelization through peace and love as against war and terror, a scheme he carried out in Venezuela and, with more success, in Guatemala. The idealistic cleric speaks as a former exploiter, for he himself was once an *encomendero,* and participated in the conquest of Cuba. Furthermore, fray Bartolomé is what we would call today a cultural anthropologist, for in order to discredit the prejudice against the Indians he demonstrates that the Indians indeed have a culture. Finally, Las Casas is a mythmaker. He is one of those responsible for the myth of the Noble Savage and the main contributor to the Black Legend.[2] All of these roles merge into his own final concept of himself as a hero: his *History* is as much a monument to himself as to the cause he made famous.

Las Casas wrote as he lived, with fervor and without respite. The *History* is characterized by long Ciceronian periods constantly jolted by unusual turns of phrase, colorful words, abrupt changes of tense, and the dramatic use of dialogue. Its power of speech is such that in 1555, the Franciscan fray Toribio de Benavente, better known as Motolinía, thought it necessary to warn the

2. In 1565, Girolamo Benzoni published his experiences of fourteen years of bloody campaigns with Benalcázar to Ecuador and Colombia. This, together with Las Casas's *Very Brief Relation of the Destruction of the Indies* and the blood-chilling scenes in the *History* (available in MS form in the sixteenth century), supplied the main ammunition to the foreign detractors of Spain who instigated the so-called Black Legend. The extent of the popularity of the *Very Brief Relation* may be judged by the number of first translations: Flemish, 1578; French, 1579; English, 1583; German, 1597; Latin, 1598; and Italian, 1626.

Emperor against fray Bartolomé's "pitiless defamation of the Spanish nation." And in 1963, a scholar as courteous and sensible as the late Ramón Menéndez Pidal lost his objectivity when, in the name of "historical truth," he denounced Las Casas as a paranoid and a pathological liar. What makes Las Casas's eloquence particularly compelling is its tone of anguished urgency: the reader must become morally involved, he must wake from his mental lethargy (*el sueño de la razón*) and oppose the colonial policy of his government by joining him, Las Casas, in the fight for the rights of the Indians, "if there are any left when I finish my history."

Thus Las Casas writes with anger and frustration toward the men who turned Columbus's "divine exploit" into a hellish performance and his own dream of Christianization into a nightmare, though it is precisely that nightmare that propels him to fame. He is indignant because the "wise and learned men" of the King's councils make up dehumanizing codes with the result that the Indians become strangers in their own land. They go about "dispossessed of their mothers' vassals, with no memory or trace of their real identity, unremembered and unnoticed." To say that Las Casas had no love for the Indians and merely used them as a means to self-aggrandizement is absurd. One has only to read his encounters with hungry, beaten and mutilated Indians or with Indian slaves in the market place waiting to be sold to see that their plight is indeed his plight. On the other hand, Las Casas also writes with pride and arrogance when he recounts his accomplishments, for he has a high sense of self, and he is capable of relating human tragedies with detached irony and scorn, as when he justifies the Indian slaughter of "innocent" Spaniards.

Las Casas hopes to unfold the narrative in chronological order. However, the stream of events and recollections constantly breaks his discourse, causing an impression of diffuseness and disorder. Any datum, however small, proliferates into cosmic proportions: a sugar mill leads to reflections on the Indian's gentleness and raises questions on economics, the morality of slavery, the vision of a world destroyed by a revengeful God and the theological ramifications of this concept. It is distinctive of Las Casas to proceed from the particular to the general and to apply abstract moral principles to real-life situations which he narrates with great vividness, often at the cost of exaggeration. But no one should expect accuracy in polemical writings, and the sweeping statements and prodigious numbers in the *History* must be taken with caution. A Spaniard on horseback may not have killed "10,000 Indians in one hour's time" but, as Américo Castro aptly puts it, Las Casas "magnifies and makes the distance between Spain and his Indies ideally abysmal" and it is in this light that both his numerical exaggerations and his love-hate relationship with Spain make the most sense.

Central to Las Casas's arguments in the *History* is his conviction that the Indians are human beings who live in an evolved culture, who have their own social, economic and religious institutions and who are "endowed with inner and outer senses not only good but excellent and far superior to those of many other nations." And, in order to invalidate the claims of those who report that the Indians are a "bestial race" and in so doing justify the aims and methods of the conquest, Las Casas takes pains to describe Indian culture.[3] He dwells on the high degree of social organization the Indians enjoy, their harmonious communism, their courtesy and gentleness, their hospitality. Las Casas has the insight to consider the problems of the conquest as stemming in the main from a clash of cultures, and his treatment of the Indians is intended to debunk the theories of those who would forcibly impose a European life style on the Indians "for their own good." Thus, he combats the stereotypes created by the apologists of the conquest by presenting Indian ways of life from the Indian point of view, and demonstrating that their so-called vices "in truth were not thought of as vices by the Indians but virtues answering to a life view much closer to natural reason than that of the Spaniards." To the charge that Indians are lazy, Las Casas answers that their rhythm of life is perfectly adapted to their climate and their delicate constitution. He denies that they are an idle lot by showing that they simply do not conceive of work the way Europeans do. If the Indians lie to the Spaniards, it is precisely because the Spaniards have taught

3. The magnitude of this task caused Las Casas to separate his description of the "perfection of Indian societies" into another volume entitled *Apologetical History*, originally conceived as an integral part of the *History of the Indies*.

them how to lie. Las Casas states flatly that the purported sodomy of the Indians is nonexistent. He sees clearly that the Spaniards are using the charge of cannibalism—the only legal grounds for enslaving the Indians—as the pretext for greedy depredations. In those cases where cannibalism does indeed exist, Las Casas justifies it by placing it in the context of the Indians' religious ceremonies.

Las Casas's enlightened treatment of the Indians as well as his tendency to ennoble their "natural" way of life are important factors in the creation of the myth of the Noble Savage.[4] His dialectic with contemporary authors[5] leads him frequently to exalt Indian virtues, while his belief in his own God-sent mission of conversion and his biblical and classical knowledge dispose him to see the Indians as possessing the innate goodness of man before the Fall. Like the Arcadians of the legendary Golden Age, the Indians are untainted by the corruptions of civilization: money and power are empty concepts for them. They are innocent because they live closer to nature: Adam simply has not sinned in them. Indian culture is good because the Indians govern their personal and social relationships according to "natural reason" and "natural law." The New World is virgin territory, unspoiled by vitiated systems and corrupt men, and it offers the chance to evangelize without changing the Indian way of life. When Las Casas compares the Indians to Greeks, Romans and Jews (as he often does) it is not because the Indians have a sophisticated civilization, but because—like their better-known counterparts— the Indians are a dignified race oppressed.

Now for the other extreme. Las Casas sees his country in the

---

4. It is important to point out that Montaigne, whose essay *On Cannibals* (I, 31) was also to play such a vital role in the creation of the myth of the Noble Savage, was well acquainted with sixteenth-century Spanish histories of the New World and that much of his information about the Americas may have come directly or indirectly from Las Casas (see Montaigne, *Essais*, ed. Maurice Rat, 2 vols. [Paris, 1962], I, 233, 712).

5. Las Casas's main target is Gonzalo Fernández de Oviedo y Valdés (*Natural History*, 1526), but others are alluded to directly and indirectly throughout the *History*, especially Cortés's biographer and historian Francisco López de Gómara (*General History of the Indies*, 1552) and the humanist Juan Ginés de Sepúlveda, who wrote a formal apology of colonialism based on the Aristotelian justification of slavery—"The Just Causes of War Against the Indians" (1548).

role of the aggressor. The fundamental fact about the conquest is that it is a military venture that includes the terroristic use of weapons, horses and trained dogs. The Spaniards are cruel; they exploit the superiority of their arms, physically and psychologically, and perform unnecessary acts of violence, killing "as for a joke," inventing horrifying means of torture. As all Indians are disinterested and humble, so all Spaniards are gold-hungry and power mad. Away from the battlefield, they are lazy, vain, arrogant. If they rely exclusively on Indian labor for their mines and plantations, it is not only because it costs them nothing, but also because they themselves abhor manual labor. If townships are not prosperous and organized, the reason lies in Spanish restlessness that drives the Spaniard to abandon the newly established town and to go on to further conquests. In short, they are materialistic beasts leading reckless lives of insubordination, adultery, rape and pillage.

The exaggeration is obvious and, stated thus crudely, might lead one to think that Las Casas failed to take into account the complexity of the enterprise. It is nonetheless true that the early years of the conquest were marked by anarchy and license. In addition, many a soldier in the Indies was a professional who had fought the Moorish wars on Spanish soil and to whom Indian-Moor was an automatic association. Las Casas's charges must also be weighed against contemporary events in Spain. The Inquisition is taking harsh repressive measures against "heretics" suspected of Erasmianism and other more personal crimes, and, around 1558, is burning people of high rank at the stake in order to inspire terror. This practice coincides with the public execution of high-ranking Indians, also to inspire terror, and Las Casas's outcry against the barbarism of such methods might well be taken as an outcry against a more general Spanish intolerance. As for Indian atrocities committed on "innocent" Spaniards, which were taken as justification for Spanish methods of war, Las Casas sarcastically declares that "a nation at war with another is not obliged to discern whether an individual is innocent or guilty. . . . The Indians had a most excellent reason to suppose that whosoever came to their islands from Castile came as an enemy and thus could rightly resolve to kill him. But let God be the ultimate judge of this." But what is most shocking about *all* Spaniards, especially the "learned men" and indeed "the whole world," is that people encourage these goings-on by their silence and credulity, for they buy the official version of the conquest and tolerate the atrocities even after Las Casas has unveiled them. Las Casas makes it plain that he wants his readers to awake to nothing less than their collective guilt.

The New World shapes the humanitarian ideas of Las Casas and his firsthand knowledge endows his descriptions with their tone of urgency and moral intransigence. The interaction between his lived experience and his ideals is best demonstrated in his evolving treatment of slavery, for, when he first came to America, Las Casas himself profited from slaveholding, both as an *encomendero* and as a participant in the conquest of Cuba. Indeed, nothing in Las Casas's writings suggests that he even thought about the problems of slavery until he heard the sermons of the Dominicans, who came to Hispaniola and began preaching against the institution in 1510. The sermons Las Casas heard were to produce a delayed reaction in him, for it was in 1514 that he dramatically gave up his Cuban *encomienda*. Over the years, as he witnessed the continuing evils of slavery, he became more and more aroused against this institution.

At the start of the *History* he still accepts slavery as an institution and believes that slave trading is legitimate as long as there is a "just" cause for enslaving people—that is, the capture of prisoners in political wars. In all other cases slavery is "damnable," even when it is the outcome of religious zeal: "What right or reason can justify so many offenses, deaths, enslavements, and the scandalous loss of so many lives the Portuguese caused among those poor people [Black Africans] even though they had become Moslems? Only because they were infidels? Surely this is great ignorance and damnable blindness." Yet Las Casas has no compunction about recommending that Spain buy Negro slaves to replace the dying Indians on the grounds that Blacks are stronger and thus better able to endure the climate and hardships of forced labor, assuming of course that those slaves are legitimately acquired. However, as more and more Black slaves keep pouring into the New World and he witnesses their plight, he comes to realize that the Black slaves' sufferings are no different from those of the

Indian slaves and he rejects slavery altogether as immoral. Indeed, Las Casas sees his former position as a result of his own blindness and he implores God's forgiveness, since he considers that he himself has been guilty of complicity in "all the sins committed by the Portuguese and the Africans, not to mention our own sin of buying the slaves."

However much Las Casas's views on Black slavery may have changed, his position on the Indians was always the same. In his mind there had never been any justification for their enslavement, since Spain's war against them was an unjust war. Cutting through the thin juridical distinction between slavery and servitude, Las Casas viewed the Spanish exploitation of native lives and labor as outright slavery. "How free is an allotted man when night and day he is subject to the orders and the will of another man who stands next to him all the time?" Las Casas therefore advocates the abolition of the *encomienda* as the system responsible for the existence of *de facto* slavery. Over the years he experiences a growing frustration with Spanish economic institutions in the New World and the toll of innocent lives they take. He is made increasingly bitter by the failure of his efforts to convince the King, the governors of the Indies, the public and the slaveholders that slavery is indeed scandalous. He is so aroused against the slavery of the Indians that, as Bishop of Chiapas, he invites the reprisals of the Inquisition when he goes one step further than the Dominicans: he enjoins the priests under his authority not only to refuse absolution to but also to excommunicate slaveholders who will not give up their slaves and make restitution to the Indians (1545).

Las Casas's criticism of slavery reflects the enlightened Spanish legal tradition, the main expression of which is found in the *Siete Partidas* (compiled in the thirteenth century), which under the code of slavery provides for slaves' civil rights. This liberal tradition is being reinforced by the strong influence of Erasmian humanism in Spain which stresses the Pauline view of humanity— *all* people are God's people. In dealing with the Indians, the Spaniards have failed to respect the God-given "natural rights of man" (*derecho natural de las gentes*). They have violated the Indians' territory, liberty and persons. Since all men are free and since they have the right to be governed for their own good, the

King, who may not dispose arbitrarily of persons and property without incurring the risk of the peoples' right to depose him, should abolish the unjust *encomienda* system. The student of the evolution of natural law theory, both in its moral and juridical applications, can only be surprised by the advanced nature of Las Casas's thought, which develops and concretizes the thought of Erasmus and of the distinguished jurist and contemporary of Las Casas, fray Francisco de Vitoria, on the rights of kings and peoples. By constantly exposing the failure to enforce existing statutes dealing with slavery and the inadequacy of new statutes concerning the Indians, Las Casas tries to salvage the humanity of the American Indian at a time when Europe is arguing about whether or not the natives are capable of being saved. And in so doing, he lays bare the European hyprocrisy which postulates the universality of humanism while denying it in the American colonies.

Las Casas also grasps the politico-economic implications of the conquest, and his writings contain a good measure of political criticism as well as positive suggestions for the government of the Indies. He predicts that the conquest will lead Spain to ruin because the Indies bring too much wealth—hence corruption—to Spain. But more practical considerations also dictate his criticisms of the conquest: first, the colonists want only to acquire personal wealth—gold, silver and pearls—and to spend it on "vain and lavish" things; second, the colonists go back to Spain with their riches and fail to invest them in other enterprises in the Indies, especially agriculture, which Las Casas considers a dangerously neglected part of the New World's economy; third, as heavily taxed as the gold is, the Crown mismanages this new-found source of income and remains militarily vulnerable and riddled with debts; fourth, despite the increase in certain commodities (sugar, for example), prices are spiraling upward and inflation is having a debilitating effect on the Spanish economy.

Las Casas's viewpoint on the government of the Indies results from his profound analysis of the political realities of the early stages of the conquest. From the beginning, the seeds of genocide and exploitation were sown, and, although he holds Columbus in high esteem, Las Casas does not hesitate to blame the admiral's "ignorance of the law" for the abuse that was to characterize the Spanish administration of the Indies. The actual institution of the *encomienda* is the work of the governor of Hispaniola, Ovando, who, acting without authorization from the Crown, introduced "the disorder of this pestilence . . . [which] spread to San Juan, Jamaica, Cuba and the continent." Las Casas also makes it clear that the early license and anarchy, together with the lack of advocates for the Indian cause in Spain, were responsible for the later spoliation and depopulation of the Indies. He reports the frequent rebellions of Spaniards against their commanders and describes the outrageous disorganization of the Spanish administration in the New World, where favoritism and personal interests pass before the interest of the nation. All these crimes remain unpunished because the King is kept ignorant of the actual situation in the Americas. Indeed, it was partly because of the influence of Las Casas that legal measures were taken to correct some of the Spanish abuses; to minimize his importance is perhaps to dismiss too easily the whole question of the role and influence of the political critic.

In the power conflict between the Crown and the colonists, Las Casas casts himself in the role of the protector of the Indians and the conscience of the King in order to oppose the colonists' destructive appetite for power. For example, in the story of Enriquillo (Bk III, Chs. 125–127) he intends to show that the civil rights of the Indians, guaranteed by Spanish law, are denied and that the Indians have no recourse in justice against the colonists. Obviously, the Audiencia—the instrument of the Crown responsible for rendering and enforcing justice in the Indies and thus maintaining the Crown's control over the colonists—is inoperative when the rights of the Indians are at stake. The story of Enriquillo also points out indirectly what Las Casas's treatment of the Dominicans' preaching points out directly: the missionaries, especially the Dominicans, do and should play a political role by pacifying colonist and native and by representing the interests of the Indian in the policy-making organs of Spain. So then, Las Casas's political criticism is in the main intended to bring about the reform of the actual administration of the Indies by redefining the King's prerogatives. The King should by no means think that his universal sovereignty is not compatible with the sovereignty of the "natural lords of the Indies" (the Indian nobles). Rather, he should consider the Indies to be a "true Spanish province," governed by native kings paying tribute and pledging allegiance to the Crown. With the passing of time, however, after years of frustrated efforts to persuade the Spanish rulers that such a program is desirable, Las Casas comes close to recommending that Spain leave the Indies alone altogether, as in his letter of 1544 to the future Philip II against the presence of Christians—old or new—in the Indies.

The interaction of Las Casas's lived experience with his high sense of evangelical mission shapes his theology, especially in its teleological manifestations. The discovery of the Indies, Columbus's "divine exploit," is an event of major import in God's scheme, comparable in importance only to the birth of Christ. Indeed, the discovery is another major step in the revelation of Christianity to the multitudes, and Las Casas envisages the New World as a vast continent ready for evangelization, an untilled vineyard of the Lord. For him the Indies are in every sense of the phrase a New World; and, as Silvio Zavala points out, he sees that history is realizing itself in the westward thrust of civilization. The discovery of America is not to be judged as the discovery of just another island in the Atlantic, nor evaluated in terms of the Crown's income; it must be seen in the light of both history and eternity. Thus Las Casas enjoins his countrymen to realize that whatever happens in the Indies—from the sinking of a ship or an ant invasion to major disasters—is not the outcome of blind chance or coincidence, but is indeed shaped for a purpose. This rather orthodox view of the existence of evil in the world includes the concept of God as the dispenser of justice, a God who permits the destructive outbreak of evil in the Indies because He intends to turn Spain away from its ambitions and iniquities or to punish Spain for them. And since all people are God's people, He may have wished to predestine the suffering Indians to sit at His right hand when the final judgment comes: "It may be that once God has exterminated these people [the Indians] through our cruel hands, He will spill his anger over us all . . . inspiring other nations to do unto us what we have done unto them, destroying us as we destroyed them, and it may be that more of those whom we held in contempt will sit at the right hand of God than there will be of us, and this consideration ought to keep us in fear night and day."

Las Casas saw in the Indies first an opportunity for evangelization similar to the one that challenged St. Paul, with whom the Spanish priest identifies, and second the opportunity to revivify the pristine form of Christianity before it became institutionalized and acquired temporal interests. Since, in all likelihood, Las Casas himself came from a family of converted Jews, he was particularly sensitive to the indignities of forced conversions. He also opposed mass conversions (such as those practiced by Motolinía in Mexico) because they are an insult to man's intelligence and interfere with his freedom of choice. Las Casas, then, develops an art of conversion based on the teachings of St. Paul, which is at the same time a bitter attack against Spanish methods. Religion is a private matter and it is imperative that Spain understand that "nobody can want to leave of his own free will that which God gave him over the ages, the religion sucked in the cradle and authorized by his elders"; or again, how can Christians be so foolish as to think that they can sell Christianity when their actions belie the very essence of Christianity: "a religion rooted in their hearts by centuries of devotion, reverence and rituals is not erased by ten words Cortés might have said, chewing and mispronouncing them at that, especially when Indians held the Spanish to be their major enemy." Las Casas would approach the Indian with love and respect for his beliefs and his rites, and reason alone could bring the Indians to the Faith, of their own free will, after years of communication with and understanding of Christians. But Las Casas was enough of this world to understand that these lofty ideals would not be carried out unless he also demonstrated that it was economically beneficial to the Crown to allot the money and resources to convert the Indians peaceably. Therefore, his schemes for conversion always contain their measure of practicality. And he says, referring to himself: "The clergyman's maxim was that unless the solution worked for as well as against the Spaniards, the Indians would never be saved, and knowing this for certain from his long experience, he founded the freedom and conversion of

Indians on the pure material interests of those who were to help him achieve his goal." We see that much as Las Casas feels himself turned toward other-worldly goals, he is deeply aware of his existence here and now. The interrelation of these two forms of consciousness creates an agonizing conflict within him: Las Casas lives simultaneously on two planes that constantly tug at each other and torment him.

The tension between now and hereafter also molds Las Casas's view of history. If God's ultimate design remains unknown to man, it is nonetheless man who by his actions determines the present, which in turn determines the future. Thus, the present takes on an all-important dimension: it is of utmost urgency that the deed be "right" and that the historian set it down in order to rescue it from distortion and oblivion. "My eyes saw all these and other things so alien to human nature that now I fear to tell them, not believing myself, as if perhaps I had dreamed them." Or: "Who will believe this? I myself an eyewitness writing this, I can hardly believe it." While Las Casas stressed the incredible horror of events, his insight into the value of the present along with his conviction that the discovery of America was a unique and dramatic moment in human history motivated him to preserve a mass of letters and manuscripts written by the makers of history themselves. But for his transcriptions, the journals of Christopher Columbus would have been lost to posterity.

The function of the historian is to interpret and judge events, for history is a court of world opinion and the act of writing history creates that opinion. The historian is not only the creator of the national image, but also of individual fame. And, while the historian must be learned in all domains, since there is unity in all knowledge, it is best that he should have lived the events he recounts. All theories, ancient and modern, crumble before the reality of experience, which, together with reason, is the criterion of truth. History, then, is a weapon of political warfare and its validity is the truth of experience. The reader must understand that, of all the contemporary accounts of the New World, Las Casas's history is the true account: he alone can claim forty-five years of participation in the American reality and at the same time he alone is moved by the right intentions.

Las Casas was exquisitely aware that the New World gave obscure men the opportunity of finding and enacting their destiny: Columbus, Cortés, Hojeda, Bernal Díaz del Castillo, Bartolomé de las Casas . . . But what distinguishes Columbus and Las Casas from the other actors who thrust themselves into the center of history is that God chose the admiral to be *"caudillo* and leader of this divine exploit" and the priest, "through whom God was fighting," to be the conscience and judge of Spain ("No one spoke on behalf of the Indians until God gave them someone to enlighten [the Spaniards] and the world"). In fact, the stories of Columbus and Las Casas—as recounted by the latter—show striking parallels: both are heroes, pioneers, hated by the majority; both win their cases at court after long battles against ignorance, prejudice, privilege; both confront kings and noblemen who see them as enemies, outsiders; both encounter the same mixture of encouragement and insults from the Spanish monarchs and grandees.

So Las Casas comes to see himself as a historical figure and to project himself as such by telling about Las Casas, seen by Las Casas. As the narration proceeds, he becomes conscious that he himself is a character in the drama, and by the third book he is decidedly writing his own story: "he" and "I" now regularly alternate when he talks about the clergyman. The "he" is used when he recounts those of his acts destined to transcend time, while the "I" telescopes past happenings into the present and expresses his conscience and emotions: "I could cry when I think that the clergyman Casas had to reproach Bono, whom he had known well." One can scarcely reproach Las Casas for being too modest: he knows only too well that he is both an intelligent and crafty man and a self-made wielder of power. He dramatizes himself as a figure who, without any of the social advantages, has risen to a position where he can chide great and powerful men and see his admonitions taken seriously enough to deserve special meetings and discussions in the highest councils of the land: "He saw himself in the midst of a most learned and illustrious group, among enemies and friends. . . . You should have seen how the clergyman answered and satisfied everyone's questions, always standing up for himself. Antonio de Fonseca was dumbfounded." And yet to say that Las Casas was a hypocrite or a madman is to ignore the fact that he was well aware of himself, as well as of the image he wanted to project to his contemporaries and across the ages. Said to be too prosperous and too diligent in the management of his *encomienda*, Las Casas—who was by then a clergyman—arranged a most theatrical renunciation of his earthly goods. Said to be ambitious of worldly honors, he refused the lucrative bishopric of Cuzco, later to accept the impoverished diocese of Chiapas (only because Charles V insisted).

The complex nature of the man is also reflected in his love-hate relationship with Spain. As Américo Castro has stated, Las Casas was torn all his life between his pride in belonging to the most powerful nation on earth and his shame at having been born a nobody and perhaps a relative of the victims of the Inquisition. We might add that when he dissociates himself from the brutality and atrocities of the Spanish oppressors, Las Casas writes of them as "they," "the Spaniards," "the Christians." But when he talks about the nation's greatness or its collective guilt, then he writes "we." As Montaigne was to say so judiciously, the living of a historical event and the writing of a history book tell you who you are.

A.M.C.

Chronology

The life and works of Bartolomé de las Casas are inseparable. However, for the sake of clarity, here is a brief chronology:

1474: Born in Seville

1502: Arrives in Hispaniola and settles as *encomendero*

1510: Becomes a priest

1512: Participates in the conquest of Cuba and is awarded a sizable *encomienda*

1514: Renounces his *encomienda* and preaches his first sermon against that system

1515: Spain: negotiates the repudiation of land- and slaveholding

1516: Hispaniola: named the official protector of the Indians and "adviser" to the Hieronymite committee of investigation

1517–20: Spain: negotiates the tract of Venezuelan coastline for an experiment in evangelization

1520–22: Venezuela: the experiment fails

1522–36: Hispaniola: enters the Dominican Order (1522), begins the *History of the Indies* (1527), and writes various anti-slavery memorials

1534: Nicaragua: fails to win converts to his cause

1536–38: Guatemala: successful experiment in evangelizing and organizing Indian communities

1538–40: Mexico: writes *On the Only True Way to Attract People to the Faith*; participates in the controversy about mass baptism and alienates Motolinía

1540–44: Spain: writes his most notorious work, *The Very Brief*

Relation of the Destruction of the Indies; is elected Bishop of Chiapas (1543)

1545: Chiapas: faces riots caused by the New Laws, in which he had been instrumental; is denounced to the Inquisition; writes *Rules of Confession* on the illegality of all conquest

1547–65: Spain: debate with Juan Ginés de Sepúlveda on "natural" servitude and the right to conquer by war; resigns bishopric (1551); prints his eight major polemical writings (1552), among which is *The Very Brief Relation of the Destruction of the Indies*; is again denounced to the Inquisition; finishes *History of the Indies*, maintains an important and voluminous correspondence on political issues, collects writings on the Indies, and writes *On the Treasures of Peru* and *Twelve Doubts* (1563) on the duty of Spain to make restitution to the Indians

1566: Dies in Madrid.

History of the Indies

Prologue

In his Prologue to the twenty books of *The Jewish Antiquities*, Josephus, that illustrious historian and most learned of rabbis, tells of four different reasons why men are impelled to write history. Some choose it as a way to self-glory, through the exercise of eloquence, polished words and sweet phrases. Others—in order to serve and flatter the princes whose deeds they determine to treat in their commentaries with the utmost study and care, sometimes exceeding the limits of virtue—do not scruple to devote to this exercise all their waking hours, even the major part of their lives. Still others, compelled by the same need, knowing that events they have witnessed and in which they took part are not being recorded truthfully, choose to put aside their peace of mind in order to elucidate and defend the truth, especially since they know that their solicitude is of great benefit to many people. Finally, others feel compelled to write history in order to rescue the great deeds of their nations from neglect and oblivion. The Greek historians belong for the most part to the first and second categories. Their natural eloquence and desire for self-esteem led each one to write, not what he saw or experienced, but what he held as opinion, incorporating fables and erroneous fictions, so that each account differed one from another, with the result that both writers and readers were confused and deceived, and injury was done to what Providence ordered for the good of mankind. . . . Because if history, which is so useful to mankind, as we shall see, is not written with utmost respect for truth, it is apt to cause as much damage as these other defective and harmful books, both in private and public domains, and for this reason the texts must be examined, scrutinized and polished before being made public.

Many ancient Chaldean and Egyptian writers were moved by the third and fourth reasons, and their histories are more creditable. After them come the Romans, but the Greeks are the last to be believed. The Jews wrote histories also, and after them many Catholics too numerous to mention. . . . It is very important that historians be learned men, spiritually inclined, fearless and conscientious, free of any private goal or passion. For when they recount the events of their day, they should not fear to blame particular individuals or excuse them from evil and despicable deeds, as some have done. And when they blame or excuse someone, they should first consider very carefully what they write, and keep in mind that their judgment will influence many people and many events in the future. . . .

Some will ask why such a long Prologue and so many citations of ancient writers? I will reply that all the above serves as a foundation for my *History*. I need not say that I was not moved by the first of the above-mentioned reasons. The paucity of words, the human quality of the style, the lack of eloquence in it speak for themselves. The fact that I am a Christian and a priest to boot, and over seventy years of age, and, though for no special merit of mine, a Bishop, shows clearly that I do not belong to the second category. When I ponder these qualities, and the fact that divine goodness has kept me free and sane of mind, it is not permissible that I should spend the little life that is left me pleasing men who, being poor mortals—though they call themselves powerful and rich—can free themselves from the rigors of divine judgment through the exercise of reason and Christian philosophy. My work itself will tell posterity how little care was paid to flattery. As for present readers, they will know I did not seek to please anyone if they are informed of the difficult state of affairs in the Indies. I can then truly affirm that I was moved to write this book by the great and desperate need all Spain has of truth and enlightenment on all matters relating to this Indian world. What damage, calamities, disruptions, decimations of kingdoms, what millions of souls lost, how many unforgivable sins committed, what blindness and torpor of mind, what harms and evils past and present have been caused to the kingdoms of Castile by the shortcomings and mistakes of Spain! I am certain that they cannot ever be enumerated, weighed, measured and lamented enough from now until the final and fearful Day of Judgment.

I see that some have written of Indian things, not those they witnessed, but rather those they heard about, and not too well— although they themselves will never admit it. They write to the detriment of Truth, preoccupied as they are with a sterile, unfruitful arid superficiality, without penetrating that which would nourish and edify man's reason, to which everything must be subordinated. They waste their time telling about things that only fill the ears with air and satisfy our craving for novelty, the shorter the better, since that is least capable of wounding the reader's mind. And because they did not work the field of controversy with the plow of Christian discretion and prudence, they planted the arid, wild, sterile seed of their human and temporal feelings from which have sprung up and grown a deadly discord, scandalous and erroneous knowledge, and perverse conscience in a multitude of people, to such a degree that the Catholic Faith and the ancient Christian customs of the universal Church have suffered irreparable harm. The reason for this lies in the ignorance of the goal for which divine Providence meant the discovery of those peoples and those lands, which is none other, since we are mortal, than the conversion and salvation of those souls, to which end all temporal concerns must necessarily be subordinated. It lies in the ignorance, too, of the dignity of any rational being, never so unsheltered and destitute of divine care that he is not singularly endowed over and above the universality of inferior creatures. Hence it was not possible that over such extensive regions so many and innumerable kinds of men should be allowed to be born naturally and all-inclusively monstrous, that is to say, without reason and the ability to govern their domestic affairs. Since nature works always, or almost always, for the perfection of all forms of inferior life, so much the more then, since we deal with men, as will be evident throughout my *History*, are they gifted with better judgment and greater ability to rule themselves. In this the Indians surpass all other infidels; they even surpass, as we shall see, other self-presuming nations which hold them in contempt.

Such historians have also ignored another necessary and Catholic principle, that is to say, there is not and there has never been in the history of mankind a nation from which, especially after the Incarnation and Passion of the Saviour, there cannot be selected and composed that innumerable multitude of St. John's vision—Chapter 7 of the Apocalypse—that body of the Elect which St. Paul called the mystical Body of Christ and Church. Consequently, divine Providence must have naturally disposed these people for indoctrination and divine grace, reserving the time of their calling and conversion, as it did and we believe will always do toward all other nations outside the holy Church, as long as it endures. . . . Since we believe that God predestined a few select ones from all parts of the world, appointing a time for their calling and glorification, and since we do not know who these might be, we must esteem and judge all men, trying to help them inasmuch as we desire their salvation. As for ourselves, we must see that our works be instrumental to their predestination as if we were all sure of being Elect ourselves. . . .

Such historians make another mistake. If they had read the ancient historians, holy and profane, they would know that there never was a people, before or after the Flood, who, no matter how politically well organized and urbane it may be now, was not in its beginnings full of wild and irrational defects and abounding in grave and nefarious idolatry. Many nations, today smoothly organized and Christianized, lived like animals, without houses and without cities, before their conversion to the Faith. Therefore, since uncultivated soil produces only thistle and thorns but possesses the innate goodness to yield useful fruit if it is cultivated, so all manner of men, however barbaric or bestial, possess the use of reason and are capable of being taught. Consequently, no man and no nation in the world, however barbarian or inhuman, is incapable of bearing the reasonable fruit of excellence, if taught in the manner required for the natural condition of man, especially with the doctrine of the Faith. . . . We could cite many examples of this, but let that of Spain suffice. All historians know the barbaric simplicity and ferocity of the Spanish people, especially those of Andalusia and other provinces of Spain, at the time the Greeks first colonized Monviedro and when the pirate captain Alceus and the Phoenicians came to Cádiz. These were very astute people; the natives were like animals in comparison. Now see the foolishness and simplicity of the Andalusians! Who could fool them! And, by the grace of God, what nation surpasses Spain in matters of faith? It should be that much easier then to induce and persuade those who govern themselves by reason in their social life and human contacts—as for the most part do all the nations of these our Indies—to cultivate the true and perfect virtues of the Christian religion, the only religion that can cleanse uncultivated nations of their faults.

The lack of knowledge of ancient customs caused many ignorant people to marvel and hold as new and monstrous . . . the Indians' natural and moral defects, as if all of us were naturally and morally perfect and very holy in spiritual and Christian matters! Secondly, if they were not so ignorant, they would realize that all people experience difficulties in being converted and in converting: pain, labor, sweat, anguish, contradictions, incredible persecutions, schisms and controversies. Even among the Christians themselves, the Apostles and Disciples of Christ suffered by preaching and promulgating the Gospels in order to bring the Christian religion at all times and in all places, and so did all true preachers because God willed it so. Spain is a good example since in all of its territory St. James could win only seven or nine proselytes to Christ's militia.

As will be obvious to anyone who cares to look into it, ignorance of the above caused learned and nonlearned men to make incomparably harmful mistakes about the inhabitants of this world. Some have inverted the spiritual end of this whole affair by making it the means; and the means—that is to say, temporal and profane things, which even pagan philosophers say must always be subordinate to virtue—have come to constitute the end of this Christian exercise. . . . From this grave transposition it necessarily follows that these nations are looked upon with contempt and their inhabitants held as beasts incapable of doctrine and virtue, used by the Spaniards with no more consideration than men use bread and wine and similar things, which merely by being used are consumed. The Indians contributed to this contempt and annihilation by being *toto genere* gentle and humble, extremely poor, defenseless, very simple and, above all, people long-suffering and patient. For this reason our Spaniards had and still have today

ample room to do whatever they wish with them, treating each
and every one in a like manner, regardless of sex, age, status, or
dignity, as my *History* will show. From this also springs the fact
that they have no scruples or fear in despoiling and deposing their
natural kings and nobles. God, nature and the common law of
men made them rulers, confirmed and authorized by divine law.
By ignoring this as well as the rules and dispositions of natural,
divine and human law, one fails to take into account the three
different kinds of infidels. One, those who usurp unjustly our lands
and kingdoms. Two, those who molest, fatigue and oppose us, not
only by disturbing or intending to disturb the temporal state of
our Republic, but also the spiritual, by seeking, as their main
objective, to overthrow our holy Faith, the Christian religion and
the whole Catholic Church. Three, those who have never usurped
anything from us and never owed us anything, who never disturbed or offended us, who never knew of the existence of our
Christian religion or of ourselves, who lived in their own natural
lands in kingdoms extremely different from ours. Whenever and
wherever in the universe one discovers this last group, no matter
how many grave sins they may possess—idolatry and others—we
can only treat them with the love, peace and Christian charity
which we owe them, attract them, as we would be attracted ourselves, to the holy Faith through sweet and humble evangelical
preaching in the form established by Christ, Our Lord and
Master. All the Indians of our transatlantic Indies belong to this
third category of infidels. To this end and to no other was the
Holy See able legally to establish, by the authority of Christ, the
kings of Castile and León as sovereign and universal princes of all
this vast Indian world. Their natural kings and nobles were to be
maintained in their own kingdoms, land and subjects untouched,
and each one required to recognize the kings of Castile and León
as superior and universal princes, because it was considered necessary for the sowing and conservation of the Christian Faith
throughout the Indies. And about this universal sovereignty, many
have erred most grievously and perniciously, by believing blindly
that it was not compatible with that of the natural lords of the
Indians, as I have shown in a special treatise I wrote through
divine grace.

Thinking, then, and many times morosely pondering the defects and errors I have just mentioned, as well as the considerable harmful inconveniences that have followed and follow every day, I decided to write this history. Jurists say that law is born from the true account of facts, and for this reason I write the principal events that I have witnessed with my own eyes for more than seventy years. I was present in many parts of the Indies, in many kingdoms, provinces and lands, and I have seen not only public and famous past occurrences, but also a great many whose effects were permanent. Just as it cannot be denied that the sun shines brightly when no clouds obstruct it at high noon, so no one can refuse to concede that in this year of 1552, the same calamities occur as have occurred in the past. And if I refer to some I have not witnessed, or that I may not remember too well, or that I heard diversely from various sources, I shall always rely on my long experience and relate them with the best possible likelihood of truth.

I undertook this rather burdensome task, adding it to my many other occupations for the following reasons. One: (and this is the principal reason) for the honor and glory of God, for the manifestation of His profound and unscrutable judgment, for the execution of His right and infallible divine justice and for the good of His universal Church. Two: for the common benefit, both spiritual and temporal, of the innumerable Indians, if there are any left when I finish my *History*. Three: not to please kings but to defend the honor and royal fame of the distinguished rulers of Castile, so that those who come to know the irreparable harm done in those regions, and how and why it was done, might not, for lack of knowledge about the decrees and objectives of the Catholic kings, past and present, believe that such things happened through lack of royal concern and justice. Four: in the best interest of Spain, for once the good and evil of the Indies are known, I am sure the good and evil of Spain itself will be known. Five: to enlighten the readers about many ancient things beginning with the discovery of this world machine, which information will delight the reader; and I affirm with certitude that there is today no man alive, except myself, who can relate them as they occurred and with such detail.

I also know many things that few people have written about.

When they have, their texts are intolerably vitiated, wanting in veracity perhaps because they did not understand the events, perhaps because, not witnessing them, they either were carried away by their imagination or received information from corrupt sources. Six: to free my Spanish nation from that gravest and most deceitful error in which it lives and has always lived by denying to Indians the condition of human beings, making beasts of them, incapable of virtue and of being indoctrinated, depraving their goodness and encouraging the faults that result from centuries of neglect and forgetfulness. And in some ways, this very false opinion concerning the Indians is reinforced by the fact that they live prostrated in their abyss because the Spaniards have terrorized them. Seven: to temper the boasting and excessive vainglory of many and to unveil the injustice, of not a few who take pride in vicious deeds and execrable evil as if they could herd heroic men of illustrious exploits like cattle. Future generations ought to be able to distinguish between good and evil, between virtue and most abominable vices. That I should reprehend and abhor the errors of Spaniards must not surprise anyone, nor must I be thought guilty of harshness or viciousness. . . . Eight: to manifest, in a different way from other accounts, the grandeur and number of prodigiously admirable things, lost in the forgotten past, whose very existence we would never have believed. All of which I intend as exemplary: the knowledge of virtuous deeds, if any—and provided the world lasts—will lead to emulation; the knowledge of guilty deeds, of the divine punishment and disastrous end of those who perpetrated them, will lead to fear. . . .

When I began writing about Indian affairs, in 1527, especially those pertaining to the discovery of the Indies and to Hispaniola and neighboring islands, there was nobody writing in Castilian or Latin who had seen what he was writing about. There was almost no one present in the Indies capable of writing about them. Everything was picked up from hearsay, and those who lived there a while are very noisy about it, although they did not remain there as long as they claim. Therefore, their knowledge must not be credited any more than if they got it from people in Valladolid or Seville. Only Pedro Martyr is to be believed on the discovery of the Indies. He wrote his *Decadas* in Latin while residing in

Castile, but he wrote under the direction of Columbus himself, and had many conversations with him as well as with members of his fleet. The *Decadas*, however, contain many falsehoods as to later developments. Americo Vespucci testifies to what he saw on his two voyages to our Indies, but he seems to have omitted some circumstances, knowingly or inadvertently. For this reason, some ascribe to him what is owed to others who ought not to be defrauded in such a way, as we shall see at the opportune time.

All other accounts in Latin must be discarded: they tell as many lies as their authors are alien in place, language and nation. Although I began my *History* many years ago, I have not been able to finish it because of my numerous peregrinations and occupations. In the meantime, histories have been written with an eye to public use. May I be forgiven for uncovering their defects since they affirm things their authors did not know. Although I have followed Dionysius of Halicarnassus and Diodorus on points six and eight of my reasons, I am sure that I have surpassed them. They saw and studied their material at the age of twenty-two and thirty respectively, but I, as I said, am almost seventy-three—for which I thank God—and I have roamed these Indies since about 1500. I have firsthand knowledge of what pertains to my *History*: the profane, secular and ecclesiastical acts committed in my day, mixed now and then with moral considerations; the quality, nature and properties of these lands and kingdoms; the customs, religions, rites, ceremonies and condition of their natural inhabitants, compared with those of other nations when cosmography and geography warrant. In this way, not only will many people, especially princes (as the ancients well knew), benefit from their reading, but my chronicle will engender less tediousness and more appetite in those who hear it.

All this pertains to both the form and content of this book. As to the form itself, the *History* will contain six parts or books, encompassing almost sixty years, each book devoted to the events of one decade (with the exception of Book I, since the Indies were not discovered until 1492). If Providence grants me more life, I shall bring my *History* up to date, provided that the new events are worthy of being turned into history. Its author—besides God—is don fray Bartolomé de las Casas or Casaus, of the Dominican

Order, Bishop of Ciudad Real on the plains of Chiapas, called Zacatlán in the vernacular, which is a province of what today is called New Spain. By divine grace, I am perhaps the oldest man alive—perchance there may be one or two others—who has spent so much time and gathered so much experience in the western Indies. *Deo gratias*. Now for the text.

Book One

1

The Scriptures tell us that God's very first concern was to create Heaven and earth, an exploit that surpasses human understanding. The heavens: that pure body of admirable clarity which is the foundation of the world and everything visible; that royal palace and delightful dwelling of angels on whom He especially sheds His glory, for although omnipresent He is said to reside in Heaven as the place best suited to His divine splendor, the radiance of His most beatific beauty of which an inspired David exclaimed: "How amiable are thy tabernacles, O Lord of hosts! My soul longeth, yea, even fainteth for the courts of the Lord" (Ps 84: 1–2) Surely, a day's rest there must excel a thousand days of rest in the richest palaces of this world.

As for the earth: we are earthlings and as such have more knowledge of it than of the heavens. We see it with our eyes, and, both the Scriptures and our experience tell us, all men were created in God's image although the Fall of our first fathers caused men to have to battle with their natural surroundings, as can be seen by the ferocity, rebellion and distress from which we sometimes suffer. The earth, then, became inhabited through the propagation of men, before and after the Flood, and their descendants spread to all parts of the world in order to ease our population and find adequate supplies of food; thus, they lost track of their lineage in distant regions and caused the formation of many diverse nations who, having lost the memory of such a remote past, forgot the existence of one another. However, human ingenuity, curiosity and malice kept pace with the march of time. Vital

13

needs, such as self-preservation and the acquisition of property, caused exchanges between nations, provinces and cities, both by land and sea. Trade relations were established, as were laws regarding political asylum, wars and territorial expansions aimed at securing safety. For this reason, men opened the doors closed by oblivion and antiquity, discovered forgotten lands and went on searching for the unknown.

These seem to be the ways of men, and the reasons behind their desire to leave their country and travel to foreign lands. It would be better to believe, however, that the Creator of the universe, who created all things for the well-being of man, inspires man to discover the wonders of the world which but confirm His perfection. . . . Far from being the basest creatures in the universe, men are the most noble users of this world machine, arranged primarily to hold the perfect number of the Elect with whom He intends to fill the kingdom of Heaven. This kingdom is without the shadow of a doubt reserved for peoples of all languages all over the world who will be selected exactly at the time appointed by His divine and infallible judgment even before He created His predestined individuals. It is then that the hidden nations will be known and revealed: each generation of men has a time appointed for its calling . . . and for the receiving of the Faith. But this is not a reason for human weakness to make daring judgments or to take bold guesses as to why this is so: the heights of His wisdom are simply beyond reach of human presumption.

The Christian religion is granted to different peoples as the universal way to salvation so that they may leave behind their various sects, which necessarily leads their worshippers to eternal exile and infinite misery, and, consequently, so that they may be guided to that unparalleled kingdom where everyone is King. As for the mass of the people, original sin has caused it to suffer cruelly and to experience misery by devious ways in order to merit goodness. . . . It is unreasonable, then, to ask questions like Why now and not before? or Why so late? It must not be thought that, because a nation is discovered later than another, its Maker denied it His support, for He ordained things as He pleased. If a nation is unknown, it is to help some and edify everyone that they are to blame if it is not in a state of grace, and that they should not attribute it to themselves if that nation basks in divine grace, but must attribute it instead to the benevolence of the Lord. . . .

3

Among his natural attributes, the illustrious Genoese Christopher Columbus de Tierra Rubia was a tall, imposing, good-natured, kind, daring, courageous, and pious man. . . .

Now let us turn to his acquired qualities, his training and occupations up to the time he came to Spain, such as we can infer from his correspondence and other writings, from the *Historia portuguesa* [by Juan de Barros], and from his exploits. As a child, his parents made him learn to read and write, and he learned such calligraphy—I saw his writing many times—that he could have made a living by it. He also studied arithmetic and drawing with the same skill and degree of excellence. He studied Latin in Pavia—the *Historia portuguesa* praises him as a good Latinist— which must have given him an unusual insight into human and divine affairs. Since God had endowed him with good judgment, a sound memory and eagerness to learn, he sought the company of learned men and applied himself to his studies with great intensity, acquiring proficiency in geometry, geography, cosmography, astrology or astronomy, and seamanship. This is clear from his writings about the Indies and from some letters I saw that he wrote to King Ferdinand and Queen Isabella. Surely, as a God-fearing man and considering the fact that he was writing to a King, he must have avoided exaggeration. I transcribe a few passages from these letters because I think they are documents of value.

Your Highnesses: I began sailing at an early age and haven't stopped yet. The art of navigation inspires the navigator to want to know the secrets of this world. I have practiced this art for over forty years, sailing all waters known today. I have known many scholars, churchmen and laymen alike, Latins and Greeks, Jews and Moors, and many others of many other sects; I found God amenable to my eagerness since He gave me inspiration and intelligence. He made me proficient in navigation, gave me some knowledge of astrology, geometry and arithmetic, and endowed me with the ability to draw the sphere, accurately placing cities, rivers, mountains, islands and harbors. By this time I have studied all the latest writings about cosmography, history, chronicles, philosophy and other arts, so that Our Lord broadened my understanding and gave me the certitude that it was possible to go to the Indies from here; He fired me with the will to do so and it is with this fire that I address myself to Your Highnesses. Everyone laughed at my enterprise and dismissed it as a joke. My knowledge and my quoting of authorities have proved of no help. And now I trust only in Your Highnesses. . . .

These are the words of Christopher Columbus, written in 1501 from Cádiz or Seville, and he had drawn a map of the sphere on the letter. He wrote another letter to the same monarchs in January 1495, from Hispaniola, in which he talks about the craftiness of navigators who act one way instead of another in order to deceive their people, thus endangering the ships sometimes, and he says:

Once, King Reynel—may God rest his soul—sent me to Tunis to seize the galley *Fernandina*. We had come to the island of St. Peter in Sardinia, and a watchman told me that with the galleass or galley there were two more vessels and one galleon, which so upset the people on board they refused to continue the voyage, saying they wanted to go back to Marseilles and get another ship and more people. Seeing that I could not prevail upon their fear, I agreed and, changing the compass point, I set sail at sunset, so that at sunrise the next morning we were clear within the Cartagena Bay, and they thought for sure we had been sailing toward Marseilles.

He annotated books, and one of his annotations verifies by experience how the five zones are inhabited. It says:

In February 1477, I sailed 100 leagues past the island of Tile, whose southern part is 73° away from the equinox, not 63° as some maintain, and it isn't within the line that includes the West, as Ptolemy says, but rather much further West. That island is as large as England. The English go there to trade, especially from Bristol. When I was there, the sea was not frozen but the tides were tremendous. In some parts high tide rose 25 fathoms deep twice a day, and receded likewise.

And it is true that Ptolemy's Tile—modern cosmographers call it Frislanda—is where he says it is. He goes on verifying that the Equator is habitable. "I was below the Equator in Portuguese territory, therefore I know they are wrong when they say the zone is not habitable." *Haec ille.* Elsewhere he states that he sailed many times from Lisbon to Guinea and noted very carefully how its degree corresponds to 56 and two-thirds miles; that he was in the island of Enxion in the Aegean Sea and saw mastic being sapped from certain trees; that he sailed East and West almost without interruption for twenty-five years and saw it all; that "I brought two ships to Puerto Santo and left one there for a day because it was taking water, but I arrived in Lisbon a whole week before that ship because I had stormy southwest winds and she had only the sparse contrary winds from north northwest."

All this proves not only that Christopher Columbus was a skilled seaman and experienced navigator but also that he studied carefully all things pertaining to the sea and knew the basic theories and principles of navigation without which pilots make dreadful mistakes, as can be seen in these Indies, where accuracy is a matter of chance. I think Christopher Columbus was the most outstanding sailor in the world, versed like no other in the art of navigation, for which divine Providence chose him to accomplish the most outstanding feat ever accomplished in the world until now.

So then, Christopher Columbus had been terribly busy before he undertook the discovery of the New World, and well he needed all that time, too, to acquire such skills. Agustín Justinianus is wrong when, in his collection of Psalms—written in four languages—and later in his *Crónica,* he says that Christopher Columbus was only an artisan. This is unlikely, almost impossible in fact, unless it happened to him as happens to those good children who run away from home and stay a while in some foreign land until they are found learning some trade or other. But it seems that Christopher Columbus had not even the time to do that, since "in his tender years he learned the principles of doctrine, and in his youth he dedicated himself to the art of navigation, studying cosmography, etc., in Lisbon," as Justinianus himself writes in his collection of Psalms, making him so busy studying that no time would have been left for apprenticeship in any of the mechanical arts. So then, Justinianus appears to have been misinformed about this and other facts of Columbus's life. For this reason, I understand that the ruling house of Genoa has issued a public decree that prohibits the having and reading of his *Crónica*, withdrawing it from circulation as an inaccurate book harmful to the reputation of a person as meritorious as Christopher Columbus, to whom all Christendom is so greatly indebted.

4

. . . We have just seen how dedicated a sailor Christopher Columbus was; let us see now why he came to Spain. It happened that the most famous pirate in those days, a man named Columbus Junior—to differentiate him from a third famous Columbus, all being of the same house—was leading an armada against the infidels, the Venetians and other enemies of his nation. Christopher Columbus decided to accompany him and stayed with him a long time. Columbus Junior heard that four Venetian galleys had gone to Flanders, and he arranged to wait for their return passage between Lisbon and the Cape of Saint Vincent so that the ships could be boarded and fighting could take place on deck. That was a terrible encounter in which both sides used iron hooks, chains, firearms and all kinds of other weapons employed in those hellish naval battles. The day's casualties were so heavy on both sides that few survived to escape to a place a league away from the battle scene. Christopher Columbus's ship caught fire, and so did the galleon to which it was attached; and since it was impossible to separate the two, all the men jumped into the sea and those who could swim survived, while the rest chose the torment of drowning to that of being burned alive. Christopher was a great swimmer; he was able to grasp a floating oar on which to catch his breath from time to time, and he swam to shore, some two leagues from where the ships that had engaged in such a blind and foolish battle had retreated. . . .

After recuperating a while from his wounds and a paralysis in his legs, he went to nearby Lisbon, where he knew he would find other Genoese, who helped him set up a business. He found a partner and acquired a good reputation as well as some means. A few days after his arrival, as he was a well-mannered, handsome man and a churchgoing Christian, he met one of the sisters in the Santos Monastery (I don't know to what Order it belonged) and had relations with her so that she had to marry him. Her name was doña Felipa Moñiz; she was the daughter of the hidalgo Bartolomé Moñiz Perestrello, who had served the house of the Infante don Juan of Portugal, the son of King Juan I of Portugal . . . and, since her father had died, they went to live with his widow.

In the course of time, Christopher's mother-in-law found out about his dedication to cosmography and the sea—a vocation occupies a man's mind night and day, and the interest that succeeds in deflecting him from it must be mighty powerful indeed— so that she was brought to talk to him about her late husband's inclinations. He, too, had devoted much of his life to the sea; he and two friends had gone to settle the island of Puerto Santo, as the Infante Enrique of Portugal had ordered; and, the island being but a recent discovery, he settled it all by himself and received good benefits in return. Since the discovery of the coast of Guinea and the islands of the Atlantic was the most talked-about news at that time, Perestrello had hoped to launch new discoveries and had navigational instruments and maps which the mother-in-law gave Columbus, much to the latter's joy. It is believed that these maps reinforced his interest in investigating the Portuguese expeditions and that his imagination was fired by the lands that were still unknown and said not to be habitable. Thus he decided to see from experience what was going on in the direction of Ethiopia, and as a Portuguese resident joined various Portuguese expeditions to those parts. He lived on Puerto Santo a while, where Perestrello had left an estate, as I remember being told by Columbus's son, the admiral Diego Columbus, in Barcelona, where King Charles of Spain was made Emperor in 1519. It was in Puerto Santo that he engendered his first son Diego, and, wanting to go on sailing, he left his wife there. There was a constant movement of ships to and from Puerto Santo and the newly discovered neighboring Madeira Island; frequent discussions about the Portuguese discoveries were on everyone's lips. This seems to have given Christopher Columbus the opportunity to come to Spain as well as to formulate his plans for the discovery of the New World.

5

We have seen how Christopher Columbus came to Spain, as well as his reasons for wanting to discover the Indies. I understand that when he tried to find a Christian Prince to sponsor him, he was already sure that he would discover new lands and peoples, as sure indeed as if he had already been there in person. I myself have no doubt about his certainty. I want to discuss the natural reasons, as well as corroborations from ancient and modern authorities, that made it logical for him to infer that new lands could be discovered to the west and south of the ocean.

First, philosophical authority supports the fact that the earth is round and that people stand at antipodes; therefore, Christopher Columbus thought it possible to circumnavigate it from East to West. Second, he knew from experience, books and hearsay that most waters had already been navigated, which left unexplored only that area from the eastern point of India (known by Ptolemy and Marino) eastward, thus making possible a return from the West to the islands of Cape Verde and the Azores, which at that time were the westernmost land points. Third, he understood that the space between the eastern point known to Marino and the Cape Verde Islands could not exceed the third part of the sphere's larger circle since, out of twenty-four hours, Marino had calculated fifteen from the West, which left out only a bare eight hours, and he had not begun that far West either. Fourth, he thought that if Marino had calculated fifteen hours of the sphere going East, he had not reached the limits of the eastern land territories which, it was reasonable to suppose, extended far beyond; consequently, the further East he went, the closer he would be to our west of the Cape Verde Islands. If that space turned out to be water, it would be easily navigated in a few days; if it turned out to be land, it would be discovered much sooner sailing West because of its proximity to the Cape Verde Islands. . . . Fifth, Alfragano and his followers added support to the theory that the space left unexplored was small since they calculated a spherical degree to be a mere 56 and two-thirds miles. If so, that space could be navigated in a very short time, and he thought further that, since the eastern point of India was still unknown, it was bound to be close to us from the West, for which reason the land to be discovered in those parts could be called the West Indies.

Maestre Rodrigo de Santaella, the Queen's Archdeacon in Seville, was wrong then, when he tried to correct Columbus by saying it should not be called the Indies because indeed that land was not India. Columbus did not name it the Indies because it had already been discovered before, but because it was that eastern part of India *ultra Gangem* which, going East, was to the west of us since the world is round. No cosmographer has ever marked out boundaries of India except those of the ocean. And since the new land is the unknown eastern part of India, which bears no particular name, he called it western Indies as the land closest to India. Besides, India was known for its great wealth, and he wanted to induce the monarchs, always doubtful about his enterprise, to believe him when he said he was setting out in search of a western route to India, which is why he sought the support of the Catholic kings. Except for a few additions, what I have said in this chapter are the words of don Hernando Columbus, son of the first admiral of the Indies, Christopher Columbus. . . .

28

. . . Christopher Columbus then decided to look for a Christian Prince who would finance his enterprise by supplying ships and equipment. He turned to the King of Portugal because of convenience: he had become a resident of that country and its King was very involved in all matters of discovery. So he proposed the following: sailing south by west he would discover islands and a continent rich in gold, silver, precious stones and innumerable peoples; he would find a new route to India, to the island of

Cipango [Japan] and the land of the Great Khan, that is to say, the King of Kings. He asked for three caravels equipped with a crew and a year's supply of food, navigational instruments and a few chests filled with objects for barter: Flemish notions such as bells, brass boxes, sheets of brass, strings of beads, multicolored glass, small mirrors, scissors, knives, needles, pins, linen shirts, pieces of coarse dyed cloth, colored caps and similar things worth little but esteemed by ignorant people. He asked for remuneration in exchange for his services and the dangers to which he was exposing his life, and in this Columbus showed his usual moderation and generosity as well as self-assurance. One, that he be knighted and given the title of don for himself and his heirs. Two, that he be appointed chief admiral of the Ocean Sea, together with all the prerogatives and privileges granted the admirals of Castile. Three, that he be appointed viceroy and governor for life of all the territories he should discover. Four, that he receive the tenth part of the King's income resulting from the gold and all other saleable items that should be found within the territory of his admiralship. Five, that he be allowed to contribute one-eighth of the cost of all ships used for trade in exchange for one-eighth of the profit resulting from such trade.

So then, he made his offer to the King of Portugal and gave him reasons. The *Historia portuguesa* says that Christopher Columbus was more talkative and self-assured, more a fantasist with his story of Cipango than a man of sound reason, and that consequently people were loath to believe him. I saw a letter from Columbus to King Ferdinand where Columbus says something of this: "God Our Lord sent me here miraculously to serve Your Highness, and I say miraculously because I appealed to the King of Portugal who more than any other King is interested in land discoveries, but God blinded him to me and made him deaf to my reasons, for in the fourteen years I was there he would not listen." It seems that Juan de Barros is trying to discredit Columbus as well as his noble enterprise by calling it a dream based on false arguments. He goes on to say—in Chapter XI, Book III, the first *decada* of his book called *Asia*—that after Columbus's success the King of Portugal felt very sorry when he saw the gold and the Indians, who were not black, and all the other things Columbus had brought back.

Thus the historian Juan de Barros contradicts himself. He adds that the insistence of Columbus caused the King of Portugal to refer the matter to Diego Ortiz, Bishop of Ceuta (a Castilian, I believe . . .), maestre Rodrigo and maestre Josephe, a Jew, both physicians who knew astronomy and were consulted about matters of cosmography and discoveries, and that both found Columbus's words full of air. . . .

Juan de Barros does not mention, if ever he knew it, that the King of Portugal wormed more and more information out of Christopher Columbus and that, together with Dr. Calzadilla and other people asked to study the case, he secretly equipped a caravel with Portuguese sailors and sent it on the ocean to follow the route Columbus had charted out for himself. This was a way to use Columbus's information gratuitously, letting nothing slip out of the King's royal hands. Thus, while Columbus was kept waiting for an answer, the Portuguese caravel sailed, pretending that the Portuguese colonizers of the Cape Verde Islands needed help, and, as I said, this was a time of feverish activities to and from Guinea, the Azores, Madeira and Puerto Santo islands, and pretexts were not hard to find to explain the departure of a caravel. But human trickeries are powerless in the face of the divine will, which had reserved the discovery of the New World for the kings of Castile and León; and when the caravel had sailed many leagues out to sea without finding anything, a fierce storm forced it back to Lisbon.

When the people of Lisbon saw the caravel in such bad shape, they asked where it came from. At first the sailors only muttered things, but soon they were spelling out the reason so that, when Columbus heard it, he knew he had been the object of a double deal and he decided to leave Portugal and come to Castile. However, to dedicate himself to God's assigned task, he first had to be free of his wife, and God provided by taking her, leaving him with his small son Diego, who was to succeed him in the office of admiral. The King of Portugal had had his reasons for rejecting Columbus's proposal: the treasury was depleted by wars in Barbary, the maintenance of the cities his predecessors had conquered in Africa and the expenses of all present discoveries along the coast of Guinea. It was difficult to find sailors willing to sail more than a day without sighting land because, in those days, losing sight of the coast was considered a frightening and horrible experience no sailor would undertake, which was why 3,000 leagues of coastline had been explored down to the Cape of Good Hope. Columbus's list of privileges appeared exorbitant but, if indeed this entered into consideration, the King of Portugal would have done better to consider the millions that were at stake in exchange for risking such a little sum and not a penny more; the discoveries in Guinea promised further discoveries that could reach India, and, seeing himself master of the vast Ocean Sea, he was inclined not to give a straw for what Columbus was offering.

However, it is best to believe the reason we already gave, namely, that divine Providence had reserved for the Portuguese the mission of saving the Elect from among the people of the territory we call India, and for the Castilians the mission of showing the way to the Truth to the peoples of the New World. And pray to God that both the Portuguese and Castilians may be brought to the knowledge of their mission and of the incomparable favor God did us by choosing us as instruments of His will, so that we may escape the rigors of His judgment with accrued interests. . . .

29

Christopher Columbus had good reasons for leaving the King of Portugal, whose ways with him had been so deceitful, which does not argue well for the great straightforwardness becoming to kings. Thinking that, should the Castilian monarchs refuse to negotiate with him, he could not waste the better part of his life looking for needed backers, he decided to send his brother Bartolomé to the court of England with the same proposal. Bartolomé Columbus was a very wise and courageous man, more careful and astute, it seemed, and less direct than Christopher. He knew Latin and other manly things, was especially outstanding and experienced in all things nautical, almost as learned as his brother in cosmography and the making of navigational charts, spheres and other instruments; in fact, having learned them from him, I presume he sometimes surpassed his brother. He was rather tall but not as stately as his brother. He went to England, and, so that such a novel and arduous venture should not lack all manner of obstacles, God willed that he be captured at sea by eastern pirates whose nationality I do not know. He fell into a state of illness and great poverty, thus taking a long time to reach England after God had first restored his health and he had somewhat got back on his feet, thanks to his wits and the work of his hands, by drawing navigational charts.

After some time in England he succeeded in notifying King Henry VII of his business. And to dispose the King in his favor he gave him a world map that was very handsomely made, on which he had drawn the lands he and his brother intended to discover. He had written some Latin verses on it, composed, as he said, by himself. I find them poorly written, misspelled, at times even illegible, but I want to transcribe the poem here, not for its elegance and perfection, but as a document of the times, considering its subject matter as well as the person who wrote it.

For those who do not read Latin, it says that the map shows everything about the borders of land and sea as demonstrated in different ways by Strabo, Ptolemy, Pliny and St. Isidore of Seville; that the ancient discoverer of the Spanish shores had proved by experience that the torrid zone was habitable, thus almost making a prophecy about America; and that the Genoese Bartolomé Columbus de Tierra Rubia drew the map in London, on February 10, 1488, Christ be praised.

The King, then, received both poem and map graciously and from then on enjoyed discussing the matter with Bartolomé Columbus. Finally, it was said that he had agreed to the enterprise and was sending for Christopher, who by that time had already discovered land and had returned with the wonderful reward for all his hardships, as, God willing, we shall see later.

Christopher Columbus was in Castile for seven years trying to win the favor of the King and Queen, and had left Portugal before his brother, as I gather from his letters to the monarchs and from other circumstances. Thus, he must have left in 1484 or early 1485; or, if they left Portugal together, Bartolomé must have returned to Portugal after being captured, then sailed with Captain Bartolomé Díaz and discovered the Cape of Good Hope with him, returning to Portugal by December 1488 and proceeding to England, where he wrote the poem in February. It follows that Christopher Columbus did not take part in the discovery of the Cape of Good Hope, and that what Bartolomé wrote in the margins of his copy of Peter Aliacus applied to him, not to his brother.

But, to go on with our history, Christopher left Portugal as secretly as he could for fear the King should order him to stay, which undoubtedly would have happened. The King was anxious to win him back, either because, having missed his chance, he wanted to try again, or because he meant to wheedle more information from him and launch an expedition on his own account, or indeed because he truly wanted to support Columbus. But the latter outfoxed the King and, taking his young son Diego with him, went to Palos, where he knew some sailors, and also, perhaps, a few Franciscan monks from the monastery of Santa María de la Rábida, approximately a quarter of a league from Palos, with whom he left his son. He set out for Córdoba, where the Spanish court was at the time because the war with Granada kept the Catholic kings very busy.

He arrived on January 20, 1485, and began his own terrible, continuous, painful and tedious battle—perhaps harsher and more horrible than a fight with material weapons—that is, to inform the many people who, presuming to understand, did not in fact understand him at all, and to answer and tolerate the many who ignored and shunned his person, insulting him with words which pained him very much. The first step in negotiations with kings is to present a lengthy account of one's goals to those people who have constant access to the King, either at council, in special meetings, or in private. Therefore, Christopher Columbus managed to speak to those men he felt could help his cause. They were: Cardinal Pedro González de Mendoza, who prevailed with the King by virtue of his faithfulness, his illustrious family and his eminent dignity—the *Historia portuguesa* says that the King accepted Columbus's enterprise through him; the Dominican fray Diego de Deza, tutor to Prince don Juan, later Archbishop of Seville; Cárdenas, a comendador mayor; Prado, the prior of the Order of St. Jerome, who later became the first Archbishop of Granada; and the Aragonese Juan Cabrero, the King's steward, a man of good heart beloved by both King and Queen.

In a letter in Columbus's handwriting, I saw how he acknowledged Diego de Deza and Juan Cabrero as having been the cause of Spain's dominion over the Indies, but long before I saw the letter I had heard it said that those two men had taken pride in being instrumental in the discovery of the Indies. Certainly, they helped a great deal, although not enough, since the Aragonese Luis de Santángel, clerk of the exchequer, an honored and prudent person, accomplished much more by being the one who finally convinced the Queen. They arranged an audience with the King so that Columbus might make his case, but the King heard the request very superficially, being so occupied with the war—as a general rule, warring kings have ears for little else but war—and they referred the case to scholars who would listen to Columbus, appraise the quality of his offer and the proof thereof, discuss it among themselves and report fully to him and the Queen. They especially entrusted Prado with the task of gathering people versed in cosmography—and in those days there were not many; in fact, it is an awesome thing to consider the ignorance in these matters all over Castile.

They met often. Columbus would present his proposal, giving reasons and authoritative support to prove it feasible, but keeping the most urgent ones to himself, for fear the Portuguese experience would be repeated. Some would ask how it was possible that, after so many thousands of years, no one had heard about those Indies and, if they existed, how was it that none of the famous wise men, cosmographers, astrologers, not even a Ptolemy, all of whom had written about such things, wrote nothing about the Indies. They said that to assert such a possibility was to pretend to know more than the next person. Others would argue that the world was infinite and that it would be impossible to reach the eastern limits even after years of sailing, as Columbus proposed, from the west. They quoted Seneca, *De las suasorias*, Book I, on the ancient doubt as to whether the ocean was navigable, supposing it infinite; or, in the event it was navigable, whether one was likely to find land on the other side; but if there were land, it was unlikely it was inhabited; but if it were inhabited, it was unlikely that one could set out to find it. They did not notice that Seneca's words were rhetorical and since Seneca's alleged authorities assumed India did not end in the East, these modern scholars inferred that the same applied to Columbus's plan to sail West from Spain.

Those who professed to know more of the mathematics related to astrology and cosmography maintained that only a small body of land in the southern hemisphere was left uncovered because the rest was under water; therefore, it was possible to sail only along coast lines, as the Portuguese had done; and those who said this had read very few books, much less treatises on navigation. And they said more: sailing straight West, as Columbus planned, would mean one could never return, for supposing the world were round, going West was sinking downhill out of the hemisphere described by Ptolemy; it would then be necessary to return uphill, which is something ships cannot do. And this genteel and profound reasoning shows how well they understood the matter! Still others called on St. Augustine who, as we said, did not believe in antipodes, so they would repeat the refrain "But St. Augustine doubts it." Some even brought in the story of the five zones, three of which are, according to many, altogether uninhabited; this was the opinion of the ancients and, when all is said and done, the ancients did not know very much. There were other reasons not worth recording, and there were those contrary minds who contradict everything, no matter how clear and good the reasons.

Finally, the subject became so enmeshed that little was accomplished. Columbus gave answers to their objections that should have satisfied them; however, to understand Columbus it would have been necessary first to unlearn the erroneous principles on which they based their reasoning, which is more difficult than teaching uncluttered minds. . . . For this reason, Columbus gave them little satisfaction and they judged his proposal impossible, useless and worthy of total rejection. They informed the King of their opinion and persuaded him not to waste money and royal prestige on a venture so flimsily founded, so uncertain and impossible as to appear thus to anyone, learned or not. Finally, the King sent a reply to Columbus that dismissed his proposal for the time being, but left hope for future reconsideration. Later, he would have the leisure he now lacked on account of the Granada war; there was no room for new transactions, but in time a more opportune occasion could present itself.

Columbus spent a long time in court before he received this reply: the monarchs were constantly moving from one place to another, and all royal transactions, whether kings move or stay in one place, normally require prodigious tediousness. The time of kings is often squandered; also, too many of their officials are indolent, careless, and give unwarranted weight to things, unaware that they must account to God for each hour they delay a businessman. All this procrastination caused Columbus much anguish and bitterness. He saw his life being spent in vain and, as a Christian, he rightly feared that God would deprive him of his role as the discoverer of those benefits he knew would result from his enterprise. He found himself lacking in the necessary things without which life at court is intolerable and little less than death itself. But above all, he suffered because they doubted both his words and his person, and this to a generous man is equivalent to death in pain and abomination. Without a doubt, such a promising offer required little risk on their part, because for the present he needed only two million *maravedís*, a mere trifle compared with the amounts they were spending every day.

The monarchs ought to have granted such a modest request; Columbus was not asking to take money out of the country or to spend it on himself; rather, he meant to buy and equip three vessels and employ only Castilians. And the favors he asked in return for his services were not absolute but conditional, not immediate but hypothetical, depending on the future, just as when rewards are contained in the very request, the initial cost is of little importance compared to the risk of losing it all, especially since Columbus looked so dignified, was so well spoken, wise and prudent. The reasons for this oversight I think are briefly these: one, ignorance of mathematical science and ancient history on the part of those in charge of examining the question; and two, the austerity of the times, which always causes austerity in men's hearts, had put Spain in a state of financial penury such that all monies were overtaxed and tightly controlled. Consequently, either because of the recurrence of costly events or of the fact that the greater a country's power, the greater the threat, expenses were regulated and appraised accordingly, and those whose duty it was to persuade the King that a large sum would be lost by risking so little, discredited the enterprise, as we have seen, through their lack of knowledge.

The excellence of Columbus's project and its inestimable value also failed to gain acceptance because the King was engaged in the long siege of Granada. When rulers are preoccupied by war, there is no peace and rest either for King or country and they care little for the necessary things in life; all people talk about is war councils, war deliberations, special meetings about the war, so that everything else is suspended and silenced by this. But the fundamental reason is the law which God established throughout the world: that no amount of good, however small, happens in life without the greatest toil, reminding us that anguish is part of winning eternity. Precious things are bought at great price, especially things pertaining to our holy Faith, as is evident from the incomparable difficulties involved, in the beginning, in the evangelization, propagation and foundation of the Church. The reason is that no individual may take pride in having accomplished the task alone, without the assistance of divine grace, since the prime mover is at the same time the final doer of God's will, that is, God Himself. And this is why He leads matters dearest to His heart to the brink of disaster and, when man is most unaware, lends His aid and brings them to a perfect conclusion, so that man will acknowledge His divine intervention. In view of this, the persons He chooses to use for such matters are the most meritorious; and also because the forces of Hell attack more fiercely whatever is meant to result in greater benefit for the Church, as we see written in the Apocalypse, and all things are so designed by God as to extract the best from all evils. Well, since the discovery of the New World was one of the most outstanding exploits reserved by God for the propagation of his holy Church over so extensive a part of the universe hitherto hidden, and for the resplendence of His holy Faith among an infinite number of nations, no wonder then that so many obstacles impeded the beginning and even the middle, as we shall see, of these negotiations.

To return to the story, Columbus resided at court for more than five years, arguing and trying in vain to persuade all kinds of potentially helpful people, suffering innumerable rejections and contradictions, varied hardships and many insults. Unable to bear such frustrations any longer, especially as he now lacked both means and hopes of finding support in Castile, he rightly decided to leave court and, heavy-hearted, departed for Seville.

30

. . . In Seville, Christopher Columbus heard of the wealth and munificence of the Duke of Medina Sidonia, don Enrique de Guzmán, a truly generous man whose copious financial aid, both on land and sea, had caused the surrender of Málaga. He also helped break the siege of Alhama, where the Moorish King of Granada held the Marquis of Cádiz, don Rodrigo de León. Columbus made his proposal to the Duke but found disbelief and incomprehension, perhaps because all the grandees of the kingdom, especially in Andalusia, were spending a great deal of money on the siege of Granada; and this was true also of the Duke who, though the wealthiest man in Spain, refused to touch his treasures for an enterprise that would have increased his estate and munificence. Next, Columbus tried his luck with the Duke of Medinaceli, don Luis de la Cerda, then residing in Puerto de Santa María, who had always lacked previous occasions to display his generosity.

When the Duke [of Medinaceli] found out that the man reputed to have offered the monarchs a golden opportunity for wealth and fame was actually in his domains, he had him called to his house and treated him nobly as became his own dignity and that of his guest. He discussed the details of the enterprise with Columbus, enjoying daily conversations with him and, won by the man's sense of prudence and good judgment, decided to sponsor him. He treated Columbus as a guest, for he knew that in those days, after many years spent at court, Columbus had not a pot to cook in—they say he even had to rely on the talent of his hands and on occasion drew navigational charts, which he did very well, and sold them to seamen. So, then, the magnificent Duke of Medinaceli was satisfied with Columbus's reasoning and set aside a sum of up to 4,000 ducats to build three ships and equip them with enough food for one year, as well as sailors and objects to be used for barter. He gave orders to begin work immediately and not to stop until the ships were finished. To give his case more weight, the Duke deliberately delayed asking the monarchs' permission until the work had already been started and in his petition he stressed that if they granted him permission to encourage such an enterprise, the result would be great prosperity for the kingdom.

But divine Providence had other plans and reserved the discovery of such magnificent new lands, not for the glory of inferiors, but for that of the most excellent monarchs themselves. The obstacles that had made discussion difficult were disappearing: the Granada war was coming to an end; the monarchs were engaged in negotiations with the Moors, who had unjustly occupied and tyrannized Granada for so many years; and, with the Cross so near to being hoisted on the Alhambra, Their Highnesses saw an end to the laborious years of their reign and showed willingness to hear the Duke's request favorably. Queen Isabella showed a particularly keen interest and took it upon herself to support the pious armada and to formulate the hope that something illustrious and worthy of renown would result from it. Some said that she had been influenced by the magnanimous Cardinal Pedro González de Mendoza and the Dominican scholar-friar Diego de Deza, who was the Prince's tutor and later became Archbishop of Seville. She wrote to thank the Duke for his heroic service, saying she was pleased to have such a noble and capable person living in her kingdom . . . and she begged him to allow her to support Columbus, for she meant to finance the expedition herself by drawing on the royal treasury. In addition, she wrote to Columbus and asked him to come to court without delay. She ordered that funds be taken from her treasury to reimburse the Duke for his expenses and that work be continued on the ships— apparently, Columbus sailed to the New World on those very ships. The Duke's annoyance was beyond belief, since the more he thought about the enterprise, the more he burned to finance it and see it terminated. But he was wise and obeyed the Queen and, as a Christian bending to God's will, decided to be patient.

The above is the substance of what Diego de Morales told me about the matter many years ago in Hispaniola. Morales was among the first people who came here—he came before I did; he was a reliable person and a nephew of the Duke's head steward, who I believe bore the same name and was the person who first approached the Duke with the news of Columbus's plans and influenced him to look upon them with favor. . . .

34

Columbus left the court of Granada on May 12, 1492, beaming with happiness since, finally, King Ferdinand and Queen Isabella had agreed to sponsor him, issuing the provisions, grants and privileges that he had requested. He went straight to Palos, where he could find experienced sailors, and where, too, he had friends and acquaintances, among whom was his good friend Juan Pérez, guardian of the monastery of La Rábida. Palos was also a town obliged to the King, for what reason I do not know, to supply him with two caravels for a period of three months.

Columbus began his preparations. There lived in Palos three wealthy seamen of status by the name of Pinzón; they were the brothers Martín Alonso—the wealthiest and most prominent of the three—Vicente Yáñez and Francisco Martínez. It could be said that almost the whole town gravitated around them since they were wealthy and had good connections. Columbus first approached Martín Alonso to induce him to join his expedition together with his brothers, relatives and friends. Although some say Columbus made no promises to Pinzón, I think he did promise him something since nobody does anything without a promise of returns. I think the Pinzón brothers helped Columbus financially, especially Martín Alonso, who had long experience in nautical matters. Columbus wanted to contribute one-eighth of the cost because the money lent him by Luis de Santángel in the name of the King—1,000,000 *maravedís*—did not suffice and because he wanted to keep one-eighth of the gain resulting from his enterprise for himself. But since he came out from his residence at court a poor man and since the cost of the expedition was recorded at 1,500,000 *maravedís*, it is likely that Martín Alonso supplied the difference.

Later, when Diego Columbus started a lawsuit against the King to obtain fulfillment of the royal privileges granted him through his father, the treasurer defended the King by maintaining that Christopher Columbus had discovered little or no continent and that Martín Alonso Pinzón had financed Columbus's first stay in court as well as received promises from Columbus, after the capitulations and negotiations were written down and terminated, to be given half of Columbus's profits. I know the documents of that lawsuit very well; these are convincingly false. The treasurer was trying to put in doubt the fact that Columbus had discovered the Indies, presenting rival witnesses, asking impertinent questions to cloud issues and discredit the most outstanding feat man has seen in millions of years, and on the whole requalifying Columbus's enterprise with such pettiness that the whole argument must be discarded as ridiculous. Had Columbus promised to share his benefits with Martín Alonso, the latter was not as simple-minded as not to have required it in writing, or else his heirs would have claimed it; or again, Vicente Yáñez, who survived his brother for many years and whom I knew personally, would have complained and publicized the fact. But not a word was said—I certainly would have heard it since I was so very much a part of those days—before the lawsuit in 1508, when the King returned from Naples.

. . . Finally, one way or another, Columbus hastened the preparations as best he could; once the Pinzón brothers had decided to accompany him, many people followed suit, and he equipped three caravels with good sails, riggings, food to last one year, and whatever else he thought would remedy the uncertainties of such a voyage. He made Martín Alonso and Francisco Martínez Pinzón captain and master respectively of the lightest and swiftest caravel, named *Pinta*; Vicente Yáñez was both captain and master of the caravel *Niña*; and he himself took command of the flagship named *Capitana*. Both crews and passengers were from Palos except for some ninety persons who had come with him, either from among his own family and acquaintances or from the King's household, some of whom were going out of sheer curiosity. . . .

76

Many is the time I have wished that God would again inspire me and that I had Cicero's gift of eloquence to extol the indescribable service to God and to the whole world which Christopher Columbus rendered at the cost of such pain and dangers, such skill and expertise, when he so courageously discovered the New World. I would also wish to praise Queen Isabella for her realization of the value of the discovery of so many good, peaceful and humble nations disposed to good by their incorruptible spiritual virtues. She believed that during and after her lifetime they would yield a copious harvest for the glory of Almighty God, the culmination of His holy Christian Faith and the propagation of His universal Church. Would that her successors equaled or exceeded her zeal, for even half of it would strengthen their political power here and now, as well as bring divine compensation hereafter for just measures taken for the salvation of these innumerable nations placed under their protection by divine Providence. Queen Isabella's holy zeal, intense care, tireless efforts and meritorious will to save the Indians are attested by the royal decrees she issued in the few years she lived after the discovery of the Indies, and these years hardly came to ten when one considers that for quite some time, information concerning the Indies was a matter of guesses and hearsay.

My limited understanding and poor eloquence prompt me to think that the fruit of Columbus's labor speaks better for itself than I do. However, I want to say enough for the wise and clear-minded reader to draw his own conclusions, and what I particularize here in a few words stands for greater principles worthy of prime consideration above all others. Is there anything on earth comparable to opening the tightly shut doors of an ocean that no one dared enter before? And supposing someone in the most remote past did enter, the feat was so utterly forgotten as to make Columbus's discovery as arduous as if it had been the first time. But since it is obvious that at that time God gave this man the keys to the awesome seas, he and no other unlocked the darkness, to him and to no other is owed for ever and ever all that exists beyond those doors. He showed the way to the discovery of immense territories whose coastline today measures over 12,000 leagues from pole to pole and whose inhabitants form wealthy and illustrious nations of diverse peoples and languages. Their rites and customs differ but they all have in common the traits of simplicity, peacefulness, gentleness, humility, generosity, and, of all the sons of Adam, they are without exception the most patient. In addition, they are eminently ready to be brought to the knowledge of their Creator and to the Faith.

It is then very clear that the boundaries of Christ's empire could be vastly extended by spreading the Christian religion to all its countless parts and by increasing the number of its worshippers to include such fine rational creatures in such great numbers. God chose the selected few even before He created the world—no Catholic would dare deny this—picking souls then, now and for ever, as He would grains of celestial wheat to enrich His divine granaries, or as more than precious living stones to build His divine house, and no amount of fiendish hordes and devices of the devil scattered over these parts would succeed in stealing away a single one of these souls. What then, can be compared to this on the whole face of the earth? And what can one say of the abundance of temporal wealth in gold, silver, pearls and precious stones? To give an idea, Indian gold is what prevails on the market all over the world (this is not the place to speak of the disorder and accidental abuses of how it gets there). If some do not acknowledge this, at least it is clear that the nations of Christendom are infinitely enriched by the gold, silver and pearls from our Indies, or would be, if God did not occasionally strike them down in punishment. If the kings of Christendom were united in peace and conformity, they would be strengthened by this treasure and the enemies of our holy Catholic Faith would not dare oppose it. Even if they should form armies as powerful as those of Xerxes or any other of that magnitude, Spain alone could smash them with God's help and with the sinews of war, that is, monies derived from our Indies. According to historical authority, wealth helps rulers keep the enemy in check and in a state of submission.

It is fitting to stress that God most sublimely favored all of Spain over any other Christian nation, when he chose Christopher Columbus to give to Spain such a golden opportunity in every sense of the word. Not only scholars, great theologians, and eloquent and witty sermonizers but any plebeian idiot can, provided he possess a steady faith, some knowledge of doctrine and the ten commandments, mediate between Christ and a vast number of infidels, provided also that he live the life of a good Christian and show it by his actions. In this way anybody has the opportunity to be a holy Apostle, should he also receive such grace from above as to be content with helping to harvest the spiritual riches of these lands, since these universal Indian nations are so simple, so gentle and so eminently ready to receive the Faith. For this reason, every Spaniard ought to ponder gravely that this illustrious gift, denied to all other Christians, is a most powerful gift for which he will be asked to account on the Day of Judgment, together with the interests thereof; and on the day of his death he will have to give a precise and exact account of it, the scrupulousness of which will be made clear from the following chapters. And of all those distinguished and incomparable goods (as well as of those discovered daily which I shall make known later), that most worthy man Christopher Columbus was the cause, second to God but first in the eyes of men, being the discoverer and only worthy first admiral of the vast territory already known as the New World. . . .

78

RETURN FROM THE FIRST VOYAGE: 1493

Christopher Columbus, now admiral, left Seville with as much finery as he could gather, taking with him the seven Indians who had survived the voyage. I saw them in Seville where they stayed near the arch to St. Nicholas called the Arch of the Images. He had brought beautiful green parrots, *guayças* or masks made of precious stones and fishbone, strips of the same composition admirably contrived, sizable samples of very fine gold, and many other things never before seen in Spain. The news spread over Castile like fire that a land called the Indies had been discovered, that it was full of people and things so diverse and so new, and that the discoverer himself was to take such and such a route accompanied by some of the Indians. They flocked from all directions to see him; the roads swelled with throngs come to welcome him in the towns through which he passed. The monarchs, who had received Columbus's message from Seville, began to take steps to launch a second expedition, and wrote to this effect to the future Bishop of Badajoz and Palencia, don Juan Rodríguez de Fonseca, then Archdeacon of Seville . . . who, for an ecclesiastic, was a most capable businessman with a talent for armadas more suited to a Basque than a Bishop. The monarchs always entrusted their armadas to him and now put him in charge of providing the vessels with such things as Columbus had requested in his message.

Columbus hastened to Barcelona, where he arrived in mid-April. The monarchs were very anxious to see him. They had organized a solemn and beautiful reception to which everybody came. The streets were crammed with people come to see this eminent person who had found another world, as well as to see the Indians, the parrots, the gold and other novelties. For greater solemnity, the King and Queen sat outside facing the public on their royal thrones and next to them sat Prince don Juan and the highest nobility of Castile, Catalonia, Valencia and Aragon, all of them beaming with happiness and anxious to greet the hero of the exploit that had caused so much rejoicing in all of Christendom. Finally, Columbus reached the royal stand. He looked like a Roman senator: tall and stately, gray-haired, with a modest smile on his dignified face betraying his pleasure and glory. He greeted them with ceremony and they stood up before him as before the highest nobleman. Then on bended knee, he kissed their hands; they kissed his hands and asked him to come sit next to them, a mark of honor Their Highnesses showed only to very few. Columbus told them quietly about the favors God had granted the Catholic kings, and in particular recounted his tribulations, the discovery, the greatness and abundance of the new land, his certainty that much more of it still lay undiscovered—thinking as he did that Cuba was part of the continent—showing what he had brought of wrought but unpolished gold pieces and nuggets of all sizes. He gave the King the assurance that the land was infinitely rich, which meant the royal treasury was replenished as surely as if all were already under lock and key. But what is more important, he described some customs of the Indians and praised them as simple and gentle people ready to receive the Faith, as could be seen from those Indians who were present.

The King and Queen heard this with profound attention and, raising their hands in prayer, sank to their knees in deep gratitude to God. The singers of the royal chapel sang the *Te Deum laudamus* while the wind instruments gave the response and indeed, it seemed a moment of communion with all the celestial joys. Who could describe the tears shed by the King, Queen and noblemen? What jubilation, what joy, what happiness in all hearts! How everybody began to encourage each another with plans of settling in the new land and converting people! They could tell how their sovereigns, especially Queen Isabella, valued the propagation of the Faith by showing with words and actions that their principal source of pleasure was having found such favor in the eyes of God as to have been allowed to support and finance (though with mighty few funds) the discovery of so many infidels ready for conversion. King Ferdinand and Queen Isabella's reign was blessed with many joys mixed with sad and bitter worries that God sent as proof of his singular care. They saw the birth of Prince don Juan, the Cross raised on the Alhambra in Granada after they had taken it at great cost, their daughters' weddings, the birth of Prince Miguel born to the Crown Princess, the arrival of Prince Philip, the birth of Philip's and Juana's son, that is, the Emperor Charles V who now triumphs over the world, and many other blessings. But I am sure that this miraculous discovery equaled any of those. Indeed, I believe it surpassed them in quality and quantity because it was founded on the glory of the divine name, the expected improvement of the holy Catholic Faith, and the conversion of infinite souls. Surely, they outnumber those in the kingdom of that small and narrow corner of Granada if one judges by the size of the New World.

Now, the pleasures caused by God, the pleasures that are founded in God and spiritual interests are always more intimate, more intense, more keenly felt and more lasting. They are greater, sweeter, more consoling and enduring when their cause is closer and more acceptable to God, resulting in more glory to His divine name, as this one is which could not be greater. What more universal pleasure had ever affected the whole Christian world, a pleasure which, surely, was caused by God's acceptance of the discovery? It was magnified by its happy coincidence with King Ferdinand's recovery from a nasty wound he had received from a madman who had stabbed him in the neck. But for the gold chain the King wore, the knife would have slit his throat, and all because the devil had given the man the notion that killing Ferdinand would make him King. His Highness came near death, and as he had just recovered, there were great feasts in the kingdom. I saw one in Seville that equaled in splendor the feast of Corpus Christi and was unparalleled in variety and novelty. Thus, divine Providence arranged it to give the monarchs and their kingdom ample material for rejoicing with the concurrence of two events of magnitude, and people of all stations celebrated them copiously. At last the admiral was given permission to retire for the day and he left for his quarters accompanied by a royal escort. . . .

80

While they awaited confirmation and approval from Rome of the Castilian King's supreme right to evangelize the Indies, the King and Christopher Columbus discussed the second expedition. The King and Queen were anxious to express gratitude for his services and they confirmed all the articles of the contract, for it was a contract, drawn up at the time of the siege of Granada in Santa Fe, before the admiral's first voyage. In exchange for the promise that he would discover new territory, Columbus received a certain sum of *maravedís* to equip his ships and promises of various privileges. The terms of the agreement are described in detail in Chapter 27. . . . Now in Barcelona, the King and Queen added a paragraph: "Since it pleased Our Lord to allow you to discover those islands and since we trust He will help you find others in that region of the Ocean, you requested confirmation of the contract drawn up in your favor, and in that of your sons and descendants. . . ." And below:

We, considering the risks you took to serve us in that entreprise, hereby confer upon you now and forever the titles of Admiral, Viceroy and Governor of the Islands and Mainland discovered and to be discovered by you. It is our wish to grant you and, later, your sons, descendants and heirs, one after the other, the title of Admiral of our Ocean as delineated by the demarcation line that goes from the Azores and the Cape Verde Islands, North to South, from pole to pole. Thus, everything beyond that line to the West belongs to us and we make you, your sons and your heirs our Admirals of it as we make you, your sons and your heirs Viceroys and Governors of said Islands and Mainland. We entrust you with all the powers—or almost all powers—you shall need to exercise your Admiralship, etc.

This document, written in Barcelona, May 28, 1493, contained all kinds of other favors and privileges as befits the generosity of such princely kings and such an outstanding servant. Columbus also received beautiful insignias, composed of the castles and lions from the royal coat of arms, as well as emblems from his own ancient lineage and others symbolizing his discovery; and all this was made into an escutcheon so handsome it stood out amongst the most beautiful in Spain. Two of the admiral's brothers were knighted and given titles of address: they were Bartolomé and Diego Columbus; the former became Adelantado of the Indies, and I knew both very well. While in Barcelona, the admiral was treated daily with great honor. They say that when the King rode his horse in the city he requested that Columbus ride on one side while on the other rode the Infante Fortuna of royal blood, and this privilege was granted to no other nobleman. The rest of the nobility followed suit, attending him hand and foot, sending him dinner invitations, some because they knew they would profit from the discovery that was affecting all of Spain, others because they wanted to hear details of the admiral's voyage, the new land, its people and its wealth.

The most illustrious Cardinal and Archbishop Pedro González de Mendoza was at that time riding the crest of his prestige in Castile. He was of high nobility like all those of his house, but he surpassed them all, for it seemed that he had the entire country united behind the King in peace, love and obedience. He especially held the nobles together, and this was most important because the King and Queen had just begun to reign after the terrible wars with Portugal; and after the death of Henry IV, the cardinal helped conciliate the diversity of opinions. For this reason, the monarchs loved and esteemed him very much and took him into their personal confidence. He was one of the handsomest and most imposing persons in Spain, being at the same time learned, hardworking, witty and sociable. His fame was such that if a nobleman bore the monarchs a grudge, the Cardinal always succeeded in placating him by solving the dispute and bringing the man back into the King's service. Sometimes the monarchs were reluctant to ignore a petitioner, pardon, or accede to a particular request. But the Cardinal resolved, reconciled and appeased everything, reducing strife to such well-regulated order that in all the kingdom he was called an angel of peace. He was understandably the most influential person at court, loved by all without the envy that so often accompanies a person so close to the most powerful men, because they knew his interventions always brought the best results for all. He kept his house with munificence, entertaining all the highest nobility sumptuously, and well he could, for he had a royal income of over 40 million which in those days was the equivalent of 100 million today.

There was not a single noble, however high-ranking, who did not feel flattered to eat at the Cardinal's table and enjoy his company and succulent food. He honored everyone according to his rank and had the God-given ability to please everyone, as he seemed to be the last word in matters of etiquette: forms of address, seating arrangements and such points of honor. It was said, and it is credible since no one criticized or gossiped about him, that he had never offended anyone. There was even a sort of proverb that said Where the Cardinal goes, there goes the court, because the court was not held without him. This most munificent lord and pontiff understood the meaning of Columbus's discovery; and as he saw that the rulers showered honor upon honor on the admiral, the Cardinal took him to his house one day, seated him in the most eminent place next to him, and for the first time Columbus was served a full course dinner with covered dishes and a food taster, and from then on everyone served him with the solemnity and pomp that his title of admiral commanded. . . .

84

The fleet sailed on Monday, October 7, 1493, passed the last of the Canary Islands and from then followed a more southerly course than on the first voyage, sailing an estimated 450 leagues by the twenty-fourth of October. The men saw a swallow, then some-what later, clouds and thunderstorms. They felt that the change in weather was caused by the proximity of land and the admiral had some sails lowered, giving orders to keep a close night watch. At sunrise on Sunday, November 3, they could see land from all the ships and were as happy as if Heaven had suddenly opened up before them. That was one of many islands; they named it Dominica, since they had seen it on Sunday. They sang the *Salve regina* as sailors do at sunrise and marveled at the scent of flowers blowing from the coast; they saw green parrots flying together like thrushes and screeching all the while. They reckoned that in the twenty-one days of their sailing from Gomera to Dominica they had traveled some 750 leagues. Dominica did not seem to have a harbor, therefore the admiral crossed over to a second island which he named after his ship, Marigalante. Columbus took possession of it in the name of the rulers of Castile and León before his crew and with due legal form.

On Monday they sailed on to a larger island they named Guadalupe. They found a harbor, anchored, and put out the boats to investigate a small village on the coast. However, they saw no one; all the inhabitants had fled to the mountains. For the first time they saw the parrotbirds called *guacamayos*, which are as big as roosters and have many colors, mostly red with a little blue and white. These birds do not speak or screech but from time to time they emit a very unpleasant shriek and one finds them only from the coast of Paria onward. They found a ship's beam in one of the huts and could not imagine how it had gotten there except by being blown all the way from the Canaries or from Hispaniola where Columbus had lost a ship on the first voyage.

On Tuesday, November 5, the admiral sent two boats to shore to see if they could take someone from whom they could learn about the island. They brought back two youths who, using sign language, indicated they had been brought from another island, called Boriquen and now San Juan, by the Caribs of Guadalupe, who meant to eat them, as was their custom. The boat returned for a group of Spaniards who had remained on shore and who were found with six women who were fleeing from the Caribs.

The admiral would not believe their story, neither did he care to provoke the natives, so he gave the women beads, mirrors and other objects of barter and sent them back. The Caribs stole these things from them within sight of the boats and the women again ran away, this time with two boys and a youth, all begging to be taken on board. From them the Spaniards learned the names of many other islands and the existence of a larger region that could be the mainland. When asked about Hispaniola—in their language *Haiti,* with the stress on the last syllable—they pointed in its direction, which pleased the admiral very much although he could have gone straight to it with the map he had drawn on his first voyage.

Columbus was ready to sail, but he was told that the inspector Diego Márquez, who also commanded a ship, had not yet returned from the shore where he had gone at sunrise with eight men and without permission. This angered Columbus but he sent a search party after him, which could not find him for the thickness of the woods. Columbus decided to wait the remainder of the day to make sure he would return and be able to find his way to Hispaniola. Again he sent men with trumpets and guns, but they got lost and finally returned without Márquez. Every hour felt like a year to Columbus, yet he could not decide to abandon his men for fear they would need protection against the Indians. He then ordered his ships supplied with wood and water and gave shore leave to those who wanted recreation or to wash their clothes. He sent the captain of a caravel, Alonso de Hojeda, with forty men to search for Márquez while at the same time investigating the territory. They said they found gum mastic, ginger, wax, incense, sandalwood and other aromatics, but to this day this has not been confirmed. They found cotton, but cotton grows in warm climate everywhere. They saw falcons, hawks, an abundance of kites, cranes, crows, pigeons, doves, flycatchers, geese, nightingales, partridge. Partridge, however, have been found only in Cuba. They said they had crossed twenty-six rivers within six miles and many times the water was waist deep, but it could have been one and the same winding river, just as the Panamá can be crossed over four hundred times. They, too, returned without Márquez.

Finally, on Friday, November 8, Márquez and his men reported back to the ship, saying they had gotten lost in those craggy mountains; but the admiral imprisoned Márquez and punished the others. Columbus went ashore and in a house there saw a lot of cotton both woven and ready to be woven, a new kind of loom, and many shrunken heads and human bones that must have been the natives' loved ones. It is unlikely that they were remnants of people they had eaten for, if they ate human flesh as much as is said, a house would not accommodate all the bones and heads—which there would be no reason to keep anyway, unless as relics of their most famous enemies, and all of this is pure guesswork. It seems that the houses were better built and better supplied than those found on the first voyage.

85

That Sunday, November 10, they sailed northwest along the coast of Guadalupe toward Hispaniola, finding islands on the way. They named one Monserrat from its resemblance to the rocks of Monserrat in Spain; another Santa María de la Redonda for being round, with straight clifflike walls that looked inaccessible; and another Santa María del Antigua, that had some twenty miles of coastline. There were many more islands to the north, elevated and green; they stopped near one they named San Martín which had so much coral that it stuck to the anchors. Columbus does not mention the color. On November 14, they anchored near an island they named Santa Cruz, and went ashore to see if they could find Indians and learn about the region from them. They came back with four women and two children, but on the way back to the ship, the boat met a canoe with four men and one woman who, seeing no other escape, fought to defend themselves and wounded two Christians; one of the woman's arrows even went through one of the shields. The boat ran into the canoe and turned it over. The Indians were captured, even though one of them kept shooting arrows from the water as easily as if he had been on dry land. They saw that one had been castrated and thought it was the work of Carib Indians who meant to fatten him like a capon before eating him.

As they proceeded toward Hispaniola, the islands became numerous; the admiral named the biggest one St. Ursula and the rest of them the Eleven Thousand Virgins. A little further on, a large island was named San Juan Baptista and this is the island we now call San Juan and the Indians, Boriquen. They anchored to the west of it and caught all kinds of fish, mostly shad, sardines and especially mullet, which is what abounds in all seas and rivers of the Indies. On land, they came to a village: the houses were well built of straw and wood; there was a plaza with a straight and clean street going down to the sea. The walls along the street were made of woven reed and above them grew a lacing of vines and greenery much like the orange or cedar groves of Valencia and Barcelona. There was a high resting place near the sea, with room for ten or twelve people and built in the same way; it must have belonged to their chief. Columbus does not mention having seen anybody there; perhaps they fled when they saw the ships. On Friday, November 22, Columbus arrived at the northern tip of Hispaniola, some fifteen miles beyond San Juan. He entrusted an Indian he had brought back from Castile with the mission of ingratiating himself with the Indians of the Samaná province by telling them about the splendor of the Castilian court. Although the Indian had volunteered, he disappeared and was not heard of any more; they surmised that he had died.

They reached the Cape of Angel, as I said in Chapter 67, and exchanged things with Indians who had come in their canoes to offer them food. When the fleet anchored at Monte-Christi and the crew went ashore, they saw the corpses of two dead men, one old and one younger; the former was found with a Castilian rope around his neck and his arms tied to a pole as if on a cross. They could not be identified as either Indians or Christians, but Columbus suspected the worst. Tuesday, November 26, he ordered another search for the thirty-nine Christians left in the fortress. Indians met them in great numbers, showing no sign of fear. On the contrary, they came up to the Spaniards and touched their shirts and jerkins, naming them in Spanish, and this Columbus took as a good sign boding well for his men.

On November 27 at midnight, they reached the Navidad harbor. A canoeful of Indians came shouting "Admiral, Admiral!" but they would not board the ship until the admiral appeared in

person and they had recognized him. Two Indians climbed on the ship, each with a *guayça* or gold mask, of fine workmanship, as presents from their King, Guacanagarí. When asked about the fate of the Christians, they answered that some had died of illness and others had gone inland, taking many women along with them. Columbus knew then that all had perished, but he kept his feeling to himself and took leave of the Indians, giving them a present of brass pots and other trivia for their King as well as a few trifling things for themselves, with which they happily took their leave.
. . .

88

Although the Marien province had good waters and harbors, it seemed to lack building materials; therefore, the admiral decided to backtrack in search of a good place to build a town. . . . He anchored in a large river port where there was an Indian village. Despite the exposure to northwest winds, he decided to leave the ships there and go ashore because the riverbanks looked green and fertile, and water could be brought to town by canals, thus making possible the construction of water mills and other commodities. Everyone was exhausted and worried, the horses were in bad shape; but everyone and everything found its way to a flat spot sheltered by a rock where they would build a fort, thus starting to found Isabela, the first Spanish settlement in the Indies named after Queen Isabella, for whom Columbus felt a deep devotion.

The admiral thanked God for the amenity of the land and rightly so, too, for the location is rich in stones, tiles and good earth for the making of bricks, besides being very fertile and beautiful. He hastened to proceed to the building of a fort to guard their provisions and ammunitions, of a church, a hospital and a sturdy house for himself; he distributed land plots, traced a common square and streets; the important people grouped together in a section of the planned township and everyone was told to start building his own house. Public buildings were made of stone; individuals used wood and straw for theirs. But the men were exhausted from such a long voyage and lack of familiarity with the sea, especially the working people, and building is hard manual labor. In addition, the climate was different, Spanish food was rationed and, because of their newness, the native products produced such ill effects that even the sturdiest peasant was ill with fever and many died for lack of medication.

All men were assigned the same manual tasks and it is hard work, as everyone knows who has been involved in the building of a town, especially in those early days. To make things worse, they were sad and frustrated, being so far from home and not having found the gold and riches everyone had longed for since the day of their departure from Spain. The admiral was sick like everyone else, for his task at sea had been immense and he had had none of the sleep so essential to pilots; nor was he a mere pilot sailing on chartered routes! His was a new route known only to himself; consequently, the responsibility for the whole fleet fell upon his shoulders, a responsibility unlike any other in that he had the whole world in suspense, waiting to see what would come of his enterprise, and he had the obligation to satisfy the King of Castile as well as all Christendom. Also, the monetary and human investment was greater this time than for the first voyage, so that the totality of these responsibilities weighed on his mind and compelled him to go on.

I am sure that all his cares, fears, torments and hardships defy all comparisons and that his illness was caused by them. All of us who followed his trials and tribulations must surely be awed by the concern God showed for this enterprise: not only did the admiral, leader of this divine exploit, sail on calm seas with favorable winds on his first voyage—which is extraordinary considering how stormy most crossings were afterwards, and I speak from experience—but he was never ill, either coming or going or when he had to negotiate at court, until after he had taught others how to navigate this ocean and until after he had deposited his people on these lands, as a pledge, so to speak, of what was to come later. . . .

92

Saturday, March 29, the admiral returned to Isabela and found everyone demoralized by the number of sick, dying and hungry, which, to the healthy among them, was a sad and tearful spectacle. The situation was aggravated by lack of food because rations shrank every day, and they blamed the admiral and the ship captains for having neglected precautions that would have kept the food from rotting on board when, in fact, the heat and humidity were as much a cause of food deterioration as anything else. Since they were running out of biscuits, the admiral wanted to build a water-powered mill to grind the wheat they had brought from Castile. But the nearest place was a good league away and the manual workers were for the most part too sick and weak to work. Thus, everyone had to pitch in, hidalgos and courtiers alike, all of them miserable and hungry, people for·whom having to work with their hands was equivalent to death, especially on empty stomachs.

The admiral had to use violence, threats and constraint to have the work done at all. As might be expected, the outcome was hatred for the admiral, and this is the source of his reputation in Spain as a cruel man hateful to all Spaniards, a man unfit to rule. Columbus's prestige declined steadily from then on, without one day of respite, until in the end nothing was left of it and he fell utterly into disgrace. This must be the reason for the Benedictine fray Buil's indignation against Columbus when, as a prelate, he freely reproached Columbus for the punishments he was inflicting on his men, as well as for the strictness of his rationing principles. The auditor Bernal de Pisa hated Columbus. And so did all other gentlemen of rank who thought of themselves as having some authority and accused him of forcing them to starve, as can be derived from the letters of explanation Columbus wrote to the King: these people had insisted on accompanying him and, once accepted by him, they brought along more servants than they could support.

As a foreigner, he had another strike against him in Castile, for Spaniards are arrogant by nature, especially when they are highborn. They had never liked Columbus; therefore, he had little credit with them. All this added to fray Buil's criticism and caused Columbus's downfall. For my part, my own observations and investigations into the matter make me wonder how in so little time—a mere three months, during which their hardships necessarily sprang from the novelty and difficulty of the enterprise itself—the admiral could have offended his Spaniards so as to deserve so much hatred and disfavor. But to return to the point, the Christians' misery grew stronger every day as the possibilities of relieving it diminished. . . . And what made it worse was the idea that they were going to die of starvation so far away, without any of the usual consolations afforded a dying man, not even someone to give them a glass of water. . . . So, then, many noblemen raised in comfort who had never known a day of hardship in their lives found their misery intolerable and some died in a state of great turmoil; even, it is feared, of utter despair.

For this reason, the residents of Hispaniola were terrified to go to Isabela after it was abandoned. Reports circulated about the horrible voices and frightening cries that could be heard day and night by anyone who happened to pass near the town. There was a story about a man walking through the deserted town and coming upon people lining the street on both sides who were dressed like the best of Spanish courtiers. The man, awed by this unexpected vision, greeted them and asked where they came from. But they kept silent, answering only by lifting a hand to their hats as a sign of greeting, and as they took off their hats, the whole head came off so that two files of beheaded gentlemen were left lining the street before they vanished altogether. The man almost died of fright, and the story was told quite frequently among the common people here.

To return to the point, the admiral received a message from Captain Pedro Margarite, of the fort of Santo Tomás, advising him that all the Indians were deserting their villages and that the Indian chief Caonabo was preparing to attack the fort. Columbus sent a reinforcement of seventy men—twenty-five as guards and the rest for the fort—chosen from among the healthiest sailors around him and given an additional supply of arms and food. Then he ordered Alonso de Hojeda to lead a squadron by land to the fort of Santo Tomás and spread terror among the Indians in order to show them how strong and powerful the Christians were. Hojeda was to take the direction of Vega Real because it was heavily populated; he was to see that Spaniards got used to the native foodstuffs, and he was to remain in charge of the fort in the post of governor.

93

On Wednesday, April 9, 1494, Alonso de Hojeda took some 400 men inland and, after crossing the river that the admiral had called Río del Oro (it must be the Mao river, for I know the land and the Indian names of rivers very well), Hojeda came upon a town, chained its cacique [native chief], his brother and one of his nephews and sent them as prisoners to the admiral. Moreover, he caught a relative of the cacique and had his ears cut off in the public square. The reason for this, it seems, is that the cacique had given five Indians to three Christians going from the fort to the ship to help them ford the river by carrying bundles of clothes. Supposedly, the Indians left the men stranded in the river and returned to the village; the cacique did not punish them but instead kept the clothes for himself. The cacique of the nearby town, trusting in the welcome he and his neighbor had given both the admiral and Hojeda on their first visit, decided to accompany the prisoners to plead with the admiral not to harm his friends. When the prisoners arrived and he with them, the admiral ordered a crier to announce their public decapitation. What a pretty way to promote justice, friendship, and make the Faith appealing—to capture a King in his own territory and sentence him, his brother and his nephew to death, for no fault of their own! Even if they were guilty, the crime was so benign it begged for moderation and extenuating circumstances. Besides, how could their innocence or guilt be proven? Hojeda captured them on arrival and nobody knew their language. The same lack of justice may be observed in Hojeda's order to cut off the ears of one of the cacique's vassals in his presence. What good tidings all over the land, and such a show of Christian gentility and goodness!

To return to the story, when the other cacique, who was perhaps related to the prisoner, heard the sentence, he begged the admiral to save them and with tears promised as best he could by sign language that nothing of the sort would ever happen again, and the admiral granted his plea by revoking the sentence. Whereupon a horseman arrived from the fort with news of insurrection: the cacique's subjects had surrounded five Christians and meant to kill them, but he and his horse managed to free them and chase some 400 Indians away, wounding some in pursuit and, I have no doubt, killing others as well. What a reputation for Christians who had been held but a short while back to be men come from Heaven! This was the first injustice committed against the Indians under the guise of justice and the beginning of the shedding of blood which was to flow so copiously from then on all over this island, as I will show later.

No man in his right mind would doubt that the cacique and his people had a right to declare a just war against the Christians, and that their behavior toward the five Christians was indeed the beginning of their exercise of that right. With their lord taken away prisoner to the ship, perhaps they meant to ransom him with these Christian lives. What convincing reasons did the admiral have when he came to this town, in the few hours he was there and especially not knowing the language, for the cacique not to believe he was acting well by allowing free passage on his land and welcoming him as he did? After all, the admiral had come without permission, and Christians were such a fierce-looking novelty, trespassing with arms and horses that seemed so ferocious that the mere sight of them made the inhabitants tremble and fear they would be swallowed alive! In truth, this was an offense which everyone in the world today would take as such and seek revenge, on the strength of natural law as well as *iure gentium*. Also, would not the cacique think himself superior to the admiral and his Christians? And to Hojeda also, who condemned the Indian thief for a dubious theft, acting as a supreme judge on foreign soil under foreign jurisdiction.

The worst and gravest crime was to capture a King living peacefully in his own domain, and to chain him was an ugly and atrocious crime. Reason itself says it was not right to trespass, not right to do it in a warlike manner, and not right that the admiral leave the ship without first sending an embassy to notify the Indian kings of his intention to visit them, asking permission to do so and sending gifts, as he had been instructed to do by the King of Castile. The admiral should have taken pains to bring love and peace and to avoid scandalous incidents, for not to perturb the innocent is a precept of evangelical law whose messenger he was. Instead, he inspired fear and displayed power, declared war and violated a jurisdiction that was not his but the Indians'; and it seems to me this is not using the door but a window to enter a house, as if the land were not inhabited by men but by beasts.

Truly, I would not dare blame the admiral's intentions, for I knew him well and I know his intentions were good. But, as I said above in Chapter 41, the road he paved and the things he did of his own free will, as well as sometimes under constraint, stemmed from his ignorance of the law. There is much to ponder here and one can see the guiding principle of this whole Indian enterprise, namely, as is clear from the previous chapters, that the admiral and his Christians, as well as all those who followed after him in this land, worked on the assumption that the way to achieve their desires was first and foremost to instill fear in these people, to the extent of making the name Christian synonymous with terror. And to do this, they performed outstanding feats never before invented or dreamed of, as, God willing, I will show later. And this is contrary and inimical to the way that those who profess Christian benignity, gentleness and peace ought to negotiate the conversion of infidels. . . .

96

The admiral decided to leave Santa María Island to explore the multitude of other islands of whose existence he had learned from an Indian there. Also, he wanted to keep out of danger; the food supply was running low; and he was anxious to see the people and the town he had left unfinished on Hispaniola, which worried him night and day. To make provision of water and food, he stopped at an island about 30 leagues in circumference called Evangelista, located some 700 leagues away from Dominica. I think that island is the one we call the Island of the Pines today, bordering Havana north to south; it is the only island of that size to the south of Cuba, which shows how close he was—a matter of 35 to 36 leagues—to completing the exploration of Cuba. He corroborates this in a letter to the King, when he speaks of the discovery of 333 leagues of Cuban coast and, measuring the trip according to the laws of astronomy, says: "From the tip of Cuba, called Fin de Oriente and by another name Alpha and Omega, he sailed westward from the South past the 10th hour, so that when the sun set for him it was two hours past rising in Cádiz (Spain). He said he could not be mistaken for there was an eclipse of the moon on September 14; he had good instruments and the sky was very clear that night." Those are his very words.

To return to the story, on Friday, June 13, Columbus sailed southward out of the crowded group of islands and, taking a channel that looked deeper and less encumbered, found it blocked and the ships surrounded by land as in a corral. The crew turned white with fear and apprehension at being exposed to danger and lack of provisions; it is likely that their anguish was great, but that of the admiral was twice as great. Yet he comforted them as best he could and succeeded in turning his course and finding a way out, steering toward Evangelista Island where fresh water was available. Wednesday, June 25, he sailed northwest to investigate a group of smaller islands some five leagues away. He came upon a sea of green and white streaks that looked like shallows, although it was two fathoms deep. Seven leagues later they came upon a very white sea which even looked all curdled; and another seven leagues further on, five fathoms deep, the water was so dark it looked like ink; and this was the path that led him to Cuba. The sailors were afraid of these color differences because they had never seen or experienced them before and they were frightened of drowning in them. From Cuba, the admiral sailed eastward, with little wind and in shallow channels, writing his diary as usual.

On June 30 his ship ran aground and because the anchors and cables could not pull the ship from the poop, it was necessary to drag her on the sand from the prow, which caused much damage. This, in addition to uneven winds, the irregularity of the course caused by the shallows and channels, and nightly downpours, made them sail the white waters at random and caused the admiral much anguish and fatigue. They returned to their starting point in Cuba, smelling the same sweet scents as they had before—and it is true that the air is more heavily scented here than near other islands. We think the scent comes from the storax tree we used to smell almost every morning when we were exploring the island; it is a wood the Indians used to burn.

On July 7, the admiral went ashore to hear Mass. An old cacique who seemed to rule the province arrived during the ceremony. When he saw the priest's rituals, the Christians' signs of adoration, reverence and humility, and the respectful way they treated the admiral, he assumed that the admiral was their chief and, presenting a pumpkin-like bowl of native fruit to him, squatted beside him—Indians "sit" in this fashion when not sitting on a dais—and held the following discourse:

"You have come a powerful man to these lands unknown to you, and you have inspired great fear wherever you have gone. I want to tell you that we believe in the life hereafter. Departing souls go in two directions: one is bad, full of darkness, where those who do evil to men go; the other is good and happy, and peace-loving people go there. Therefore, if you feel you must die and believe that every man answers for his deeds after death, you will not harm those who do not harm you. And this ceremony is very good, because it seems to me you are giving thanks to God by means of it."

They say he added that he had been to Hispaniola, Jamaica and southern Cuba, and had seen their native lords dressed like priests. The admiral understood the speech through his Indian interpreters, especially one named Diego Columbus, an Indian he had taken to Castile and brought back with him. The admiral marveled at the Indian's wisdom which, to be sure, excelled that of any pagan philosopher. He answered he had learned this a good while back, that is, how the soul is eternal and evil ones go to Hell while good ones go to a place Christians call Heaven, adding how pleased he was to find out that the Indians believed it also. He said he had been sent by his King and Queen, the wealthy and powerful rulers of Castile, for no other purpose than to gather information about these parts, especially if it was true they were inhabited by man-eating cannibals or Caribs and if so, to prevent them from doing such evil, while defending and honoring the good people who lived in peace.

The wise old man heard these words with tears of pleasure and said that, if it were not for his wife and children, he would go to

Castile with the admiral. He was given some trinkets and sank to his knees with signs of admiration for men of such quality that he was not quite sure whether they had been born on earth or in Heaven. I took this from the writings of Hernando Columbus, the admiral's son, and from the more lengthy account in Pedro Martyr's *Decadas*, for Don Hernando was only a small boy at the time of the event. It is likely that Pedro Martyr heard it directly from the admiral himself, as he heard many of the things he describes, because he resided at court and was one of the King's protégés. The old man's speech is not surprising either since all Indians believe in life after death, especially the Cuban Indians, and we will have occasion to return to this topic later, if God wills. . . .

107

Columbus arrived in Isabela on September 29, 1494, and before his return to Spain, fray Buil, Pedro Margarite and other noblemen went to Castile on the ships that had brought the admiral's brother Bartolomé. They informed the King that he should not entertain any hopes of acquiring wealth in the Indies, for the whole affair was a joke, there simply was no gold on the island. They spoke so well that the King began to conceive of Columbus's enterprise as a waste of money, which was reinforced by the fact that these gentlemen had not brought any gold with them. He was not thinking, of course, that gold does not grow on trees but in mines under the ground and that nowhere in the world has gold ever been extracted without toil unless it be stolen from someone else's chests. Columbus had brought ample proof of the existence of gold both when he returned from his first voyage and when he dispatched Antonio de Torres back to Castile with the gold his men had extracted and the gold given him by Guacanagarí. He was busy founding Isabela when fray Buil and Pedro Margarite left for Castile, and he had been there four months and a few days; how, then, could he have mistreated the Spaniards and what was his bad government; why did his star begin to decline? God only knows.

In the four ships taking Antonio de Torres back to Castile with 500 Indian slaves, there were Spaniards angry with Columbus who worked hard against him at court. And while Columbus was busy unjustly harming the Indians, a scheme was being prepared that meant his first severe reprimand and, indeed, the first and bitter trick against him. He left Isabela on March 24, 1495, at the precise time when the King was sending one of his servants, the Sevillian Juan Aguado, to spy on him, giving Aguado strong letters of recommendation. Aguado began by throwing cold water on the admiral's pleasure and prosperity so that, while Columbus was tyrannically offending the Indians instead of converting them, Aguado was arranging the beginning of his punishment. That is how God operates and that is why all of us must take care not to offend Him, praying that He enlighten us as to our sins so that we may mend our ways. So then, the King equipped four ships with the things the admiral had requested for the people who earned the King's money on the island, and he made Aguado their captain, giving him instructions and a letter that read: "The King and Queen.—Knights, squires, and all of you in the Indies: we are sending our servant Juan Aguado who will speak for us to you. We command you to trust and believe him. From Madrid, April 9, 1495. I the King.—I the Queen. By order of Their Highnesses, Hernandálvarez."

Aguado arrived in October 1495, when the admiral was engaged in the war against King Caonabo, in the province of Maguana where later on a Spanish town was built which still exists today, named San Juan de la Maguana. Aguado took on airs of authority and liberties he did not have when he meddled in juridical matters such as taking prisoners, reprimanding the admiral's officers, and treating the admiral's brother Bartolomé, then acting governor, with little respect. Then Aguado went looking for the admiral. They say that whenever they met Indians he would tell them a new admiral was coming because he had come to kill the old one. And since Indians around Isabela and Vega Real had been much aggrieved by the admiral's slaughters and the gold tribute he had imposed upon them—work which they found unbearable—it seems likely that the Indians rejoiced at hearing this. Poverty, unjust servitude and oppression cause people to thirst for novelties, because they are so intent on leaving their misery and so hopeful that something new will better their lot that they fail to think how that something new might bring about worse disasters.

For this reason, there were large gatherings of Indian chiefs, especially in the house of Manicaotex, a chief I knew very well and for a long time, who ruled the land near the great Yaquí river, about three leagues from the present city of Concepción. They discussed the benefits that might result from a new admiral since the old one so mistreated them; but they were mistaken, for every Spaniard who ever went to the Indies added new injuries to the old ones and drove them infernally until they were extinguished.

It happened also that in 1495 some Sevillian sailors and other people asked permission to come explore the Indies. The King granted it but specified: one, that every ship leaving for the Indies must pass through the King's officials in Cádiz for the appointment of one or two overseers per ship; two, that each one transport the tenth part of royal cargo free of charge; three, that said cargo was to be unloaded on Hispaniola; four, that they pay the King one-tenth of everything they should happen to bring back; five, that each leave a security with the King; six, that the admiral must be allowed one out of every seven ships for his personal use. There was also a clause specifying that merchants selling goods to the Spaniards on Hispaniola were not to tax their merchandise. The document was dated from Madrid, April 10, 1495. . . .

112

Return: Second Voyage, 1496

Columbus leaves Hispaniola in charge of his brothers Bartolomé and Diego, appoints Francisco Roldán chief mayor of the island, and sails for Cádiz.

No sooner had the admiral arrived in Cádiz that he started for Burgos via Seville. The King was in Perpignan, where Spain was fighting the King of France. The Queen was in Laredo or in the Basque country, taking leave of the Infanta doña Juana, who was on her way to Flanders as Archduchess of Austria for her marriage to Prince Philip, son of the Emperor Maximilian; the royal couple returned to Castile later, their son Charles is now our lord and

Emperor. Doña Juana had a fleet of 130 ships for the occasion. The King and Queen returned shortly to Burgos where they prepared for the arrival of Prince Philip's sister Margarita who was to marry the Infante don Juan. The admiral paid his respects to Their Highnesses; they were very glad to see him and honored him greatly. He gave them a detailed account of how he had left the island, how he had discovered Cuba, Jamaica, etc., and where the gold was to be found in grains of all sizes varying from gold dust to grains the size of a walnut. He also gave the monarchs Indian masks with eyes and ears made of gold, parrots and other things which pleased them very much.

The monarchs asked many questions; Columbus satisfied them —we shall not waste time mentioning Aguado's reports since little attention was paid them. Columbus said he hoped to sail again, this time to discover the continent although, to tell the truth, he thought he had discovered it already when he found Cuba. The monarchs said they would be pleased to see the list of his requirements for the third voyage. They were: eight ships, two for carrying merchandise to Hispaniola—he was anxious to please the Christians there so that the whole Indian enterprise would prosper and become famous—and six for his own use; a plan to leave 330 persons on Hispaniola on a permanent, though voluntary, basis (all in the King's pay), who would be distributed as follows: 40 squires, 100 peons as soldiers and laborers, 30 sailors, 30 cabin boys, 20 goldsmiths, 50 farmers, 10 gardeners, 20 handymen and 30 women—these were to receive wages of 600 *maravedís* and a fanega of wheat per month, plus 12 *maravedís* a day for food; a plan to establish trade so that merchants would receive a loan from the King if they guaranteed to engage in trade and nothing else, the King to bear the risks of transportation and the merchants to keep the proceeds after reimbursement of the loan; as for the merchandise itself, it was to be taxed according to the admiral's judgment—the wine tax was fixed at 15 *maravedís* an azumbre [approx. 2 liters] and the meat tax at 8 *maravedís* per pound; a plan to maintain friars and clergymen to administer the sacraments to Christians and engage in the conversion of Indians, as well as maintain a physician, a pharmacist, an herbalist, and musicians to provide entertainment to the residents of the island.

. . . To replace those who were unhappy on the island and wanted to return to Castile, the admiral thought of recruiting people in Spain. But he feared that the King would restrict the funds reserved for wages and he invented a plan designed to save the King money by not paying the recruits. Thus, he requested that the King pardon Spanish criminals in exchange for a few years' service on Hispaniola, and the King issued two letters on the subject. One said that since, hopefully, the presence of Christians would spread the Catholic Faith in the Indies, and since it pleased him to show clemency, he entreated all delinquent men and women to join the admiral and these were the criminals committed for homicide, assault and other offenses except heresy, lèse-majesté, treason, arson, murder with fire and arrows, counterfeit, sodomy and contraband. The death penalty would be lifted in exchange for two years of service; other penalties required only one year, after which time they would be allowed to return acquitted to Castile. I have met some of these people on Hispaniola; I even knew one whose ears had been cut off for a crime in Castile, and his conduct here was beyond reproach. The other letter notified the courts of the kingdom that prisoners condemned to exile or work in the mines should be exiled to Hispaniola instead of the ordinary places.

The two letters were signed from Medina del Campo on June 22, 1497; they also specified that the admiral was entitled to distribute land, forests and rivers to the residents, who promised to remain on Hispaniola for a period of four years, and that these grants were to be used for residences as well as the cultivation of vineyards, olive groves, cane fields, etc., and the construction of mills and other private and public buildings. Except when a fence surrounded a property, the rest of that land was to be free from civil and criminal jurisdiction and used as public pasture or the raising of common crops. Brazilwood, gold, silver and other metals found on such land was the King's property. The costs of the war and royal weddings made the grant of six million *maravedís*—four million for expenses, two million for wages—very difficult indeed, but it was nothing compared to the difficulties the admiral experienced in drawing that amount when the time came for him to use it [on his third voyage, 1498]. . . .

163

Before proceeding any further, let us return to the point when Columbus discovered the continent at Paria and dispatched five caravels to Castile with the news and some samples of pearls found there. Alonso de Hojeda was in Castile then and so was my uncle, Francisco de Peñalosa. Hojeda learned that Columbus had discovered the continent and saw the map representing Paria, together with its description as an "island" that was likely to be the continent. The Bishop of Badajoz, Juan de Fonseca, granted him the permission to come and explore this land and affixed only his own signature to the document, omitting that of the King—it is difficult to believe that the King had given the Bishop that much power. In 1495, Columbus had complained to the King about the unrestrained granting of visas to the many who were asking for them. Therefore, I am surprised that the Bishop failed to consult the King with respect to Hojeda, unless it be that he was an impulsive man and had always disliked the admiral, which is not a good enough reason, since no one, however powerful, would have dared to act over the King's head. Be that as it may, the Bishop granted Hojeda a visa, restricting his travel to territory other than that belonging to the King of Portugal as well as that discovered by Columbus up to 1495.

Here is another problem: given that restriction, why did the Bishop not include Columbus's latest discovery of Paria, the land described on the chart sent to the King? Surely, I can give no answer for that. Hojeda easily found people in Seville to equip four ships for his journey; many were greedy and anxious to follow the thread the admiral had placed in their hands when he opened the tightly shut doors of the ocean. According to Americo Vespucci, Hojeda sailed from Santa María or Cádiz on May 20, 1497; but this is a lie—he sailed in 1499—told in order to claim the discovery of the continent for himself, thus usurping the glory and honor due to Columbus alone, as I have already proved in Chapter 139. I was trying to establish whether Vespucci had tacitly denied the admiral's discovery of the continent by attributing it to himself alone, but I had not yet seen Vespucci's writings nor had I any of the documentary proofs I was to find later. Now I can state with certainty that Vespucci was in bad faith and deliberately sought to steal the admiral's glory. It was already clear to me from the number of eyewitnesses that Columbus had discovered Paria; consequently, no one had been there before him, as Pedro Martyr corroborates in his *Decadas*, I, 8, 9. In addition, Hojeda himself reports that, having seen the chart in Castile, he explored Paria, the land already discovered by Columbus. Vespucci figures among Hojeda's list of pilots, together with Juan de la Cosa, and as I conjectured, he went also as a merchant who had invested money in Hojeda's armada. I then supposed what Vespucci confirmed in the account he wrote of his first voyage, namely, that he landed on the territory the Indians call Paria and in an encounter with the Indians there they lost one man and twenty-two were wounded.

This incident occurred in 1499. The admiral discovered the continent at Paria; Hojeda followed and Vespucci was with Hojeda who said they landed on Paria. The admiral had sailed from San Lúcar on May 30, 1498; Hojeda and Vespucci must have sailed from Cádiz in 1499, because if Columbus left on May 30 and Hojeda on May 20, and Columbus sailed first, it is impossible that Hojeda should leave in 1498. It cannot be argued that Hojeda sailed first, since Columbus was the first to arrive and discover Paria, which proves that Vespucci was mistaken when he said he sailed in 1497. He sailed in 1499, and it is clear that Columbus discovered the continent.* It surprises me that the admiral's son, Hernando, who is such a wise man, did not notice how Americo Vespucci usurped the glory of his father, especially since he had documentary proof of it, as I know he does.

164

This, then, was the long premeditated plan of Americo Vespucci to have the world acknowledge him as the discoverer of the largest part of the Indies. Let us continue the story of Hojeda, who

---

* "Which should have been called Columba and not as it is unjustly called, America" (Ch. 139, p. 40).

left Cádiz with the pilot Juan de la Cosa and other people who had gained experience in the admiral's various expeditions, as well as with Americo Vespucci who, as I said, went either as a merchant or an experienced seaman. They sailed West to the Canaries and proceeded South until, twenty-seven days later, they spotted land which, as it happened, was the continent. They anchored about one league from the shore, put out the boats, armed themselves and rowed to shore, where an infinite number of naked people stood gaping before fleeing to the woods, despite the Christians' signs of peace and friendship.

Since they had anchored on the beach, they returned to the ships to look for a safe harbor and found one two leagues down the coast and saw people lining the banks, gathered there to see such a novelty. Forty armed men went ashore, calling to the people and flashing mirrors and Castilian beads until some of the Indians dared approach to take what was offered them. At nightfall the Spaniards returned to the ships and the Indians to their villages, but the next morning the beach was full of Indians, men, women and children happily staring at the ship. And when the Christians put the boats out to sea, some swam up to meet them. The trusting Indians welcomed our men, milling around them as if they had known them all their lives. Those Indians are a people of medium height and well proportioned; their faces are too wide to be handsome; their color is reddish blond like that of a lion's mane, and if they had worn clothes, they would have looked almost as white as we. They shave all the hairs off their body and are such an agile people they can swim two leagues at a stretch, especially the women. Our people thought they were a warrior tribe because they had very sharp weapons and were excellent marksmen; they always took their wives to battle as cooks and carriers. They have no kings or captains but call on one another when they need to fight an enemy, who is usually an Indian of another language group who has killed one of them. In that case the aggrieved—the oldest member of the family—convokes his neighbors to help him against the enemy.

They eat whenever they feel like it, a little at a time, sitting on the ground, and they eat fish or meat in clay dishes. They sleep in cotton hammocks of the same kind we described when speaking of

Hispaniola. They treat women so decently no one in the world would mind seeing them together; but, on the other hand, they think nothing of urinating and passing wind in public. Marriage laws are nonexistent: men and women alike choose their mates and leave them as they please, without offense, jealousy or anger. They multiply in great abundance; pregnant women work to the last minute and give birth almost painlessly; up the next day, they bathe in the river and are as clean and healthy as before giving birth. If they tire of their men, they give themselves abortions with herbs that force stillbirths, covering their shameful parts with leaves or cotton cloth; although on the whole, Indian men and women look upon total nakedness with as much casualness as we look upon a man's head or at his hands. In addition, they bathe frequently and keep very clean.

They do not seem to have any religion; at least, they have no temples or prayer houses. They live in large communal bell-shaped buildings—housing up to 600 people at one time, and eight of the buildings have a capacity of 10,000 people—made of very strong wood and roofed with palm leaves. It seems that they change locale every eight years to avoid illness caused by the vapors of an excessively heated atmosphere. They prize bird feathers of various colors, beads made of fish bones, and green and white stones with which they adorn their ears and lips, but they put no value on gold and other precious things. They lack all manner of commerce, neither buying nor selling, and rely exclusively on their natural environment for maintenance. They are extremely generous with their possessions and by the same token covet the possessions of their friends and expect the same degree of liberality. A sign of great friendship among them is the sharing of wives and daughters; parents think it an honor when someone indicates that he wants their daughter, even though she may be a virgin, because it seals a friendship.

They bury their dead in various ways. Some place water and food at the head of the grave for the journey of the dead, and show no emotion whatever—they do not even cry—for the departed. Others examine the sick and when it seems to them that someone is nearing death, they lay him in a hammock and hang it between trees in the woods, dancing and singing around it the whole day. At nightfall they place water and a bowl of food at the head of the hammock, enough for three or four days, and leave there never to return again. If the sick man recovers and comes back home, they receive him with great ceremony, but I suppose they are very few since they are left sick and unattended. They cure the sick by waiting until fever reaches its highest point, then dipping the sick man in cold water, washing him well, then warming him for a good two hours near a huge fire built for that purpose. When the body is warm, they force the person to run back and forth for a while and then put him to sleep. Many are saved and cured this way. They are given to fasting, sometimes spending three or four days without food or drink, and to bleeding themselves. Not in the arm but in the calf of the leg and in the back. They induce vomit by chewing certain herbs, and have a rich blood and a phlegmatic humor caused by their diet of herbs, roots and fish. They make bread with the yucca root; they seem not to know grain. They seldom eat meat unless it be the flesh of their enemies; they were astonished to see that Christians do not eat their enemies.

The Spaniards did not find much gold or other valuable metals there, but they attributed this to their inability to speak the various languages spoken in that province, whereby they might have asked about gold; they did, however, praise the natural beauty of that land very much. Americo Vespucci relates all this in the account of his first voyage. I doubt that he understood so much in the few days he was there, especially since he admits to not having known the language—about the eight-year migrations for example, or the voluntary abortions by women tired of their men, or the absence of laws governing marriage and the ruling of the tribe. Consequently, he is credible when he describes what he saw, such as exterior characteristics—the color of the Indians, their food, their nakedness, their agility as swimmers; as for the rest, it reads like pure fiction. . . .

174

When we examine this world, experience shows us the truth of what the Scriptures teach us about God's infallible Providence, that is to say, all things aim at proving and preserving the Truth, as we can see from David: *Qui custodit veritatem in saeculum,* and Esdras: *Veritas manet et invalescit in aeternum et vivit et obtinet in saecula saeculorum.* The Indians are a docile and good-natured people, accustomed to the practice of moral virtue more than any other nation; and this makes them better suited to indoctrination in the Catholic Faith, provided it be taught them according to the principles established by Christ. For this Truth to become manifest, divine Providence ordained not only that Castilian servants of God as well as secular explorers greedy to amass temporal wealth prove it by experience, but also that the Portuguese—friars, laymen and people of all stations and professions—admit to the world that the Indians descend from Adam our father, and this suffices for us to respect the divine principle of charity toward them, since we were so privileged as to be brought to Christianity before them.

So then, the Portuguese realized the moral and spiritual disposition of the natives on the continent as soon as they arrived in 1500 and they testified to it in writing, as our Castilians do. In this and the next chapters, let us see what the Portuguese priests of the Company of Jesus—who came many years later—had to say about it in letters to their fellow priests in Portugal.

The information I can give you about Brazil, my dearest brothers, is that it has 1,000 leagues of coastline and is inhabited by naked people except in some remote regions, where I am located, where women wear cotton clothes like gypsies to protect themselves against the cold. The climate is quite temperate but frequent torrential rains make it humid and keep the vegetation green, which accounts for the coolness. Some regions are harsher than this. The natives eat the various fruits growing wild here and I think we could cultivate some Old World plants with great success; I've seen vineyards that yield two crops a year, yet the grape is scarce because of ants and other vermin. Citrus fruit, on the other hand, grows abundantly and tastes as good as the ones over there. The food staple is mandioca; they grind it into a flour which we all eat and which, mixed with corn flour, takes the place of wheat bread. Fish, seafood, *matos,* geese, oxen, cows, sheep, goats and chicken are also plentiful.

There are various castes of heathens: the *goyanazes* and *carijos;* the latter is the best of the coastal tribes. Two Castilian friars lived among them not too long ago and the Indians learned the doctrine so well that they had convent-like houses for women and retreat houses like monasteries for men, until the devil sent a ship full of raiders and most of them were taken captive. We tried to apprehend the raiders and actually caught a few whom we intend to send back home; one of our own fathers was caught with the group. Another caste is the *caymures,* who inhabit the mountains and live isolated from the Christians; when they have an occasion to see us, they are surprised and call us brothers because, like them, we wear beards— other Indians shave the eyebrows, and even their eyelids. They have pierced underlips and nostrils and look like devils because they wear bone ornaments in the holes. Some, especially the sorcerers, have these things all over their faces. They are a giant tribe who use the strongest bows and clubs; with a bow in one hand and a club in the other, they make mincemeat of their enemies and run back to the woods at great speed; thus everyone fears them very much.

Two castes so far communicate with us: the *tupeniques* and the *tupinambas.* They live in large palm houses, up to fifty families per house. They sleep in cotton blanket-like nets near a fire they keep burning all night to protect themselves against the cold and evil spirits, which is the reason they always carry lit torches when they have to travel in the dark. They worship no gods other than thunder, which they call *tupana,* meaning something like "divine object"; therefore we have no other word to use to make them understand God but "Father Tupana."

These Indians have the following ritual: every few years sorcerers come from far away and pretend to bring holiness. The streets are cleaned before their arrival and while groups are out to meet them with songs and dances, women go from door to door by twos and confess their marital failings to one another, asking forgiveness of their neighbors in this manner. The sorcerer arrives with great fanfare, goes to a dark house and dons a mask—a pumpkin with a painted face—because it facilitates his trickeries. He changes his voice to that of a child and tells them that work is unnecessary: food will grow and come to their houses by itself, tools will go out digging and arrows will fly out to the woods and bring back the game. He predicts victory over their enemies, promising abundant captives to supply them with meat. He promises longevity and eternal youth: old women will turn into maidens and daughters will be free for all. And so he goes on, promising and deceiving them to the point that they believe a divinity is actually in the pumpkin. The sorcerer ends his monologue and people in the assembly—women especially—begin to shake in such a way as to appear possessed by the devil, and indeed they are. Foaming at the mouth, they throw themselves on the ground until the sorcerer soothes them by giving them holiness. They think it wrong not to have these reactions, and the ritual ends by showering gifts on the sorcerer. They use much witchcraft in cases of illness too.

Sorcerers are our worst opponents. Sometimes they persuade the sick that we put scissors and knives in their bodies to kill them. When Indians assemble for battle, they take omens from birds as well as consulting sorcerers, and when they bring home a captive enemy tied by the neck, they rejoice a great deal. The prisoner is given the girl of his choice or the chief's daughter, and is fattened like a pig until judged ripe for killing, at which time everyone comes from the neighboring villages to see the fiesta. On the appointed day, they bring him out to a clearing with a rope tied around his waist, after having bathed him well the day before. An Indian in full regalia goes out to speak with him about his ancestors and the captive replies that valiant men do not fear death, that in his day he too killed his enemies, and that his relatives remain to avenge his death. They kill him and cut off his thumb, it being the finger he used to shoot his bow; then they cut him to pieces and eat them roasted or boiled.

When someone dies, they place food and a clean blanket on the grave site. They believe the dead return to eat and sleep upon their graves, usually a rounded cave or, if the person is of high rank, a straw hut. They have no knowledge of Heaven and Hell, but instead believe that the body rests in a beautiful place subject to the laws of nature. They own everything in common and share all they have, especially in matters of food, and they live from day to day making no provisions for the future and amassing no wealth. Daughters bring no dowry to their husbands, but rather it is the husband who is forced to work for his in-laws. When a Christian visits them, they feed him well and give him a clean cotton blanket. Wives are faithful to their husbands. They remember the Flood but have a false idea of it: They think that water covered the earth, a woman and a man climbed a pine tree and waited until the water receded before coming down to procreate the human race. Their scarcity of words makes it difficult for us to explain our religion to them but we manage as best we can, even though sometimes we must take roundabout ways to explain things. They have trouble understanding abstractions; they often ask me whether God has a head, a body, a wife, and whether he eats and dresses.

They claim that St. Thomas, whom they call Zome, was here once; their ancestors told them so and showed them his footprints near the river. I went to look at them and I saw them, four footprints, toes and all, with my own eyes; the river swells but never washes them away. The story is that the footprints were caused as he fled from pursuing Indians. But the waters divided to let him pass, and so did the forests, until he reached India, leaving his pursuers on the other side of the river shooting arrows that turned back upon themselves. They say he promised he would return, and others tell this story as if in mockery. I wish that he might look upon them now from Heaven and intercede for them with God so that they may come to know Him, as we wish they would.

All this is from the letter of a Portuguese priest. . . .

181

RETURN: THIRD VOYAGE, 1500

The admiral and his brothers were taken as prisoners to two caravels that left Santo Domingo for Castile in early October 1500 and, after an unusually fast voyage, arrived in Cádiz on November 20 or 25. Columbus and his brothers were treated well on board the ship; Alonso de Vallejo and the master of the caravel *La Gorda*, Andrés Martín, even tried to remove their iron chains, but the admiral refused, saying only the monarchs could do this. It seems that André Martín dispatched a secret message to the King from Cádiz, hoping to counterinfluence the reports of Bobadilla by presenting Columbus's letters before the formal procedures got under way. I have been unable to find any of these letters written from Cádiz to the King and Queen. He might have thought that the King himself had ordered his imprisonment, or again, it is possible that he wanted the King to learn of his affront from other sources. However, he [Columbus] did write a long letter to the governess of Prince don Juan [doña Juana de Torres], who liked Columbus and protected him by influencing the Queen in his favor. The letter shows the plain and simple quality of his style, as well as how little attention was paid at that time to the vanity of titles which are so much in use in Spain today.

Most virtuous lady:
If complaining against the world is unusual for me, the world's practice of mistreating me is not new. It has given me a thousand

battles and I have resisted them all until now, when neither arms nor warning have availed me. I have been cruelly cast down by it. Hope in Him who created all men sustains me; His aid has always been at hand; and not too long ago, when I had succumbed, He lifted me with His right hand, saying "O man of little faith, arise, for it is I; fear not." I came with such love to serve these princes and I have offered them a service unheard of and never seen before. Our Lord made me the messenger of and showed me the way to the new Heaven and earth which He had announced to Isaiah, and of which St. John speaks in the Apocalypse. Incredulity struck everyone except our lady the Queen, who was enlightened and made to inherit it all as His beloved daughter; I went to take possession of this in her royal name. They sought to hide their ignorance behind petty arguments, inventing obstacles and fussing at the expenses. Her Highness, on the other hand, defended the enterprise as best she could. Discussions lasted seven years, and it took nine years to accomplish outstanding and memorable things which are not being recognized.

Now I am here, and I am in such trouble that the basest man thinks nothing of abusing me and the world will in time praise the man who abstained from abuse, thinking it virtuous to abstain. If I had stolen the Indies and the territory next to them from St. Peter's altar and given them to the Moors, I would have made no greater enemies in Spain. Who would believe this from such a noble country? I would give up the whole business if it were not for the honor of the Queen and God, and for their encouragements that I should continue. I went again to this hitherto unknown world to soothe somewhat the grief death had brought upon her [caused by the death of Prince don Juan], and no wonder this is held in little esteem since I am the one who discovered it! I thought my discovery of Paria would ease things a bit because of the gold and pearls I had already found on Hispaniola: I had people fish for pearls who agreed that I would return for them; I understood they would be measured by the bushel. But this turned out like everything else. Had I sought my own interest, I would not have lost them, nor would I have lost my honor nor the gold I had gathered and brought back at the cost of so many deaths and painful labor. Going to Paria, I found almost half the people in Hispaniola in a state or rebellion against me; they pursued me as if I were a Moor, and for their part, the Indians attacked me most seriously.[1]

1. Why did you oppress the Indians so unjustly?—Las Casas's note.

Then Hojeda arrived and upset everything. He said the monarchs had sent him with promises of gifts, privileges and money, and many joined him, for in Hispaniola there is little else but vagabonds, and no one has a wife or children. This Hojeda caused me a great deal of trouble; he had to be sent away and he promised that he would return with more people and more ships, and he said he had left the Queen at the point of death. Then, Vicente Yáñez [Pinzón] arrived with four caravels, causing excitement and suspicions but no damages. Then, a friend of Roldán's was said to be bringing six caravels, but this news was sheer malice and came at a time when I had given up hope that Their Highnesses would ever send a ship to the Indies, and rumor had it that the Queen was dead. A certain Adrián [de Moxica] tried to rebel again, as before, but Our Lord turned him away from his purpose. I had determined never to touch a hair of anyone's head, but this fellow's ungratefulness was such that I could not save him; I would have acted in the same way toward my own brother if he had tried to kill me and steal the power invested in me by my King and Queen.

For six months I had been ready to leave to come to Their Highnesses with good news about the gold; I wanted to escape from governing these dissolute people who fear neither God nor their King and Queen, a people full of vice and malice. Before leaving I begged Their Highnesses again and again to send someone at my expense to administer justice, and after the mayor's [Francisco Roldán] rebellion I implored them again to send someone or at least some servant bearing official letters, for my reputation is such that if I build a church or a hospital they say I am building a lair for thieves. Finally, they did send someone, although he turned out to be unfit for what the situation called for, but let him be since it pleased them to send him. I was there two years without being able to secure anything for myself or for my men, but he [Bodadilla] came with documents by the trunkful; whether they will result in his favor or not, God only knows. He began by granting gold franchises for twenty years, which is a man's lifetime, and they are gathering gold. Someone found five marks' worth in four hours; I will refer to him again later. If Their Highnesses were to punish the worst of these ruffians who know my sufferings, they would be doing an act of charity; these people have caused me great harm with their evil tongues, and my services, my estate and power have proved of no advantage against them. If Their Highnesses would indeed punish them, I would regain my honor and it would resound in the whole world, for mine is an enterprise of quality that will increase with time in fame and appreciation.

When Comendador Bobadilla arrived in Santo Domingo I was in La Vega and my brother the Adelantado was in Xaraguá, Adrián's stronghold; only by now things were calm, the land was rich and everyone lived in peace. The day after he arrived he constituted himself governor, appointed officials, performed executive acts, and announced gold franchises and the remission of tithes and other obligations for a period of twenty years, which is a man's lifetime. He also announced that he had come to pay everybody, even those who had not served very well up to that day, and that he would have me and my brothers in chains, as he did, sent back to Castile never to come here again, nor any other member of my family, and he talked about me abusively. As I said, this was the day after his arrival, and I was absent; I had no knowledge of him or of his arrival. He filled in and sent royal letters signed in blank to Roldán and company, with compliments and privileges, but to this day he never wrote to me nor did he send me any messages.

Consider what a person in my position was to think of these honors bestowed on those who had tried to cheat Their Highnesses by causing such great harm and of the humiliation done to me who was upholding the rights of Their Highnesses.[2] When I heard of this, I thought it was only something mild like the Hojeda affair; I restrained myself when the friars told me for certain that Their Highnesses had sent this man here. I wrote to welcome him, to tell him that I was ready to leave for Spain and had put up my belongings for sale, and to warn him against haste in this business of franchise, because I would give him a clear account of what was to be done. I gave this letter to the friars but neither he nor they answered it. On the contrary, he reacted with hostility and forced everyone to recognize him as governor under oath, for a period of twenty years, as they told me. When I heard about the franchise, I wanted to correct such a grave error, thinking he would be pleased since he was issuing permits too generous by far even for a married man with a family, let alone for these vagabonds. I announced by letter and in public that he was not qualified to use his credentials because I had the higher authority, and I showed the grants Juan de Aguado had brought. I did this hoping to delay Bobadilla, to have time to notify Their Highnesses so that they could give new orders the better to serve their interests.

2. The admiral's reasoning is certainly very correct.—Las Casas's note.

Such franchises were not designed for the Indies: the residents here profit too much; they are given the best lands, that will be worth up to 200,000 *maravedís* in four years, and they do not even take a hoe to them. I would speak differently if the residents were married, but there are not six in the whole lot who would not grab all they can in a minute and speed out of here.[3] It would be good if honorable people came from Castile to settle and if one knew who they were and what they were like. I had agreed to these settlers' request that they should pay tithes and a third of the gold, an agreement they accepted as a great favor from Their Highnesses. I reprimanded them when I heard they were complaining about this to Comendador Bobadilla and I expected the comendador to reprimand them also; but, on the contrary, he provoked them against me by saying I wanted to deprive them of what Their Highnesses had granted them, and he incited them to blame me, which they did. He persuaded them to write to Their Highnesses and ask that I should be forbidden to come back again.

Indeed, I myself beg this as a favor to me and to my household, as long as no one is sent to replace those people. He ordered an investigation into my evil deeds, the likes of which were never known in Hell. But Our Lord exists, who saved Daniel and the three young men, and He displays His wisdom and power when He pleases. Well, I could have remedied this and all that has happened since I came to the Indies if I had been willing to look after my personal interest, but I have hit bottom for having looked after justice and gain for Their Highnesses. So much gold is being exploited today that opinion is divided as to what is more profitable: to steal or to work in the mines. They find 100 castellanos to pay for a woman, as for a farm, and this has become such a practice that there are merchants who go out to look for women; nine- or ten-year-old girls are at a premium but any woman gets a good price, regardless of her age.

I state that the evil tongues of those discordant people have caused me more harm than my services have caused me profit, a bad example for present and future. I swear that a quantity of people came to the Indies who are now returning and did not deserve baptism before God or the world. The comendador aroused them against me, and his methods show that he had intended this all along; they say he spent a great deal of money to get this job. I know only what I hear, and I never heard that an investigator gathered rebels and other nontrust-

3. This is why the Indies are lost to us; no one stays long enough in one place but leaves as soon as he has amassed his gold.—Las Casas's note.

worthy people to use as witnesses against the person in charge of governing them. If Their Highnesses ordered a general investigation here, I tell you they would be astonished to find that the island is still standing. I think you will remember the time a storm drove me to Lisbon without sails and I was accused of having gone there to offer the Indies to the King of Portugal; later, Their Highnesses learned the truth and knew it had been the work of malice. Although I have little knowledge, I am not so stupid as not to know that, even if the Indies were mine, I could not do without the support of a Prince. If this is so, where could I get better protection and security than from the King and Queen, our lords, who have raised me from nothing to a high estate, who are the greatest princes in the world, who safeguard and increase my privileges even when someone like Aguado tries to discredit me? As I said, I have rendered many services to Their Highnesses and my sons serve in their house, which could never happen with another Prince, for where there is no love, everything else is lacking.

I have spoken against malicious slander unwillingly, because it is something that I should never recall even in my dreams. Comendador Bobadilla is striving to explain his conduct but I will easily show him that his scant knowledge, great cowardice and exorbitant greed are the motives that pushed him into it. I have already mentioned that I wrote to him and to the friars, and that I came very much alone because everyone was with the Adelantado and I wanted to avoid suspicions. When he learned this, he had [my brother] Diego put in chains in a caravel; he did the same to me when I arrived, and afterwards to the Adelantado when he arrived. I spoke to him no more; nor did he consent that anyone speak to me, and I swear I could not tell why I was arrested. His first concern was to take the gold while I was away; he said he wanted it to pay the people, but I heard that he kept the first part for himself and sent for new traders. I had set aside certain samples of gold nuggets the size of a large egg and of various shapes which had been found in a very short time. I thought these stones would please Their Highnesses and make them better understand my enterprise. But he maliciously kept them for himself so that Their Highnesses would not think too highly of the enterprise until he had feathered his nest, which he did in great hurry. Unmelted gold dwindles in the fire, and chains weighing as much as 20 marks were never seen again. I was much aggrieved by this, and even more by his taking the pearls, because I could not bring them to Their Highnesses.

The comendador did everything in his power to harm me. There was no need to steal or touch the gold, he could have used the 600,000 *maravedís* to pay everyone, and the tithes and fees had brought in four million. He was prodigal to the point of ridiculousness, though I think he began with himself: Their Highnesses will know this when they order him to give an account, especially if I am present when he gives it. He repeats that great sums are owed, but it is the amount I have mentioned. I have been much aggrieved that an investigator should be sent who knew that if he discovered something serious against me, he would govern. Would to God that Their Highnesses had sent him or someone else two years ago; I know I would have been untouched by scandal and infamy then, and no one would have taken my honor. God is just and he will see that the truth is known.

They judge me as if I were a governor in Sicily or of a well-regulated town or city where the laws can be observed in their entirety without fear of losing all, and I suffer. I should be judged as a captain who left Spain for the Indies to conquer a warlike nation,[4] whose customs and religious rites are very different from ours, where by divine will[5] I have placed under the sovereignty of the King and Queen, our lords, another world whereby Spain, which was reputed to be poor, is now the richest nation in the world.[6] I should be judged as a captain who for a long time bore arms without an hour's rest and by another conqueror, not by a man of letters, unless they be scholar-soldiers, like the Greeks and Romans, or again by those modern jurists of whom there are so many and so noble in Spain. Otherwise I suffer great injury, since there are no towns or governments in the Indies.

I have opened the doors to great quantities of gold, pearls, precious stones, spices and a thousand other things. I said I would speak about the gold: on Christmas Day I was very downhearted, seeing myself attacked by mean Christians and Indians alike, and I was about to give up everything and escape with my life if I could. Our Lord miraculously consoled me by saying, "Take heart, do not be afraid. I shall provide for the seven years of the term of the gold which are not yet passed; I shall help you with this and with the rest." That day, I learned there had been measured 80 leagues of land, all of it full of mines; it now seems that there is still gold there. Some found 120 castellanos in one day, others found 90, and it has gone as high

4. He did not call it warlike when Guacanagarí saved his life when his ship sank; the admiral's ignorance on this subject is astonishing.—Las Casas's note.
5. Permissive will only.—Las Casas's note.
6. This ill-acquired wealth will cause Spain to be the poorest nation in the world.—Las Casas's note.

as 250. From 50 to 70 is considered a good day's work, and many get from 20 to 50. The average is from 6 to 12, and he is unhappy who walks away with less. These mines seem to be like the others, yielding different amounts every day; they are new and so are the men who work them. Everyone is of the opinion that, should all Castile go there, everyone, no matter how slow, would get no less than 1 or 2 castellanos per day. It is true that each man has an Indian[7] but it is the Christian who does the work.[8]

Consider Bobadilla's discretion when he gave all for nothing, and the four millions of tithes, without having been asked to do so, without first notifying the King! And this is not all the damage he caused. I know that my errors do not stem from wrong intentions and I believe that Their Highnesses know it too. I see that they use mercy toward those who serve them with malice, and I firmly believe that their mercy will be twice as great toward me since I innocently fell into error and was forced to it, as I will make clear later. Furthermore, I am a product of their creation, and they will look upon my services and realize how privileged they are. They will weigh everything in the scales, as the Scriptures tell us happens with good and evil on Judgment Day. If they persist in appointing someone to judge my conduct in the Indies (I trust that they will not), I humbly implore them to send two honorable and conscientious persons there, at my own expense, and I believe they will have no trouble finding two such persons now that 5 gold marks can be found in four hours. With or without this, it is imperative that it be done.

When the comendador arrived in Santo Domingo, he took up residence in my house and he took everything just as he found it. Well, let him have it, it may be that he needed it; but no pirate ever robbed a merchant thus. I resent more bitterly how he treated my writings: he took them, and I have been unable to retrieve a single document, and those which would have cleared me are the ones he keeps most hidden. See then, what an honest and fair investigator he is! They tell me he acted in the name of justice; that is, absolute justice. Our Lord God still exists in His power of old, and He will punish all in the end, especially the ingratitude of injuries.

And this is the letter the admiral wrote to the governess of Prince don Juan.

---

7. They had not one but many Indians who sweated and perished doing this.—Las Casas's note.
8. The Christian's work consisted in keeping the Indians there by force, in beating them and in lacking pity.—Las Casas's note.

Book Two

1

Once the two caravels on which Comendador Bobadilla was sending Columbus and his brothers as prisoners to Castile had sailed, he [Bobadilla] tried to please the 300 Spaniards who remained on the island. This was the number Columbus had informed the King as being necessary to subjugate the island and its natives; therefore, the King had ordered the admiral to maintain this force. It was more than enough not only to keep the Indians pacified, had they treated them differently, but also to subdue and kill them all, which is what they did. Indeed, twenty or thirty horses were enough to tear them to pieces, especially since they had trained dogs for this purpose and one Spaniard with one dog felt as safe as if accompanied by fifty or a hundred Christians. This is clear even to the dullest minds. How can a people who go about naked, have no weapons other than bow and arrow and a kind of wooden lance, and no fortification besides straw huts, attack or defend themselves against a people armed with steel weapons and firearms, horses and lances, who in two hours could pierce thousands and rip open as many bellies as they wished? This proves Oviedo's error (*History*, Bk III, Ch. 4) when he says that the Christians would have perished if Columbus, on his way to discover Paria, had not dispatched three ships from La Gomera Island to Hispaniola, and when he presents as a fact that the reinforcement saved the lives of Spanish men as well as their hold on the island, since they said they dared not leave the town or cross the river.

Here and elsewhere Oviedo exaggerates in order to justify Spanish tyranny and accuse the poor and forsaken Indians. Endless testimonies and the above argument prove the mild and pacific temperament of the natives, as well as the fact that we surpassed them in arms so that, had we lived among them as Christians, we would have had no need of weapons, horses or fierce dogs to attract them to us. But our work was to exasperate, ravage, kill, mangle and destroy; small wonder, then, if they tried to kill one of us now and then (the only way to catch a group of even thirty of us was if that group was fast asleep). This is a fact: Indians seldom killed groups of fifty or forty men anywhere in the Indies, especially if they had horses and sentries. So then, a group of 300 could certainly defend itself and kill all the Indians on this island, and this was their number before the arrival of Columbus's reinforcement. He brought more men, not because they were needed, but because he had to dispose of the weak, the sick and those homesick for Castile, as I have already said.

But to return to the point, Comendador Bobadilla wanted to please the 300 men who remained on the island, and his first decision dealt with the trial of those men condemned to be hanged. As far as Francisco Roldán and his followers were concerned, I saw them a few days later, as if nothing had happened, safe and sound, happy and living as honored members of the community. I heard nothing about their having been punished in any way because in those days I took no notice nor did I care to know about them. Comendador Bobadilla granted the 300 men liberties and privileges. He taxed their gold at only 1 peso on 11 and they, having no mind to work and excavate, asked him for Indian labor both for the mines and the making of bread. He ordered—rather, he advised—them to form partnerships of two to share all the profits and assigned Indian tribes to them, thus making them very happy. You should have seen those hoodlums, exiled from Castile for homicide with crimes yet to be accounted for, served by native kings and their vassals doing the meanest chores! These chiefs had daughters, wives and other close relations whom the Spaniards took for concubines either with their own consent or by force. Thus, those 300 hidalgos lived for several years in a continuous state of sin, not counting those other sins they committed daily by oppressing and tyrannizing Indians. They called these women servants and shamelessly spoke of them to one another as "My servant so and so" and "X's servant," meaning "My wife so and so" and "X's wife." The comendador didn't give a straw for all this; at least he took no measures to remedy or avoid the situation. He would frequently tell them: "Take as many advantages as you can since you don't know how long this will last"; he cared even less for the hardships, afflictions and deaths of the Indians. The Spaniards loved and adored him in exchange for such favors, help and advice, because they knew how much freer they were now than under Columbus.

The admiral, it is true, was as blind as those who came after him, and he was so anxious to please the King that he committed irreparable crimes against the Indians. However, if he did not report the harm that certain Spaniards caused them, and if he assigned a tribe of Indians to Francisco Roldán and a few others to do work for them or find gold, it seems the occasions were very, very rare, and he acted as if forced to it by his own men, on account of past rebellions. At least he did abominate the free and easy life of those sinners who called themselves Christians. Sin leads to sin, and for many years they lived unscrupulously, not observing Lent or other fasts and, except at Easter, ate meat on Fridays and Saturdays. They saw themselves as masters of lords, served and feared by tribes of nobles and common people who trembled at the sight of them because of past cruelties renewed in the present whenever they felt the whim, and who especially trembled if the chief's wife, daughter or sister was thought to be a Spaniard's "wife." Thus they grew more conceited every day and fell into greater arrogance, presumption and contempt toward these humble people. They no longer felt like walking any distance. Having neither mules nor horses, they rode the backs of Indians if they were in a hurry; if they had more leisure, they traveled as if by litter, stretched on a hammock carried at a good speed and with relays. In this case they also had Indians carry large leaves to shade them from the sun and others to fan them with goose wings. I saw many an escort follow them loaded like a donkey with mining equipment and food, many of them with scars on their shoulders like working animals. Whenever they reached an Indian village, they consumed what to fifty Indians would represent abundance, and forced the chief to bring them whatever he had, to the accompaniment of dances. Not only were they exceedingly vain in these matters, but they had other women as well who would serve in other capacities such as chambermaid, cook and similar offices. I once knew an organ maker who had such maids.

There were two kinds of servants. One, all the boys and girls taken from their parents on their plundering and killing expeditions, whom they kept in the house night and day; these were called *naborías,* meaning "servants" in the vernacular. And two, seasonal workers for the mines and the fields, who returned to their own homes starving, exhausted and debilitated. And it was a laughing matter to see the Spaniards' presumption, vanity and air of authority when they had not even a linen shirt to their names, nor cape, coat or trousers but wore only a cotton shirt over another shirt from Castile if they had it; if not, they wore their cotton shirt over bare legs and instead of boots they had sandals and leggings. To console them for their services, they beat and insulted the Indians, hardly calling them anything but "dog." Would to God they treated them as such, because they would not have killed a dog in a million years, while they thought nothing of knifing Indians by tens and twenties and of cutting slices off them to test the sharpness of their blades. Two of these so-called Christians met two Indian boys one day, each carrying a parrot; they took the parrots and for fun beheaded the boys. Another one of these tyrants, angry at an Indian chief, hanged twelve of his vassals and eighteen others all in one house. Another shot arrows into an Indian in public, announcing the reason for punishment as his failure to deliver a letter with the speed he required.

Cases of this sort are infinite among our Christians. Having failed in their attempts to defend themselves, these gentle and patient people fled to the hills but, since experience had taught them the impossibility of escaping from Spaniards anywhere, they suffered and died in the mines and other labors in desperate silence, knowing not a soul in the world to whom they could turn for help. And this is at the root of the doubt as to whether they were animals or human beings. Soulless, blind and godless, these Spaniards killed without restraint and perversely abused the patience, natural simplicity, goodness, obedience, gentleness and services of the Indians. They should have admired and pitied them and tempered their own cruelties; instead, they despised and belittled them, discrediting their humanity and believing them to be nonrational animals, and so it was thought throughout the world. The lamentable error to believe them incapable of Catholic indoctrination sprang from this first error and may he who persists in it burn for such beastly heresy.

There were other improprieties, such as saying the Indians needed tutors like children because they could not govern themselves and because, if left to their own resources, they did not work but died of starvation, and all this was said in order to keep power over them. Since nobody spoke on their behalf, but rather ate of the same dish, this pernicious infamy took such roots that for years Castilian kings, their councils, and all manner of men believed it and treated them like animals, until God gave them someone [i.e. Las Casas] who enlightened them and the world as to the truth that lay behind the lethargy—after he had ascertained the stupidity and falseness of that opinion, as well be shown below.

The falseness in itself was not so obscure as to require miraculous light—any rustic mind could have seen it and taken pride in telling others. But having found greed as the prime mover—vehement greed, blind, wild and the root of all evils—it became apparent that the original tyrants and all who followed in their damnable beliefs, confirmed by dismal actions, had been numbed by greed; and a glimmer of hope of stopping it became possible, what learned person does not know that the minds of the wisest and most generous men can degenerate to pusillanimity when subjected to harsh and lasting servitude? Oppressed, afflicted, threatened, tormented and mistreated in various ways, unable to raise their thoughts above their bitter misery, they can forget their own humanity. And this is the first plan of tyrants: in order to sustain themselves on usurped territory, they continually oppress and cause anguish to the most powerful and to the wisest so that, occupied by their calamities, they lack the time and courage to think of their freedom; thus the Indians degenerated into cowardice and timidity, as I amply demonstrated in Chapters 27 and 36 of my *Apologetical History*. Well then, if the wisest of the wise, whether Greek or Roman (history books are full of this), often feared and suffered from this adversity, and if many other nations experienced it and philosophers wrote about it, what could we expect from these gentle and unprotected Indians suffering such torments, servitude and decimation but immense pusillanimity, profound discouragement and annihilation of their inner selves, to the point of doubting whether they were men or mere cats? And who, down to the lowest idiot, will not think blind and downright malicious those who dared spread this belief and defame so many people, saying Indians need tutors because they are incapable of organization, when in reality, they have kings and governors, villages, houses and property rights, and communicate with one another on all levels of human, political, economical and social relations, living in peace and harmony?

Finally, the following argument makes even more apparent the evil design of those deceivers and counterfeiters of truth. They say that without tutors Indians would not work and would die of starvation; let us ask, then, if Spain sent food to the Indians all those thousands of years people lived there and if, when we got there, we found them wanting and thin? Also, did we give them the means to find food—since they lived on air and we brought food to them all the way from Castile—and did we satiate them or, on the contrary, did they satisfy our own hunger and free us from death many times by giving us not only the bare essentials but many superfluous things as well? Oh, vicious blindness! Wicked, insensitive and detestable ungratefulness! So consequently, these first sowers of destruction are responsible for the infamous lie which spread throughout the world that harmed the cause of multitudes of men, the sons of Adam, without cause and without reason by misinterpreting their natural goodness, gentleness, obedience and simplicity. They should have loved and praised the Indians, and even learned from them, instead of belittling them by publicizing them as beastly; instead of stealing, afflicting, oppressing and annihilating them, making as much of them as they would a heap of dung on a public square. And let this suffice to account for the state of affairs on this island under Bobadilla's government, after he had sent Admiral Columbus as a prisoner to Castile. . . .

3

In that year of 1500, in order to investigate Columbus's claim for justice against Bobadilla, as well as for other reasons, the King determined to send a new governor to Hispaniola, which at the time was the only seat of government in the Indies. The new governor was fray Nicolás de Ovando, Knight of Alcántara, and at that time comendador of Lares. When, some years later, the mastership of the Order of Alcántara fell vacant in Castile while Ovando was here, the King honored him with the title, so that we called him comendador mayor instead of Comendador Lares. He was a most prudent man worthy of ruling over many, except Indians, because his government caused them inestimable harm. He was of middle stature and had a light reddish beard. There was an air of authority about him and he was a friend of justice. He was honest in person, deeds and words, and a great enemy of greed and avarice. He did not seem to lack the pearl of all virtues, humility, which he showed both in his appearance and in his actions, in the management of his house, in his clothes and at table, in public and private conversations. He was grave and authoritative. Even after he was made comendador mayor he would not allow anyone to call him señoría. All these virtues we surely recognized in him.

This man, then, was sent by the monarchs to govern Hispaniola and the Indies, and he took with him full provisions and instructions concerning the two years of his government, including the right to investigate Francisco Bobadilla and the cause of Francisco Roldán's subversion; also, the faults imputed to Columbus and the cause of his imprisonment, all of which was to be reported to Spain. Among his instructions there was a very specific clause: all the Indians of Hispaniola were to be left free, not subject to servitude, unmolested and unharmed and allowed to live like free vassals under law just like any other vassal in the kingdoms of Castile. He was also to see that they were instructed in our Catholic Faith; in this respect our Queen always sought fair treatment in the conversion of these people. He brought with him as justice of the peace the lawyer Alonso Maldonado of Salamanca, an honest and prudent man, a humanitarian and lover of justice.

The monarchs sent this governor from Granada where the court was at the time. The fleet consisted of thirty-two ships, large and small. The passengers numbered 2,500 men, mostly nobles, knights and officials. Antonio de Torres, the brother of Prince don Juan's tutor, was captain of the fleet, a post he held in all subsequent voyages. Twelve Franciscan brothers and a Franciscan prelate, Alonso del Espinal, all pious persons, accompanied him. It was at that point that the Order of St. Francis settled here. The fleet left from San Lúcar on February 13, the first Sunday of Lent, in 1502. A week later, a strong south wind blew so fiercely near the Canary Islands and the sea became so rough that it endangered the whole fleet. A large ship with 120 passengers, sailors excepted, was lost; I think it was the *Rábida*. The remaining thirty-one ships were scattered and jettisoned as much as they could to save lives. The wind forced some to Barbary and Cape Aguer, in Moorish territory near the Canaries, and others to the islands of Tenerife, Lanzarote, La Gomera and Grand Canary. Two caravels loaded with sugar and other things sailing from the Canaries had been lost; and because the storm had scattered their debris and that of the *Rábida* along the coast of Cádiz, everyone thought the whole fleet had sunk.

The news reached the monarchs in Granada. We found out that, incredibly aggrieved, they had withdrawn into their private quarters and allowed no one to see them for a week. Finally, God willed the fleet to be saved at the cost of great perils and all thirty-one ships gathered at La Gomera Island. They added another ship from Grand Canary Island to accommodate the people there who wanted to join us, I do not remember for what other reasons. The fleet was split because some of the ships were badly damaged. Fifteen or sixteen of the fastest ships went with the new one; Antonio de Torres piloted the others. The first half arrived at the port of Santo Domingo on April 15; Antonio de Torres anchored in the river with the other half some fifteen days later.

The Spaniards and inhabitants of this township flocked to the banks with great joy. Recognizing each other—some had been here earlier and were returning—they exchanged news about the

island, Castile and the new governor. The newcomers said all was
well in Castile and told them the new governor was the comendador Lares, Knight of Alcántara. The island residents said all was
well here and gave the reasons for such well-being: there was much
gold; they had found a nugget that weighed many thousands of
gold pesos, the Indians were rebelling and many Indians had been
made captive slaves. I heard this with my own ears since I had
sailed with Lares. And they called it good news that the Indians
were rebelling and made it a matter for rejoicing! This way they
had a reason to fight them and, consequently, to seize Indians to
send to Castile and sell as slaves. God willing, I will speak of the
causes of the rebellion and of the war the Spaniards waged a few
days after our arrival.

The gold nugget I mentioned was a unique marvel of nature.
Never had eyes seen such a thing wrought by nature alone: it
weighed 35-pounds-worth or 36,000 gold pesos, each peso being
worth 450 *maravedís*; it was as big as the bread loaves they make in
Alcalá and Seville, of such a size that they weigh 3 pounds, and I
saw it with my own eyes. They thought 600 pesos of stone (which
no doubt time meant to convert into gold) might be mixed with
the gold, but it looked like solid gold because stone makes only
minute lines in it. It was a remarkably beautiful piece. An Indian
girl found it. Governor Bobadilla had given the Spaniards so much
license in exploiting the Indians that they were sent to the mines
at the rate of fifteen to forty men and women for each pair of
Spaniards.

Francisco de Garay and Miguel Díaz were partners. They took
their crew of Indians to the mines called Nuevas to differentiate
them from the older ones, on the far side of the Hayna river,
approximately nine leagues from Santo Domingo. One morning,
while eating lunch, an Indian girl of theirs was sitting near a brook
eating and resting, perhaps meditating upon her sad lot, her captivity and misery, idly poking the ground with a stick or perhaps a
pick or a hoe or some iron tool, without thinking of what she was
doing. She had scratched the ground and the gold nugget began to
gleam. Her eyes fell on it, she unearthed it and called her Spanish
victimizer. She said to him: *"Ocama guaxeri guariquen caona
yari."* (*Ocama* translates as "listen," *guaxeri* as "Sir," *guariquen* as

"look" or "come and see," *yari* as "jewel" or "gold stone"; *caona* is their word for gold.) The miner rejoiced with his friends; all were beside themselves at seeing such a new, such an admirable and such a rich stone. They celebrated the discovery by roasting a suckling pig. They carved and ate, all the while imagining a gold platter so fine that kings themselves had not the like of it. The governor took it for the monarchs and gave its value in money to the two partners, Francisco de Garay and Miguel Díaz. But we may presume without fear of sinning that the poor girl who found the nugget did not receive as much as a farthing for it. Would that they had even given her a single bite of the suckling pig! . . .

6

Let the admiral sail his four ships from Puerto Hermoso or the port of Açua, also called by some Puerto Escondido, and fare well on the high seas until we speak of him again. Now, let us return to the events that followed the arrival of Comendador Lares on the island. Bobadilla had come to greet him with the people of this town and, after the usual ceremonies, they took him to a fort of adobe where they had prepared his lodgings. He presented his credentials to Bobadilla in front of the mayors, aldermen and the town council; they acknowledged them and, according to custom, solemnly swore to honor them. He then began to govern with prudence and began his investigation of Bobadilla's case. You should have seen Bobadilla! He remained alone and disgraced, going to and from the governor's house to appear for judgment, unaccompanied by any of the men he had favored by saying: "Take advantage of this, you don't know how long it will last," "advantage" meaning Indian sweat and labor. Truly, he must have been a plain and humble man by nature. I never heard anyone criticize him; on the contrary, all spoke well of him. Since he had given his 300 Spaniards license to exploit the Indians, he gave them cause for esteeming him. If he had any defects, nobody spoke of them even after the investigation, his departure and his death.

Comendador Lares also investigated the case of Francisco Roldán and his supporters. I believe (I do not remember too well) he had him sent to Castile, a prisoner but not in chains, so that the monarchs might determine the punishment he deserved. But divine Providence intervened by calling him first for a higher and subtler justice. I mentioned in Chapter 1 how Bobadilla ordered that anyone exploiting the mines with Indians should pay the King 1 peso on 11. However, either the monarchs resented this as an action taken without their consent and gave orders to Lares to this effect, or Lares took it upon himself to tax all gold miners a third of their profit, regardless of their previous payments. Since the mines were rich and new then, everyone wanted tools and cassava bread to be able to put more and more Indians to work. A pickax cost from 10 to 15 castellanos, a 2- to 3-pound crowbar cost 5, a hoe from 2 to 3 castellanos, 4,000 to 5,000 cassava plants cost 200, 300 or more pesos. Those most eager to mine gold would spend 2,000 or 3,000 of their gold pesos for these things; and when asked to pay a third of their harvest, or rather, that of the Indians they oppressed, they would find themselves penniless. Thus they would sell for 10 pesos what they had bought for 50, and the more gold they found, the greater their loss. Those who chose to farm fared much better since they paid nothing.

In general, then, miners lived in need and even in prison for debts, while farmers would have lived in peace and abundance had they not been given to excess in matters of dress, trappings and other vanities which in the end prevented them from prospering. They spent money like air since they acquired it unjustly through Indian sweat and labor, with little or no thought of punishment. At that time, farms raised only pigs, cassava and other edible roots like *ajes* and potatoes. From then on the monarchs levied a 50 per cent tax on the gold mined. And since nobody came to the Indies except for gold—in order to leave the state of poverty which plagued all classes in Spain—they had no sooner disembarked than they set out for the mines, eight leagues from the city, thinking there was no more to it.

You should have seen each of them fill his pack with Spanish biscuits and carry it on his back with picks, pots and pans. The roads to the mines were like anthills. If they had no servants, they carried their own packs but some caballeros had servants to carry things. Once at the mines, since gold does not grow on trees but underground, lacking knowledge and experience they grew tired of digging and washing dirt because, in the first place, they had never dug anything in their lives. They rested and ate too often. Hard work made them digest quickly, so they would eat again; in the end nothing came of their labor. A week later, having exhausted their food supply, they returned to town emptyhanded and ate the remnants of their Castilian provisions. Discouraged and frustrated at not finding what they had come for, they caught fever from the climate, which was aggravated by the lack of food, of care and shelter; and they died at such a rate the priests barely managed to bury them. Out of 2,500 men, more than 1,000 died, while 500 cases of illness were made worse by anguish, hunger and need; and from then on, this was the lot of whoever came to the New World to find gold.

Those who had brought clothing, tools and other valuables sold them to survive a while to the 300 men on the island who were half-naked, wearing a shirt of cotton instead of linen and neither coat, cape nor trousers. Others formed partnerships with these 300 men, buying half or a third of their holdings, and paid them partly with clothes and other Spanish items, owing a balance of up to 2,000 castellanos. They did this because the 300 owned the land and servant maids; thus their power was food, and their abundance, servants and land. They were lords and kings, although, as I said, they walked about with bare legs.

At that time, the Indians were peacefully resting from the tyranny and anguish they had suffered under Francisco Roldán, all except those who served the 300 Spaniards and a lot of work they had, too! Only one province was at arms, preparing for an attack, as we shall see. A Sevillian hidalgo named Luis de Arriaga, who had come here with Columbus, sent a proposal to the monarchs. He asked permission to bring 200 Castilian couples in order to populate and settle four townships, and further suggested that they be given free passage as well as exemptions. Mainly, they were to be given land and terms favorable both to the settlement of such townships and to the cultivation of land. They would remain under the civil and criminal jurisdiction of the King and his successors, be exempted from the taxes raised by the King by permission of the Pope and from any other duties for a period of five years. They would have limited rights to the mining of gold, silver, copper, iron, tin, lead, quicksilver, sulphur, etc.; to brazilwood, salt, etc.; to seaports and anything pertaining rightfully to the Crown but found on their territories. They should pay the monarchs half the gold mined by them and the Indians who accompanied them, but could not buy any from the Indians; all the brazilwood they should cut, even though cutting brazilwood was forbidden; a third of whatever they obtained from the Indians in the way of cotton and other materials from outside the town limits, except gold and edibles; half the gold taken from the mines after deducting operational costs, plus the mining rights to mines discovered by them—and I believe this clause referred to mines found within the limits of the new towns; half of the gold and pearls from as yet undiscovered islands or the mainland, if they happened to discover them, but a fifth of everything else. Free passage applied only to persons, not to their belongings, however numerous or few.

Another privilege stipulated that no person could remain and live in such towns who had gone into exile from Castile to the Indies or who had been a Jew, a Moor or a convert; this was to safeguard the honor of the said 200 couples. They would have to reside five years on the island, obey the King's orders through the governor, and serve without remuneration. If any of the colonists disobeyed, if a province rebelled, or if the Indians refused to serve, they would assume the prosecution costs. If someone wished to return to Castile within this five-year period, he could do so but he would lose all property given him by virtue of his citizenship, and said property would be disposed of according to the King's wishes.

This was the agreement the monarchs made with Luis de Arriaga; it was to be extended to all Spaniards settling on the island. Later, Arriaga could find only forty couples and, while in Seville, he asked that they be granted these privileges. The monarchs consented. Back on the island, Arriaga and his forty couples found that instead of leisure and the prospect of returning wealthy, they had to work and sweat; therefore, they founded neither cities nor castles but mixed with the island population and the rules that applied to all Spaniards applied to them. A few days later, the 300 gold prospectors and the newcomers complained to the governor about the excessive royal dues and asked him to request that the King be satisfied with a third, instead of half, the value of the gold they extracted at such cost. The governor wrote, and the King conceded in a royal letter addressed to the governor. At another time, they asked the King to reduce to a fourth the third they owed on cotton and other nonmetals; it was granted from Medina del Campo, on December 20, 1503. Later still, finding a third on gold too onerous, the Spaniards requested a further reduction and sent a spokesman, a Sevillian named Juan de Esquivel, who negotiated a successful fifth on all metals. The decree began with "D. Ferdinand and doña Isabella, by the grace of God, etc.," dated February 5, 1504, in Medina del Campo. I mention these trifles, of which no other historian could give such details, so that it may be seen how loath the King was to relax his hold and grant favors, however small, because poverty plagued Castile at that time and the Catholic kings, as well as their kingdom, lacked wealth and abundance, which fact however did not restrict their activities both in and out of Spain.

7

At that time, the storm that sank the fleet having subsided, the governor had good reason to decide to settle a town in La Plata Harbor, in the northern part of the island. The chief reason was that sailing to and from Castile offered less difficulties than from this harbor, La Plata being conveniently located about mid-island, ten and sixteen leagues respectively from the two important townships of Santiago and Concepción and ten or twelve leagues from the Cibao mines, considered the richest and yielding more and finer gold than the mines of San Cristóbal or any other. Moreover, many Indians lived there and only one Spanish farmer from Santiago who raised pigs and chickens. The governor sent a few citizens by ship who, once at sea, sailed to Saona, which almost touches this island, is thirty leagues from Santo Domingo and, together with a neighboring small island, forms the province of Higuey, then in a state of insurrection; these are the people about whom I said the Spaniards rejoiced when we disembarked.

It happened that when eight men went ashore to walk and rest a while, the Indians, thinking they belonged to another crew that had done something a short time ago to which I shall presently refer, ambushed the eight men and killed them. They had legal justification which I have from good sources and relate without additions; I believe I even spare many words and leave out exaggerations about the essence of the case. There existed ample communication and friendship between the people of Saona Island and those of Santo Domingo; therefore, whether they needed it or not, the citizens here would send a caravel every now and then which the Indians would fill with bread.

One day, just before our arrival with Comendador Lares, the caravel went out for bread and the Indian chief, surrounded by his people, received the Spaniards as usual as if they were angels or their very own parents. They began to load the vessel with great joy. Just as Spanish civilians never take a step without girding their sword, so these always brought along dogs trained to tear Indians to pieces and of such ferocity that the Indians feared them more than the very devil. The Indians, then, were loading cassava onto a small boat that was to take it to the caravel, while their chief, staff in hand, walked to and fro in order to expedite matters and please the Christians. One of the leashed dogs saw the chief wave a stick and walk with agitation and, since he was so well trained in attacking Indians, pulled and strained at the leash, wanting to attack. The Spaniard who held him could hardly restrain him and he said to another man, "What if we let him loose?" Then for a laugh he and his friend, both devils incarnate, told the dog to attack, thinking they could control him. But the dog charged like a mad horse and dragged the Spaniard behind him; he was unable to hold his grasp and let go of the leash. The dog jumped on the cacique and with his powerful jaws tore at the man's stomach, pulling out the intestines as the cacique staggered away. The Indians rushed to their unfortunate chief but he died shortly thereafter and, carrying him away for burial, they wailed and lamented their sorrow to the winds. The Spaniards returned to the caravel with their good dog and his master, then sailed to Santo Domingo, leaving such a good deed behind them.

The news spread rapidly in the province of Higuey and came to the ears of Cotubano or Cotubanamá (the penultimate syllable of the first name and the ultimate of the second are pronounced long), who was the nearest and also the bravest chief around. The Indians armed themselves and resolved to take their vengeance at the first opportunity; as it happened, those eight men, all sailors I believe, going to La Plata were the first victims. Such was the Indian rebellion, the news of which greeted us, and it was happy news because we now had a reason to get slaves.

Now, any sensible and God-fearing reader can judge for himself and without difficulty whether the Indians were right in killing eight men who themselves had not harmed them at that time, and I say at that time, because perhaps they had harmed them before, as is likely, from what I saw from my acquaintance with some who had already been there. That time they were innocent, yet they were not killed unjustly since a nation at war with another is not obligated to discern whether an individual is innocent or guilty, unless he wears innocence on his face or manifests it right away in brief discourse. Thus no one doubts the innocence of a child, or of a farmer busily tilling his fields, or of a people separated, by an island, from their master engaged in an unjust war, since they are ignorant of the said war or at least do not participate in it and are not responsible for it. But this case is exactly the opposite, since there was not at the time one single Spaniard on this island who did not offend or harm the Indians; consequently, the Indians had a most excellent reason to suppose that whoever came to their island from Castile came as an enemy and thus could rightfully resolve to kill him. But let God be the ultimate judge of this.

8

When Comendador Lares found out how the Indians of Saona had treated those eight Christians, he determined to fight them. Indeed, like all Spaniards at that time, he seized the slightest pretext to provoke war, and in this case he added war to a previous injury since he had already tortured the Indian chief to death. The Spaniards on Saona Island knew how the Indians there were bound to feel injured and bitter, and knew enough to expect revenge. But after causing them irreparable harm through insult, plunder and murder, they had a legitimate reason to declare war upon them: they called it rebellion and publicized it as such, when in reality the Indian rebellion consisted of no more than a run to the woods in search of a hiding place.

The comendador notified his four townships of Santiago, Concepción, Bonao and Santo Domingo to send a contingent of soldiers, and he ordered the ablest men who had come with him to prepare for war, which they all did readily out of their greed for slaves. An all-out war was announced publicly. I believe some 400 men assembled for it, and the same Juan de Esquivel whom we just mentioned in the preceding chapter was named cacique general, although each contingent also had its own captain. In these sallies it was customary to take along a good number of armed Indians from among those already conquered, and they fought strenuously, such was their fear of the Spaniards whom they accompanied and their desire to please them; and this custom was generalized later all over the Indies. They arrived in the Higuey province—as we call the whole easternmost territory of Santo Domingo—and found the Indians ready to defend their land, if only they could have defended it as they wished. Actually, their wars are like child's play, having only naked bellies to shield them from the Spaniards' mighty steel weapons, and only bows, poisonless arrows and stones—where stones are available—to use against the Spaniards. A Spaniard's sword and strength were such that he could cut an Indian in half, and I won't mention the horses since in one hour's time a single horseman could spear 2,000 Indians.

It happened, then, that Indians would resist a while in their villages and, seeing their formations scattered and their companions mangled, would flee to the woods. Naked and unarmed as they were, sometimes they performed outstanding exploits. Valdenebro and Pontevedra, two expert horsemen I knew very well, once saw an Indian in an open field and one said to the other, "Let me go and kill that man." He raced up to the Indian, who turned about and faced him; whether he shot his arrows I do not know. Valdenebro pierced him with his lance, the Indian grasped the lance with his bare hands and hoisted himself up to the horse's reins. Valdenebro drew his sword and struck the Indian with it, the Indian snapped up the sword from the Spaniard's hand. Valdenebro stabbed him with his dagger, the Indian caught the dagger from the Spaniard's hand and Valdenebro was disarmed. Pontevedra spurred his horse to run to his friend's rescue and speared the Indian. The Indian repeated his feat with Pontevedra's lance, sword and dagger. The two Spaniards were disarmed, the Indian had six weapons stuck in his body and would have fought on, when one of the Spaniards dismounted and kicked him over to snatch a dagger from his body and the Indian fell dead instantly. This exploit was much celebrated.

Once the Indians were in the woods, the next step was to form squadrons to pursue them, and whenever the Spaniards found them, they pitilessly slaughtered everyone like sheep in a corral. It was a general rule among Spaniards to be cruel; not just cruel, but extraordinarily cruel so that harsh and bitter treatment would prevent Indians from daring to think of themselves as human beings or having a minute to think at all. So they would cut an Indian's hands and leave them dangling by a shred of skin and they would send him on, saying "Go now, spread the news to your chiefs." They would test their swords and their manly strength on captured Indians and place bets on the slicing off of heads or the cutting of bodies in half with one blow. They burned or hanged captured chiefs; I believe they hanged the old Indian lady chief Higuanamá (the last syllable is long).

They had anchored a caravel nearby to have it ready to cross over to Saona Island. The Indians fought a while and fled but, although the region has thick forests and a number of caves, they were unable to escape from their pursuers who captured some 700 men, gathered them in a house and stabbed them to death. The gentleman Juan de Esquivel ordered all the corpses taken outside to line the plaza in order to count them; there were, as I said, between 600 and 700 dead, which is how the Spaniards avenged the eight Christians whom the Indians had had good reason to kill but a few days earlier. All the Indians taken alive were enslaved since this was the principal goal of Spaniards here and everywhere in the Indies, the goal to which they devoted all their thoughts and energies, their words and their good deeds. The small island of

Saona was razed in this fashion, made barren when once it had been so fertile.

When the people of that kingdom understood themselves to be so injured, so persecuted and so hopelessly desperate about finding a hiding place, their chiefs sent peace messengers to the Spaniards, offering their services. Juan de Esquivel and the other captains received them with benevolence and promised not to harm them if they came out to live in Spanish settlements; but after deliberation, they agreed to have the Indians farm the King's bread in a large plantation there in exchange for their not being transported to the city of Santo Domingo and not being molested by any Spaniard. Among those who came to make peace with the captains was an important Indian chief of renowned courage—Cotubanamá or Cotubano was his name—whose kingdom faced Saona Island and whose tall and noble bearing betrayed his noble rank. To such an outstanding person the captain general Juan de Esquivel gave his name in exchange for Cotubanamá's, and this exchange of names, making *guatiaos* of the two parties involved, was esteemed as a bond of perpetual brotherhood and confederation. Thus, the captain general and the Indian chief became *guatiaos*, friends and brothers forever, and the Indians called the captain, Cotubano, and their chief, Juan de Esquivel.

The captain had a wooden fort built in an Indian village near the sea, leaving nine Spaniards under Captain Martín de Villamán to guard it; then they all returned to their settlements with their share of slaves. While this war was being fought, the comendador removed the township of Santo Domingo to this side of the river, where it stands today. His reason was the following: all the Spanish towns in the island of Santo Domingo were on this side and he thought it more convenient to be here to avoid the delays caused by projected ferryboats to transport the inlanders coming to the city for business purposes; and I say projected ferryboats because at that time, passage to Santo Domingo was possible only by canoe. However, the admiral's choice of the eastern shore had been the wiser choice: the rising sun lifted the fog away from the town while now it blows it all on the town. Likewise, the eastern shore has good spring water, while here, water is found only in wells and is not too pure at that, and not all residents can afford to go for spring water to the other side of the river. Those who do so find it difficult, having to wait for a canoe both ways unless they own one themselves, and even then it is a precarious operation that is always subject to weather conditions and rain swells.

For these reasons, the old site of Santo Domingo was more salubrious. When the residents moved to this side, they started to build houses with wood and straw and, a few months later, with stone since this section of Santo Domingo has the finest stone and the finest earth with which to bake bricks and erect walls. Comendador Lares was among the first to have his honest dwellings built along the shore on both sides of Fortaleza Street; he willed them to his Order as well as to the hospital of San Nicolás which he had founded. The pilot Roldán built a row of houses on all four streets, both to rent and for his own use. Then, a merchant named Hierónimo Grimaldo, and another named Briones, followed suit so that every day buildings were springing up and increased by the year, though with some setbacks. There were terrible storms at times that destroyed the whole town and left not one single house intact except the few sturdier ones built of stone.

Later, the wars with France and the increase of Negro slaves made it necessary to wall the city. The Franciscans were the first to build their monastery; they were followed by the Dominicans, and, much later, by the Mercedarians. The residents began the fort and did not stop work until it was finished; Comendador Lares appointed one of his nephews, the capable and honest man Diego López de Saucedo, as its chief bailiff. Lares also founded the hospital of San Nicolás, endowing it generously in order to enable it to take in, not only a number of poor people, but in fact I think all cases of illness. This was in the year 1503. The mastership of the Order of the Knights of Alcántara fell vacant and because the monarchs named Comendador Lares to fill it, we will refer to him as comendador mayor from now on.

9

Francisco Roldán's supporters were then in the town and province of Xaraguá where King Behechio and his sister Anacaona, a courageous woman who succeeded Behechio after his death, resided. These Spaniards took Indians whenever they could and forced them to build towns with the kind of freedom to which Francisco Roldán had accustomed them. Lady Anacaona and the many noble chieftains of the province, all very dignified, generous and a far more polite virtuous people than the people of this island, felt the presence of the Spaniards to be excessively onerous, pernicious and altogether intolerable. As a result, they must have had some words with the Spaniards; either they refused to obey or their chiefs argued and threatened. The slightest resistance to the vilest and most wicked Spaniard, even to a one-time Castilian criminal, was enough to cause the rumor that the Indians were this and that and were in a state of uprising.

The comendador mayor decided to visit that province, either because he had had wind of this from his people there—an undisciplined bunch of savages unaccustomed to following orders except for their own vicious pleasures—or because he felt that that region was more out of control, it being more remote and famous for its distinguished people and rulers and especially celebrated for Lady Anacaona. He went with 300 people on foot and 70 on horseback. There were few mares then, and fewer stallions, and he was a wealthy man who acquired a mare to ride, took part in jousting tournaments and fought in battle, for horses were trained in all these things; among those seventy, there was even one that could dance, bow and jump at the sound of a guitar.

When Queen Anacaona knew of the governor's visit, she, being prudent and courteous, sent for all her dignitaries and people of the villages to meet in Xaraguá in order to greet and feast the *guamiquina* (the penult is long) of the Christians, which in her language means "the lord of the Christians." There came a marvelous crowd of people so well groomed it was a pleasure to see: I have already said how outstanding the people of this island were in matters of elegance. Anacaona and her people came in great numbers to receive the governor and his 300 men, celebrating joyfully with songs and dances as they had done when greeting Christopher Columbus's brother, the Adelantado. The comendador mayor was housed in a *caney*, a large building finely wrought and beautifully made of wood and straw—such as I described in my *Apologetical History*—while his men stayed in nearby houses with other Spaniards. Anacaona treated them like royal guests, having game brought from her forests and fish from the sea, cassava and whatever else they had, in addition to servants to tend their tables and horses, and beautiful dances, fiestas and games.

The comendador mayor chose not to appreciate this very much. For, shortly afterwards, he decided to perform what Spaniards always perform on arrival in the Indies, that is to say, when they come to a heavily settled area, being so outnumbered that they make sure all hearts tremble at the mere mention of the name Christians; therefore they terrorize the natives by performing a large-scale and cruel massacre. This lord-governor decided to follow the custom and to do something famous, although certainly not in the manner of Romans, much less of Christians, and I have no doubt that he was led to it by those Romans, the spawn of Francisco Roldán. One Sunday after dinner he ordered some of his men and horses out under the pretext of putting on a jousting show and kept the others inside and fully armed. Anacaona says that she and her chiefs wish to see the games and this pleases the comendador very much. He asks them all to come inside, saying he wants to speak to them. Now, the plan was for the horsemen to surround the house and wait for the signal inside: the comendador was to put a hand on a gold piece he wore around his neck and his men would then draw their swords, tie up the Indian princes—including Anacaona—and wait for further orders. *Ipse dixit et facta sunt omnia.* Queen Anacaona comes in, so noble and fine a lady, so gracious to the Christians and long-suffering of their insults; some eighty of her people follow her; simply and unsuspectingly they stand and wait for the comendador to speak. But the comendador does not speak; instead, he puts his hand on the jewel on his chest; his satellites draw their swords; Anacaona and her people tremble like leaves and think they will be cut up to pieces right then and there. They start to cry and ask why such evil-doing; the Spaniards answer by hastening to tie them; Anacaona alone is let outside; armed men guard the door of the *caney* to keep anyone from leaving; they set fire to the house, burning alive all those kings who, together with the wood and straw, were soon turned into burning embers.

When the tying up began, the horsemen outside ran through the town and speared as many Indians as they could while those on foot ripped bellies open. Since a large crowd had come to a reception that proved so fatal for them, great were the ravages and cruelties done to men, old people and innocent children, and great was the number of people killed. It happened that if a Spaniard, from pity or greed, snatched a child away to save him from slaughter by lifting him to his horse, someone would come from behind and pierce the child with a lance. Or again, if the boy was on foot, even though someone held him by the hand, another would slash his legs off with a sword. As for the Queen, they hanged her as a mark of honor. Those who escaped this inhuman slaughter fled to the small island of Guanabo, eight leagues from here, on small boats and canoes. To punish them, the Spaniards enslaved them, and I had one given me as a slave.

This was the exploit of the comendador mayor of Alcántara, fray Nicolás de Ovando, and this was the way he repaid the chiefs and subjects of the Xaraguá province for the reception and services they had given him and for the endless insults they had suffered under Francisco Roldán and his allies. The cause they made public was that the Indians wanted to rebel and kill the seventy Spanish horsemen. But this is ridiculous, considering that seventy horsemen are enough to raze a hundred islands and all the continent provided it has no great river, swamps or impossible mountain passes to cross. Ten horsemen could devastate it all, especially since these poor people are not armed and walk about naked and unprotected, without suspicion or thought of evil. If it were not so, why then hadn't they killed the forty or fifty Spaniards who had stayed there and wronged them continually and had no horses? In the two or three years they were there, they certainly could have done it. Yet these are the people they said would attack 400 men, 70 of whom had horses, knowing they had come on 30 odd ships, a thing never heard of before, and all those 30 ships full of Christians! The lamblike innocence of these people is clear and the injustice and cruelty of those who uprooted and killed them is also clear.

To make it even clearer, consider the following: when in 1505 King Philip and Queen Juana succeeded Isabella, rumor spread that they were preparing to send a new governor to this island.

Then the comendador mayor, fearing an investigation of this incident, arranged a "trial" for those chiefs he had burned without trial, defense or prosecution, and for that great lady who had been hanged by the Christians. He arranged this "trial" months, perhaps a whole year after the event, here in Santo Domingo, in Santiago, and in other parts of the island, and the witnesses were those very men who had done the killing, the archenemies of the Indians and the authors of those and similar crimes. See then, how rightful, how lawfully substantiated a trial this was! They say that Queen Isabella had heard of it before her death and had been much aggrieved. People also said that Don Alvaro of Portugal, president of the royal council at that time, had threatened the comendador with these words: "We'll have an investigation about you the likes of which you've never seen." It seems that he had no other reason than the massacre to say this since, in truth, during the many years I was here under Lares's government, I never heard or knew of any complaints against him from the Spaniards.

What I have shown here will also serve to judge the truth of Oviedo's *History*. He is always condemning the Indians and excusing the Spaniards for the decimation they brought about in the Indies, for, in reality, he was one of them. Relating this particular case, he says the Spaniards found out about an Indian plot and secret uprising, for which reason the Indians were sentenced to death. I pray to God I may never take part in similar justice or sentence, but that all my efforts may be to the contrary. Oviedo also praises the comendador mayor for his goodness toward the Indians, among other things. He speaks like a blind man and his writing is padded in all sorts of ways. The "love" this gentleman felt for the Indians will be made much clearer as I unveil the truth in the course of my *History*.

10

After this pitiless deed, termed "punishment" in order to inspire terror in the poor Indians, the survivors and those Indians who had heard about it fled to the woods. Chief Guaorocuyá (the last syllable is long), one of Queen Anacaona's nephews who had survived the slaughter, took to hiding with a handful of men in the sierra of Baonuco, facing the sea. The Spaniards told the comendador mayor that Guaorocuyá had rebelled—to flee from Spanish cruelties is still today termed refusal to pay allegiance to the King of Castile. And to make the punishment complete, the comendador ordered pursuit, and Guaorocuyá was hanged. The news spread to the neighboring finger-shaped provinces of Guahaba to the north and Hanyguayaba to the west (the middle syllable is long in both cases), and the Indians, fearing for their lives, took their pathetic weapons and armed themselves in self-defense.

The comendador mayor named two captains experienced in the shedding of Indian blood, Diego Velázquez and Rodrigo Mexía Trillo, to head troops to Hanyguayaba and Guahaba respectively, Guahaba being the beautiful region which Columbus had discovered. The two captains imposed the usual treatment and the usual punishment on both provinces: Velázquez even captured the Indian chief and had him hanged as a mark of distinction; as for Mexía, I did not find out at the time the details of his exploits. But since Indians are not equipped to fight the Spaniards, it is likely that they lost and suffered. It seems that the Indians attacked first in an attempt to fend off the Spanish blades. Oviedo says that the Indians of Hanyguayaba were savages who lived in caves, but this is not the case. Those Indians lived a well-organized communal existence suited to the amenity of the land which, being like a garden, does not lend itself to savagery. There were no caves either, nor *spelea* as he calls them to show off his knowledge of nominatives, but rather generous fields and orchards with villages and cultivated land—I often ate the natural products there. Oviedo calls Guacayarina a different province (this is not so) because the tip of the island has rocks jutting out to sea. Indians call these rocks *zagüeyes*, as in the province of Higuey; they are large enough to accommodate a village, although Indians used them as such only when the calamitous Spaniards drove them into hiding. Whoever told Oviedo he had found Indians there meant it this way, unless of course Oviedo is inventing things, as he usually does, to fill up pages.

The comendador mayor founded the township of Vera Paz in

Xaraguá. Diego Velázquez founded another in the province of Hanyguayaba on the coast of the South Sea and he called it Salva-tierra de la Çabana, which gave its name to the province since *çabana* means lowland [savannah] in the Indian tongue and indeed the coast there is flat and very beautiful. By order of the comendador, Velázquez also founded the seaport of Yaquimo (formerly called Brasil by Columbus, where Hojeda, handcuffed, had jumped out and swum to shore) and built a small fort not quite as strong as the fort of Fuenterrabía. The comendador founded San Juan de la Maguana in King Caonabo's territory, thirty leagues from Xaraguá . . . as well as other towns some thirty leagues from Santo Domingo, between the two mighty rivers Neiba and Yaquí. Some fourteen leagues closer to Santo Domingo, he settled the township of Açua en Compostela in honor of a Gallegan comendador who had been there before the official settlement. Açua (short u) is the Indian name of the town. The comendador favored Velázquez so much that he made him lieu-tenant of those five townships.

As for Rodrigo Mexía, he founded and became lieutenant of Puerto Real and of Lares de Guahaba on the fork of Guahaba. Puerto Real is still alive today but is becoming a ghost town. Do not think that settling townships was done with Spanish labor; far from it, since not one Spaniard could do as much as bend over a hoe. Instead, it was the result of coercion: the Indians were forced to build towns and cultivate the land to maintain the Spaniards. This is how the comendador mayor imitated the practice which Francisco Roldán had initiated, which Columbus had tolerated and Bobadilla had developed by allowing his Spaniards free use of Indian labor for building and maintenance work, not only for the strictly necessary, but for all kinds of secondary chores as well with which a Spaniard measured his status. They lorded it over the Indians as if they themselves had been the natural rulers of the land, treating Indians not like vassals or subjects but worse than slaves bought on the market place. The comendador mayor nailed this practice down, so to speak (and it had the worst results), without any authority whatever since the instructions he had re-ceived from the King specified that Indians were free men who should under no circumstances be forced to servitude. Not only did he approve of the ways of the 300 Spaniards we found here on arrival, which were tolerated because of the fact that the Indians greatly outnumbered the Spaniards. He also added his own Spaniards and more than doubled the burden of the Indians in places as far apart as Çabana de Hanyguayaba and Guahaba, making the burden excessive and intolerable. I wish to God the bad luck of the Indians had stopped there. It was a desirable lot compared with what was to come, as this *History* will show.

11

The comendador mayor realized very early that the provision of flour and biscuits brought from Castile was being exhausted and that starvation, death and illness were taking a tremendous toll amongst his people. According to the King's instructions, Indians were free men (he should have guessed it without that) and the King had given him no authority to force them to work (even God had not that power). Except for the province of Higuey which, as I have mentioned, was in a state of insurrection, the Indians were peacefully going about their work and caring for their women and children without offending anyone, serving their natural lords as well as those Spaniards who had taken their women as servants and "wives" (at least the women thought of themselves as married), despite the vexations and anguish they endured as a humble and patient people. Thus, when the comendador mayor realized the difficulties arising from having brought more people than he could maintain—allowing too many people to emigrate from Spain has always been one of the principal reasons behind the devastation of the Indies, as we shall see—he wrote to the King explaining much too much for a man of his wisdom and conscience, supposing his conscience dictated his words. I will, however, give him the benefit of the doubt and believe that he was mistaken and blind, an evil from which very few Castilians escaped.

I say he wrote a letter, not because I saw it or because the King made it known, but because he was the only person here to whom the King gave credit before making any important change in policy. Anyway, the King was informed that making Indians free men was the cause of their fleeing the Christians as well as of their avoidance of conversation and communication with Christians, so that, even when offered payment, they refused to work and preferred to roam idly, making it impossible to indoctrinate them in our holy Catholic Faith, etc. Before going any further, it must be noted now that this freedom was really nominal: the Indians were never informed that the King had decreed their freedom. They were not avoiding the Spaniards more than before on account of this freedom but rather fled to avoid the infinite and implacable vexations, the furious and rigorous oppression, the ferocious and wild condition of the Spaniards which was frightening to all Indians, just as young birds flee when they see a hawk. This, not freedom, was and always will be the reason why Indians flee from Spaniards to hide in the entrails and subterranean paths of the earth; for they were never given their freedom, even after their acquaintance with the Christians, and this is the honest-to-goodness truth, and the King's information was falsified evil and evil falseness. For this reason, they would choose to suffer any pain rather than converse with tigers, rather than appear before them to receive payment for their servile labor, even if they had been persuasively invited to a feast and spoiled with a thousand gifts.

Did we show them any law that conformed to reason that they should be convinced and know themselves under an obligation to leave home, wife and children and come fifty or a hundred leagues to work for Spaniards, even for wages? Did the admiral and Adelantado fight a just war against them by any chance? And what of sending slave ships to Castile? And putting iron chains on the two major kings of this island, Caonabo, the King of Maguana and Guarionex, the King of Vega Real, causing them to drown at sea? And the insults and tyranny of Francisco Roldán and his followers over a great part of this island? In view of this, I believe no wise and Christian man would dare affirm that the Indians were forced by natural or divine law to work the Spanish farms for wages.

The same falseness applies to the statement about indoctrination into the holy Catholic Faith, for, upon my oath, the truth is that in those days and many years later there was no more concern for their Christianization than if they had been horses or working beasts. As for this being the cause of the Spaniards' inability to find labor for their plantations and gold mines, the Indians could ask why they were complaining. If they wanted plantations, let them work the fields, and if they wanted to get rich, let them dig the gold instead of being idle and lazy, which is something Indians were not, since they lived by the sweat of their brow and more than anyone else lived by God's second precept.

Thus, the Spaniards fell into the vice they imputed to the Indians and ought not to have required the Indians to dig for gold at the cost of intolerable labor and death. They deceived the King when they said Indians refused to help them in the mines, as if the Spaniards ever worked at anything but the beating of the unfortunate Indians to make them work faster and produce gold to satisfy their insatiable greed. Supposing they had actually preached the Faith—if indeed, except for the King, this was anyone's intention—instead of decimating the Indians by cruel wars and causing them irreparable damage, then the Indians should have contributed something to maintain the Spaniards, not all but only a sufficient number of Spaniards, thus helping to alleviate the King's expenditures. But this contribution should not have consisted in depriving them of their freedom, depriving natural lords of their domains, destroying and disrupting their order, their towns, their ways of life and their government, delivering them into the hands of Spaniards who used them in mines and on plantations absolutely and universally whether they were men, women, children, old people, pregnant or nursing mothers, as if all were herds of cows, sheep or other animals. Such a contribution should have been very modest, causing the least amount of anguish and danger for their persons, houses and cities, in order to avoid decimation and make the Faith less onerous and less odious to them.

But, since the Spanish entry into this island was so violent, bloody and destructive of so many people, so full of manifest injustice and wrongs that were never redressed, so scandalous to the Faith which was the final objective and the reason for allowing Spaniards to reside in this land, Indians were never under an obligation, and would not be now if they were alive, to contribute a single *maravedí*. I know for certain that no person who possesses a moderate understanding of the laws, natural, divine and human, would doubt this but on the contrary would affirm and would subscribe to my statement. I wanted to write this here because these are the principles and foundations of Indian affairs, the ignorance of which caused the destruction of the Indies.

12

Now it is well to note what the Queen decreed after the King had been informed of the above. Oh, kings, how easily you are deceived by the appearance of good works and reason, and how much more incredulous and aware you ought to be when you deal with ministers and other people whom you entrust with the arduous negotiations of government! You believe everyone shares your simple and clear senses, unaware of a lie because you would not tell one, which is why you hear the truth least of all men; scholars have written about this, and it is also in the Scriptures, toward the end of the Book of Esther. So then, Queen Isabella was convinced of the truth of the reports and answered with a warrant saying she held the conversion of the Indians dear to her heart and thought it preferable to achieve indoctrination by making it possible to open relations between Indians and Spaniards who would help one another and work fields and mines together for the prosperity of the island, the islanders and the Crown of Castile. She ordered the comendador mayor,

. . . from now on to compel and urge the Indians to relate to the Spaniards, as well as work for them in construction, extraction of gold and other metals, farming and the maintenance of Christians, residents and inhabitants of the island, and that the day's wages be established in accordance with the individual quality of the land, the person and the work. Each cacique will be assigned a certain number of Indians whom he will take to work and, on holidays, to hear about the Faith in certain places designated for that purpose. In order to entice the cacique and his men to work as freemen and not as slaves, they must be given wages, they must be treated well (Christians should receive better treatment than non-Christians), allowing no one to harm or displease them in any way, etc.

These are the exact words of Queen Isabella's warrant, which I transcribe here from memory but will copy later from the warrant itself. Surely, the intention clearly shows the Queen's concern for the well-being and conversion of the Indians, a concern she kept to the day of her death, as I will show by copying the relevant clause from her will. If she ordered measures contrary to their well-being, the blame falls on the erroneous and ignorant information she received from the members of the council, who should have known the law since they professed it and were paid in this capacity and not as gentlemen or caballeros. Many years later I gave information to the members of the council who had signed the warrant, yet they favored a contrary opinion attending more to the law than to facts. The warrant, it seems, contained eight points relevant to the principal aim of the Queen, hence and by obligation, to the principal aim of the comendador mayor, namely, the conversion and Christianization of the Indians.

1. " . . . the better to achieve the conversion to our holy Faith, Indians should communicate with Christians" is a phrase that presupposes that the Spaniards were Christians, which they were not. Had they been Christians, the Queen's judgment was good: the Saints recommend the proximity of Gentiles, infidels and Christians so that Christian deeds may speak for the Christian law as pure, upright, mild, gentle and holy, and consequently lead to the glorification of its founder Jesus Christ as well as to speedy conversion, as St. Matthew testifies in Chapter 5. However, since our Spaniards committed so many unjust and vicious deeds contrary to the law of Christ, it follows that this requirement was never fulfilled and is not being fulfilled, as our *History* will amply demonstrate, if Christ, for whose glory this is written, gives us time to finish it. So then, the most Christian Queen and the council were deceived in their belief that it was convenient for their conversion that Indians converse with Spaniards.

2. It is clear that when the Queen said caciques should be entrusted with a certain number of Indians to offer their services for wages, she meant only a number of Indians who could work, and not whole villages, nor older people, children, women or noblemen, and not all together but in shifts. The comendador should have understood, for it is obvious that, had she ordered the contrary, it would have been unjust and against natural law, in which case he was under obligation, in the name of that law, to disobey.

3. Indian men and their wives, houses and ways of life were to be respected, which means: workers should work near enough their homes to permit them to return to their families in the evening, as they do in Castile, and nobody ought to be forced to go from one city to another; but if work should demand a prolonged absence, it should not exceed a period of one week from Saturday to Saturday, and this is unjust enough.

4. Hired workers ought to be seasonal, not permanent, as the Queen's words imply (you will pay a worker according to the "day's work"), and they ought to be persuaded slowly in order to promote willingness and good feelings and make the work less harsh, although the Queen does use the word "compel," which she did under the bad influence of those who testified against the Indians and called them idle vagabonds.

5. The Queen could not possibly have recommended that labor be of such a nature as to have Indians perish at it; hence labor was intended to be moderate, to be done on working days only, with Sundays and holidays off for rest.

6. Wages were meant to be commensurate with the type of work involved so that a man would be rewarded for his sweat and be able to provide for his family, thus finding compensation for the days absent from home and the neglect of the daily work of maintenance of his property.

7. Indians were to be treated kindly as free men and not as slaves; and by freedom it was clearly understood that hired men had the same privileges as free men in Castile, that is to say, they are free first to attend to the necessities of their houses, choose not to give their services for hire and to abandon their wives if these happen to be the bad kind, and to rest if they are tired and be cured if they are ill. Otherwise, what good is their freedom if, having these obligations, they are still forced to be hired? Even slaves are not compelled to it without the risk of committing a grave sin on the part of the compellor.

8. It must be understood that the Queen's warrant, based on false information, was pernicious and impossible to follow without the total destruction of the Indians. The comendador mayor should have seen that supplying Spaniards with gold was not meant to cost the Indians such oppression and captivity and he

should not have tolerated it one single day, for it had not been the Queen's intention. But even if the Queen had ordered it, he should have disobeyed because it is manifest that, had the Queen known the quality of the land, the fragility and gentleness of the Indians, the harshness of the work, the difficulties of extracting gold, the bitter life of desolation and despair which they lived dying, and finally, the impossibility of dying with the sacraments, she would never have written such a warrant. And if she had lived long enough to know how the comendador mayor implemented her warrant, and how it was pernicious to the Indians, she would have detested and abominated it. But, for the Indians' misfortune, she sent it on the twentieth of December 1503 and died a few months later, leaving the Indians without protection and without the hope of human remedies.

13

That was the substance of Queen Isabella's warrant; now it is well to mention how the comendador mayor executed the eight points it contained.

1. I have already said and I repeat, the truth is that in the nine years the comendador governed the island, no measures were taken for the conversion of Indians and no more was done about the matter nor any more thought given to it than if the Indians were sticks, stones, cats or dogs. This applies not only to the comendador and those who owned Indians but also to the Franciscan friars who had come with him. These were good people but they lived religiously in their houses here and in La Vega and had no other aspiration. One thing they did was brought to my knowledge: they asked permission to have the sons of some caciques (few of them to be sure), perhaps four, and taught them to read and write and I suppose their good example taught Christian doctrine, for they were good and lived virtuously.

2. He disrupted villages and distributed Indians at his pleasure, giving fifty to one and a hundred to another, according to his preferences, and these numbers included children, old people, pregnant women and nursing mothers, families of high rank as

well as common people. They called this system "Indian grants" (*repartimientos*) and the King had his grant and his manager in each town who worked his land and mined his part of the gold. The wording of the comendador's Indian grants read like this: "Mr. X, I grant you fifty or a hundred Indians under the cacique X so that you may avail yourself of their services and teach them our holy Catholic Faith," by which was meant, "Mr. X, I grant you fifty or a hundred Indians together with the person of the cacique X, so that you may use them in your lands and your mines and teach them our holy Catholic Faith." And this was the same as to condemn them all to an absolute servitude which killed them in the end, as we shall see. This, then, was the nature of their freedom.

3. The men were sent out to the mines as far as eighty leagues away while their wives remained to work the soil, not with hoes or plowshares drawn by oxen, but with their own sweat and sharpened poles that were far from equaling the equipment used for similar work in Castile. They had to make silo-like heaps for cassava plants, by digging 12 square feet 4 palms deep and 10,000 or 12,000 of such hills—a giant's work—next to one another had to be made; and they had other tasks of the same magnitude of whatever nature the Spaniards saw as fittest to make more money. Thus husbands and wives were together only once every eight or ten months and when they met they were so exhausted and depressed on both sides that they had no mind for marital communication and in this way they ceased to procreate. As for the newly born, they died early because their mothers, overworked and famished, had no milk to nurse them, and for this reason, while I was in Cuba, 7,000 children died in three months. Some mothers even drowned their babies from sheer desperation, while others caused themselves to abort with certain herbs that produced stillborn children. In this way husbands died in the mines, wives died at work, and children died from lack of milk, while others had not time or energy for procreation, and in a short time this land which was so great, so powerful and fertile, though so unfortunate, was depopulated. If this concatenation of events had occurred all over the world, the human race would have been wiped out in no time.

4. The comendador provided continuous work for them. If he imposed a limitation later I do not remember it, but this is certain, he gave them little rest and most of them worked ceaselessly. He allowed cruel Spanish brutes to supervise Indians: they were called *mineros* if the work was done in the mines and *estancieros* if it was done on plantations. They treated the Indians with such rigor and inhumanity that they seemed the very ministers of Hell, driving them day and night with beatings, kicks, lashes and blows and calling them no sweeter name than dogs. The Spaniards then created a special police to hunt them back because mistreatment and intolerable labor led to nothing but death and the Indians, seeing their companions die, began escaping into the woods. In towns and Spanish villages, the comendador appointed the most honorable caballero as inspector, with a salary of 100 Indians to serve him in addition to his normal Indian grant. These were ordinary victimizers who were that much more cruel as they were honorable. Escapees were brought before the visitador and the accuser, that is, the supposedly pious master, who accused them of being rebellious dogs and good-for-nothings and demanded stiff punishment. The visitador then had them tied to a post and he himself, with his own hands, as the most honorable man in town, took a sailor's tarred whip as tough as iron, the kind they use in galleys, and flogged them until blood ran from their naked bodies, mere skin and bones from starvation. Then, leaving them for dead, he stopped and threatened the same punishment if they tried it again. Our own eyes have seen such inhuman conduct several times and God is witness that whatever is said of it falls short of reality.

5. "Moderate labor" turned into labor fit only for iron men: mountains are stripped from top to bottom and bottom to top a thousand times; they dig, split rocks, move stones and carry dirt on their backs to wash it in rivers, while those who wash gold stay in the water all the time with their backs bent so constantly it breaks them; and when water invades the mines, the most arduous task of all is to dry the mines by scooping up pansful of water and throwing it up outside. Finally, to have an idea of what mining gold and silver requires, consider that it was next to capital punishment among the pagans when martyrs were condemned to mine metals.

The Egyptian kings used to send to the gold mines only criminals, prisoners of war and the dangerous rebels who had incurred the King's wrath, and the work was such that they were chained to prevent escape; the mines were full of workers who were driven day and night without respite, flogged and whipped, as Diodorus says in Book IV, Chapter 2. He also says they were supervised by executioners like our mineros, and mentions examples that are closer to us, that is, the very people of Spain: after the Romans had defeated Spain, they bought a great number of slaves to send to the mines (in all likelihood, many, if not all, were Spaniards) and they were an incredible source of wealth, although at the cost of anguish and calamities suffered from excessive work and only the strongest could survive the labor and the blows; otherwise death was a more desirable state, as Diodorus says. It seems, then, that by its nature, gold is the cause of death; consequently, it is proven that the calamities I have described are not at all impossible. Would to God they were not necessary, for in truth they occur wherever the Spaniards send Indians to the mines.

14

At first, the Indians were forced to stay six months away at work; later, the time was extended to eight months and this was called a shift, at the end of which they brought all the gold for minting. The King's part was subtracted and the rest went to individuals, but for years no one kept a single peso because they owed it all to merchants and other creditors, so that the anguish and torments endured by the Indians in mining that infernal gold were consumed entirely by God and no one prospered. During the minting period, the Indians were allowed to go home, a few days' journey on foot. One can imagine their state when they arrived after eight months, and those who found their wives there must have cried, lamenting their condition together. How could they even rest, since they had to provide for the needs of their family when their land had gone to weeds? Of those who had worked in the mines, a bare 10 per cent survived to start the journey home. Many Spaniards had no scruples about making them work on

Sundays and holidays, if not in the mines then on minor tasks such as building and repairing houses, carrying firewood, etc. They fed them cassava bread, which is adequate nutrition only when supplemented with meat, fish or other more substantial food. The minero killed a pig once a week but he kept more than half for himself and had the leftover apportioned and cooked daily for thirty or forty Indians, which came to a bite of meat the size of a walnut per individual, and they dipped the cassava in this as well as in the broth. It is absolutely true that while the minero was eating the Indians were under the table, just like dogs and cats, ready to snatch a bone, suck it first, then grind it and eat it with cassava. This ration applied only to mine workers; others never tasted meat in their lives and sustained themselves exclusively on cassava and other roots. In Cuba (I mentioned this here in case I forget it when I come to the subject of Cuba) it happened that certain Spaniards provided no food at all but instead sent their Indians every two or three days to the fields to feed on fruit that was to last for another two or three days of constant work. Once, a farmer harvested a crop worth some 600 gold pesos and he told that story in my presence and boasted of it.

6. The comendador arranged to have wages paid as follows, which I swear is the truth: in exchange for his life of services, an Indian received 3 *maravedís* every two days, less one-half a *maravedí* in order not to exceed the yearly half gold peso, that is, 225 *maravedís*, paid them once a year as pin money or *cacona*, as Indians call it, which means bonus or reward. This sum bought a comb, a small mirror and a string of green or blue glass beads, and many did without that consolation for they were paid much less and had no way of mitigating their misery, although in truth, they offered their labor up for nothing, caring only to fill their stomachs to appease their raging hunger and find ways to escape from their desperate lives. For this loss of body and soul, then, they received less than 3 *maravedís* for two days; many years later their wages were increased to 1 gold peso by the order of King Hernando, and this was no less an affront, as I will show later.

7. I believe the above clearly demonstrates that the Indians were totally deprived of their freedom and were put in the harshest, fiercest, most horrible servitude and captivity which no

one who has not seen it can understand. Even beasts enjoy more freedom when they are allowed to graze in the fields. But our Spaniards gave no such opportunity to Indians and truly considered them perpetual slaves, since the Indians had not the free will to dispose of their persons but instead were disposed of according to Spanish greed and cruelty, not as men in captivity but as beasts tied to a rope to prevent free movement. When they were allowed to go home, they often found it deserted and had no other recourse than to go out into the woods to find food and to die. When they fell ill, which was very frequently because they are a delicate people unaccustomed to such work, the Spaniards did not believe them and pitilessly called them lazy dogs, and kicked and beat them; and when illness was apparent they sent them home as useless, giving them some cassava for the twenty- to eighty-league journey. They would go then, falling into the first stream and dying there in desperation; others would hold on longer but very few ever made it home. I sometimes came upon dead bodies on my way, and upon others who were gasping and moaning in their death agony, repeating "Hungry, hungry." And this was the freedom, the good treatment and the Christianity that Indians received under the comendador's execution of this point of the warrant.

8. This order was difficult or impossible and not designed to bring Indians to the Faith; indeed, it was pernicious and deadly and designed to destroy all Indians. Obviously, the Queen had not intended the destruction but the edification of the Indians, and the comendador would have done well to consider this, as well as the fact that, had the Queen been alive to see the results of her order, she would have revoked and abominated it. It is amazing how this prudent man did not realize what a deadly pestilence his order was when, at the end of each shift, he found out how many Indians were missing and how the rest suffered. And it is amazing that he did not change or revoke it, for it was impossible that he should have remained unaware of its iniquity; and, consequently, he was not excused before God or before the King. Before God, because it is in itself evil and contrary to divine and natural law to enslave free rational beings so harshly, especially when he could see from experience that his order was the cause of it; before the

King, because he completely went against what had been told him. To remedy the loss of lives that were being consumed in mines and plantations at the end of each shift, the Spaniards asked the comendador to replace the Indians of the island and the comendador granted their request, favoring the principal and most privileged Spaniards, leaving the others unsatisfied and making new distributions every two or three years. As I said, the Queen died shortly after sending her warrant and therefore never found out about this cruel decimation. Philip and Juana succeeded her, but Philip died before he could appraise the situation in the Indies and Castile was two years without the presence of a King. Thus, the decimation of these poor Indians had begun and could be kept silent, and when King Hernando came to rule Castile they kept it from him too. About eight years passed under the comendador's rule and this disorder had time to grow; no one gave it a thought and the multitude of people who originally lived on this island, which, according to the admiral, was infinite, as we said in Book I, was consumed at such a rate that in those eight years 90 per cent had perished. From here this sweeping plague went to San Juan, Jamaica, Cuba and the continent, spreading destruction over the whole hemisphere, as we shall see. Thus, from the disorder that this comendador mayor, Knight of Alcántara, established on the island by distributing Indians among Spaniards in the way we have described there followed, through diabolical delusion and craft, the violent and raging perdition which was to sterilize and consume the greater part of mankind in these Indies.

15

Now that we have given an account of the evil practice so solemnly called *repartimiento* by its originator, who had acted on his own mandate and not the King's, it is time to tell the story of the war that broke out about then in the Higuey province. When we arrived at this island with the comendador, Higuey was in turmoil over the death of the cacique of Saona Island and had rebelled, as the Spaniards call it, causing the war we described in Chapter 8. This one had another reason: we have already mentioned that Juan de Esquivel had ended the first war with a pact of sorts, forcing the Indians to work the fields and supply great provisions of bread—which was worth a lot then and was the island's principal source of wealth—in exchange for the privilege to stay home instead of being brought to Santo Domingo, which is what Indians dread the most. We have also said that a man named Martín de Villamán had been put in charge of a wooden fortress with nine other Spaniards well trained to use an iron rule. They forced the Indians to transport the King's bread to this city and to stay there for labor, and, as my long experience of these things tells me and as everyone knows who has been here, the rigors of the Spanish demands—especially hard to take were the raids for women—were such that the Indians got together, unable to tolerate this any longer, and they attacked the fort, burned it and killed those Spaniards. If I remember correctly, only one Spaniard escaped, bringing the news to Santo Domingo.

The comendador then declared war against the province and mobilized all the Spaniards; Juan de Esquivel was the captain in command as well as captain of the contingent from Santiago; Juan Ponce de León, of whom there is much to write later, headed the Santo Domingo contingent; Diego de Escobar, who is the man we mentioned in Book I in connection with Francisco Roldán's insurrection, was made captain of the contingent from La Vega, that is to say, Concepción; and I do not recall who headed the one from Bonao. Altogether they came to about 300 men, which is less than the first time. They followed various routes and assembled in the province of Ycayagua (the middle syllable is long) next to Higuey, where the citizens endure Spanish rule with more patience and equanimity.

The Spaniards recruited Indians there who proved very good warriors against the Indians of Higuey, and whose towns were located inland on mountains as flat as mesetas, terraced every 50 *estados* or so, the climbing of which was so difficult a cat could hardly have made it. Those mesas measure about 10 or 15 square leagues and are paved with slabs of natural stone so evenly that it looks hand-made, and the stones are as rough and sharp as diamond slivers. They are full of holes 5 or 6 spans round filled with red earth where they grow cassava; and it is so fertile—which is why Indians build their towns in those mountains—that one shoot of the plant produces a root as big as the hole itself, and the same happens with a few seeds of our melons, yielding a fruit about the size of a 2-gallon jug and the meat is blood-red and delicate and fragrant. They would fell enough trees in the forests of these flat mesas to make a plaza, large or small according to the size of the town, and in the middle they cut four very wide alleys in the shape of a cross, about a stone's throw in length. This was used for fighting, it being impossible to fight in the woods because of the denseness of the trees and the rough surface of the flat rocks.

When the Spaniards reached the border of the province, the Indians sent smoke signals from one town to the next and took their wives, children and the elderly to the safest place in the woods. The Spaniards came closer and encamped in a clearing in order to take full advantage of the horses and they outlined their tactics, first planning—as is the practice in wars—to apprehend individuals from the enemy camp and torture them to learn their strategy and strength, which they did with some success although there were those who did not give information and died with their secret as their chief had commanded. They arrived in a town where Indians had assembled, ready to fight but stark naked, with no other shields than their bellies, and they [the Indians] gave a war cry designed to inspire fear; and truly, if their weapons had been as extraordinarily frightening, they would have fared much better than they did. Awaiting the first charge, the Indians shot their arrows but from such a distance that when the arrow hit the mark, it was so weak it could not have killed a beetle. The Spaniards discharged their arbalests upon those naked bodies (they used few muskets then), killing many and causing others to retreat rather than wait for the sword. It happened too, that some were pierced by arrows down to the quills and they pulled them out and broke then in two with their teeth, and, spitting out one half, they threw the other half with their hands in the direction of the Spaniards in a gesture of contempt before expiring.

After the arbalest attack, Indians could only try to run back to their respective villages but, given the sharpness of the ground, the Spaniards overcame them in no time. Either then or on the battle-ground, some Indians were caught alive and were tortured incredibly to find out where people were hidden, and the Spaniards used them as guides also, tying them by the neck with a rope, and some would hurl themselves down a cliff to drag the Spaniard along with them and kill him as their chief had ordered. The Spanish squadrons arrived in this way to the place where the Indians had put their possessions into safety and you should have seen how they worked their swords on those naked bodies, sparing no one! After such a devastation, they set out to catch the fugitives and, catching them, had them place their hand on a board and slashed it off with the sword, and on to the other hand, which they butchered, sometimes leaving the skin dangling; and they said, "Go and deliver that message," meaning, "Go tell the others what we have in store for them by showing them your arms." And the poor Indians howling and crying and bleeding to death, not knowing where to find their people, their wounds untended, fell shortly thereafter and died abandoned.

16

Leaving the place deserted, the Spaniards went to another village where they knew Indians had gathered. Among others, they went to the town of one of the most important kings in the region, King Cotubanamá or Cotubano, who had traded names with Juan de Esquivel once (there was name-trading as part of a peace pact), as we said in Chapter 8. He was not only the most esteemed and most courageous man in the whole province, he was also the most handsome by any standards, regardless of nationality. He was taller than most Indians, had very wide shoulders and a narrow waist, a large hand span and well-proportioned members; his countenance was not elegant but fierce and very stern; his bow and arrows were twice the size of ordinary ones; in short, he was so striking that all the Spaniards who saw him could not help but admire him. I waited until now to describe him in detail because it was during this second war that I saw him; I had not seen him when I spoke of him in Chapter 8.

So then, the Spaniards decided to march upon Cotubanamá's town where a large gathering of Indians was preparing to resist.

They arrived at a fork in the road leading to the town: one of the paths was cleared of branches and other obstacles, which was a trap designed to attack them from behind; the other was closed and so full of cut trees and branches a cat could not have passed through it. But the Spaniards are always very careful and, suspecting an ambush, they chose the closed route. Of the league or league and a half from the shore to the town, half a league was encumbered in this way, which made passage very difficult and fatiguing. The rest of the way was clear, which confirmed their suspicion that the Indians had set a trap by leaving the other road open. They were very much on the alert as they walked forward and suddenly they came upon the Indians, who were watching the other road, waiting to attack from the rear. They discharged their arbalests and the Indians ran to the streets of the town, shooting arrows from afar to put as much distance as possible between themselves and the Spaniards' swords; but it was child's play and they [the Indians] suffered more damage than they caused. Nonetheless, they came closer and fought with stones, throwing them by hand because they do not use slings, and yelling their war cries, showing a great desire to fight back those who in their opinion were destroying their nation. Their courage did not falter when they saw their companions fall at their sides; on the contrary, they seemed to draw more strength from it and surely, it would have been a different story altogether if they had had equal weapons.

I will relate an exploit worthy of praise that I saw myself, one so outstanding I wish I could describe it adequately with words. A Spaniard by the name of Alejos Gómez was there, a tall and sturdy man so experienced in killing Indians he could slice them in two with one stroke of his sword. He told the others he wanted to fight an Indian alone and kill him alone. His weapons were a sword, a dagger, a lance and a good leather shield. When the Indian saw him walk away from the group he charged upon him, as a man armed to the teeth would attack a cat. Alejos Gómez hung his lance on his shield and started to fight with stones. The Indian threatened him with his arrow, as if about to shoot it, jumping from one spot to another and ducking the stones with the agility of a hawk. Both Indians and Spaniards stopped to watch them: the Indian would jump on Gómez as if to nail him on the spot and Gómez used his shield to absorb the shock; Gómez would hurl a stone and the Indian ducked it and kept menacing with the arrow, naked as the day he was born, with a single arrow to his bow, and this went on for a good while, Gómez never succeeding in hitting him despite their occasional physical proximity. Once the Indian thought so little of Gómez that he ran full force toward him and placed his arrow in the rim of Gómez's shield, which made Gómez curl up like a ball behind the shield and, seeing the Indian close to him, he dropped his stone and threw his lance at him. But the Indian jumped sideways and walked away laughing, mocking Gómez with his bow and unused arrow, his naked body untouched.

The Indians surrounded him with shouts and laughter, mocking Gómez and his company, congratulating their fellow soldier for an agility and courage truly worthy of praise. The Spaniards marveled and Gómez himself was as happy as if he had killed him, and all praised the Indian greatly. Surely, that was a merry spectacle worthy of being seen by any Prince of Spain or of any other nation and worthy of a generous reward for the Indian. All of this is true: I saw it just as I have described it. On the whole the battle between the Indians and Spaniards lasted from two o'clock in the afternoon to sunset.

17

The next day there was not an Indian in sight; they had fled to the forest where the people unfit for war were waiting, for they realized that they were powerless against the Spaniards. Since Cotubanamá was reputed the strongest King in the region and since he had not been more successful than the rest, from then on nobody dared await the Spaniards and they all fled to the most inaccessible and hidden parts of the woods. The Spaniards formed scouting parties to track them down, aiming always and principally to catch the caciques, Cotubanamá especially. These parties would search the paths for tracks of Indians; the paths were blind and narrow but some Spaniards were so adept at tracking down Indians they could tell that an Indian had passed that way by looking at a rotten leaf on the ground. Indians walk in the woods with great lightness since they go barefooted and naked, thirty of them leaving no more visible track than that of a cat—but apparently that was one track too many. Other Spaniards could smell fire—Indians always built fires, no matter where they are—from a great distance and thus were put on the right track. As they went, it often happened that an Indian was caught, tortured, then tied to lead the way; and, taking the Indians by surprise, they swiftly killed all those who met their blades, their first concern being to inspire terror. Those who were caught alive, such as male adolescents and adults, had both their hands severed and were told to go and spread the message, and the number of the mutilated and the dead was infinite.

The Spaniards found pleasure in inventing all kinds of odd cruelties, the more cruel the better, with which to spill human blood. They built a long gibbet, low enough for the toes to touch the ground and prevent strangling, and hanged thirteen of them at a time in honor of Christ Our Saviour and the twelve Apostles. When the Indians were thus still alive and hanging, the Spaniards tested their strength and their blades against them, ripping chests open with one blow and exposing entrails, and there were those who did worse. Then, straw was wrapped around their torn bodies and they were burned alive. One man caught two children about two years old, pierced their throats with a dagger, then hurled them down a precipice. My eyes have seen these acts so foreign to human nature, and now I tremble as I write, not believing them myself, afraid that perhaps I was dreaming. But truly, this sort of thing has happened all over the Indies, and more cruelly too sometimes, and I am quite sure that I have not forgotten.

It happened also that Spanish squads found Indian hiding places without a guide and that the Indians resisted mightily. Once a group of thirteen, with four arbalests, lances, swords and shields, found a place where 1,000 or 2,000 Indians with wives and children had gathered. The Indians attacked; the Spaniards shot their arbalests but the strings snapped; the Indians showered arrows and stones on their shields, but could not get close enough to the Spaniards to hit them with their macanas because a clever soldier manning an arbalest kept them at bay, threatening to shoot at any moment, saving Spaniards' lives for the two or three hours of the fight. It chanced that in the afternoon the main body of the Spaniards had encamped nearby, and when they heard the war cries, they came to the rescue, frightening the Indians and causing slaughter and taking a great many captives among the men, women and children.

During all these sallies the Spaniards suffered from hunger; the general rule here is that they erupt on the scene fighting, the Indians run away, and since they bring no Castilian food with them and are too lazy to provide for themselves, they starve and often die. So the captains distribute the captives as slaves, chained or unchained, depending on the availability of chains, and groups of two or three Spaniards take their ten or twenty slaves to the woods to look for a root called *guáyagas* (the middle syllable is short) from which a certain paste is made in that province. Once, three or four of the Spaniards being careless, these slaves killed them with the chains, then freed one another and brought both chains and swords as a token of victory to Cotubanamá. The Indians released after torture were told to return to their people with a message to come and surrender or else suffer the same torments; and the Indians answered yes, they would surrender, but they were afraid of Cotubanamá who had ordered them to stay away from the Spaniards or he would have them killed. For this reason, and also because Cotubanamá was so valiant, it was impossible to subjugate the province while he remained free and alive; and thus the Spaniards' major concern was to apprehend him.

They found out that he and his family had gone to Saona Island without any of his people but well guarded nevertheless and very much on the alert. Captain Juan de Esquivel decided to go to Saona since he had done so well here, and they marched toward the point closest to Saona, where from island to island the ocean is only two leagues wide. It was during that time that the Spaniards caught at least three—I think it may have been four—Indian chiefs and burned them alive: they built a bed of branches on top of four or six forks and tied the caciques securely to a pole across them. They set fire underneath and as they began to be roasted, they gave such cries I think even animals could not endure to hear them. Meanwhile, the captain was resting at some distance and, hearing those lamentable cries, gave orders to strangle them and finish them off, either from pity or because they were disturbing his rest. But the alguazil in charge of executing the sentence, who was the author of that act, had his men put sticks in the open mouths of his victims to stop the noise, and so they died parched and burned to death, as if their whole race had been killed because they were its chiefs. And I have seen all this with my very own eyes.

18

The Spaniards knew they could never subjugate the Indians of the province as long as Cotubanamá was free, but now they knew he was on the small island of Saona and Captain Juan de Esquivel set out to follow after him. Caravels were used to transport cassava, wine, cheese and other Castilian things from Santo Domingo to Higuey province; therefore, he arranged to meet one at a certain place and embark his men at night to avoid Cotubanamá's spies. Cotubanamá lived in a large cave in the middle of the island with his wife and children and as soon as he saw a caravel, even if there was nothing extraordinary about its being there, he sent spies to watch for the point of disembarkation while he himself went before dawn with twelve valiant Indians to the spot where the Spaniards were most likely to land.

One night, then, Esquivel embarked with fifty of his men and arrived on the opposite shore at dawn. But the two Indian spies had been delayed and some thirty men had already climbed a high rock before the spies could get there and set watch, and a few light-footed Spaniards who had gone ahead caught them and brought them to Esquivel who found out where Cotubanamá was hiding. Esquivel drew his dagger and killed one of the spies while he kept the other to serve as guide. A small group of Spaniards, eager to seize Cotubanamá, darted ahead in disorder and soon they found two roads: only one man took the left fork because, the island being full of hills, they could not see one another despite their physical closeness. That man was Juan López, a tall and sturdy peasant used to killing Indians, having participated in many raids from the old days on Hispaniola. He came upon twelve Indians walking single file as is their custom (they could not walk any other way for the narrowness of the paths and the thickness of the forests), naked, strong, with bows and arrows, the last of whom was Cotubanamá. His bow, as I said, was a giant's bow, equipped with a tip made of three fish bones like a rooster's foot, which would have made his life easier if the Spaniards had not worn armor.

When the first Indians saw the Spaniard, thinking that others were following him, they froze instead of killing him and getting away. López asked where Cotubanamá was, they answered he was right behind them and stepped aside for López. Cotubanamá saw him too late and started to arm his bow but López was upon him with his sword and Cotubanamá, having no experience with swords, thinking it a dull-edged weapon, seized it with both hands; López pulled on it and slashed the chief's hands, then he charged again. Cotubanamá said, *"Mayanimacaná, Juan Desquivel dacá"* (*"*Don't kill me, I am Juan de Esquivel": we mentioned in Chapter 8 how he and Esquivel had changed names), whereupon the rest of the Indians fled, leaving Cotubanamá alone with López, when it would have been so easy to kill him and run away to safety with their chief. López placed the tip of his sword on Cotubanamá's belly and a hand on his shoulders or in his hair, and since he was alone, he was at odds wondering what to do next. Cotubanamá kept pleading for his life saying he was Juan de Esquivel and, though he had deep cuts on his hands and bled profusely, he made a movement with his right hand and pushed the sword away from his body, then he jumped on López, who as I said was a very strong man. Both rolled on the rocks, Cotubanamá on top of López and the sword underneath both; and Cotubanamá forced his large hand against López's throat in order to strangle him. Choking and making sounds as best he could, López was heard by the Spaniards who had taken the other path; they ran back, found the left fork, arrived on the scene and struck Cotubanamá with the arbalest; he fell on López with all his weight and almost knocked him out, then he got up and so did Juan López, half dead, and there Cotubanamá was apprehended.

They handcuffed Cotubanamá and took him to a deserted town

while the rest looked for his wife and children, who, having been notified by the twelve fugitives, had left the cave and gone into hiding; but the Spaniards caught some Indians and brought them to Cotubanamá and made him give orders to have his wife and children brought to him. And so they did, arriving with their scant belongings such as hammocks and things of little value because the natives of Hispaniola do not own or care to own anything beyond the strict necessities. In the cave the Spaniards found the chains and swords acquired in the way we described above, and they used the chains on Cotubanamá, whom they first intended to roast alive as they had the other chiefs. But, thinking better of it, they decided to subject him to the torture of having his flesh torn to shreds with pincers, as if he had committed an atrocious crime by trying to defend both himself and his people from the oppression Martín de Villamán and company had started to inflict upon them, which was the beginning of the oppression of which Cotubanamá was well aware, as well as the cause of many deaths. They brought him in chains to Santo Domingo, but the comendador used less cruelty than Esquivel would have wished by sparing him the pincers and having him hanged instead. Juan de Esquivel liked to boast that he had accomplished three good things on this island: bringing a royal privilege from Spain which accorded only the fifth part of all gold to the King, the slaughter he committed on Saona Island which we described in Chapter 8, and the apprehension of Cotubanamá. . . .

After Cotubano's death and the cruelties of that war, which lasted eight to ten months, the strength of the island was gone; gone too were the thoughts and hopes of seeing an end to Spanish oppression, and the island was pacified, if indeed it is fitting to speak of peace when the Spaniards were left warring against God by practicing oppression without restraint of any kind, large or small, annihilating the natives to the degree that newcomers ask whether Indians are white or dark-skinned. The whole world knows and admits this lamentable annihilation of so many people; even those who never set foot in the Indies know it, for it is notoriously and justly famous, but the truth of what actually happened was greater than any account one can make of it. As Christopher Columbus informed the King, it is a fact that innumerable people inhabited this land, and the Archbishop of Seville, Diego de Deza, told me one day that he had heard the admiral mention he counted a million and 100,000 heads. This must have referred only to the people in the vicinity of the Cibao mines on whom he had imposed a gold tribute per capita, as we said in Book I, and perhaps he included in this number part of the Xaraguá province which paid tribute in cassava and raw and spun cotton. I think without fear of erring too far that there lived more than three million people on this island, because a number of areas had not yet been explored, like Higuey, Hanyguayaba, Guaycayarima, Guahaba and various other parts. To secure the province, the comendador ordered the establishment of two Spanish towns, one near the sea called Salvaleón, the other inland called Santa Cruz de Aycayagua, and he interspersed Indian towns in between so that they could serve the Christians who annihilated them in the end. And so this island had altogether seventeen Spanish towns from which to destroy Indians. They were, in this order: Santo Domingo, Buenaventura (eight leagues from here and near the old mines), Bonao, Concepción, Santiago, Puerto de la Plata, Puerto Real, Lares de Guahaba, Arbol Gordo, Cotuy, Açua, San Juan de la Maguana, Xaraguá, Yaquimo, Salvatierra, Salvaleón and Santa Cruz de Aycayagua, the penultimate syllable long.

19

The King and Queen had a royal decree forbidding all Spaniards to aggrieve the Indians in any way, to capture them, to remove them to Castile or other regions unfamiliar to them, or to tamper with their persons and/or possessions. Disobeying carried a heavy penalty commensurate with the monarchs' desire that Indians receive good examples and good works from the Spaniards in order to facilitate their Christianization. With this in mind, they gave permission to some Spaniards to establish peaceful trade relations with the Indians, hoping that love between the two parties would make the Faith attractive and desirable. However, Alonso de Hojeda and Cristóbal Guerra had already wrought havoc among the Indians, and others had done the same who had asked for a trade license for many of these islands and part of the continent, especially in the region we call Cartagena, where Guerra's violence had been particularly fierce. The Indians, then, either traded peacefully with the Christians or, if they knew better, tried to prevent them from landing on their shores; and it would happen sometimes that in the fighting they killed anywhere from one to ten Spaniards. There were loud complaints to the King about this. The Spaniards claimed that these people were cannibals—we call them Caribs today—and ate human flesh and would rather kill than allow them to disembark and establish communication. Naturally, they kept silent about the type of thing they did to the Indians, for which they got their just reward, even when Indians ate their flesh and drank their blood, as some treat their enemies.

Since no one ever spoke the truth on the Indians' behalf and no one was ever present to defend their cause, the monarchs listened to their misinformants and were deceived into acting against the Indians' interests. The Queen issued a second decree that invalidated the first and gave permission to anyone with a mind to conquer to use force whenever conversion to the holy Catholic Faith and allegiance to the Crown were not immediately forthcoming. In this case, the Spaniards were allowed to capture Indians, send them to Castile or anywhere else they pleased, sell them at slave markets and use them without incurring the penalties reserved for such acts. The Queen mentioned specifically the old island names of San Bernardo, Fuerte and Barú; since they have lost these names I cannot ascertain which islands they are, except perhaps that the Barú Islands must be the ones near Cartagena. She also mentioned the two harbors of Cartagena and, I think, Santa María. She says that she submitted her decree to the members of the council for examination and they found that, since the monarchs had duly enjoined the cannibal Indians to convert to the holy Faith and to behave civilly toward their neighbors, the fact that they had refused and were defending themselves against indoctrination, that they continually waged war against other Indians, and that they had killed many Spaniards, justified the decree as a necessary measure against a people hardened in their evil ways, idolatry, eating human flesh, etc.

These are the very words of doña Isabella's decree, and it shows how kings are usually deceived even in matters of the law. Jurists like to pretend that legal statutes naturally abide in the hearts of princes because, as they say, a Prince is surrounded by great men whose legal competence flourishes in his proximity. It is clear also that blindness characterized the members of the Castilian royal council from the early days of the discovery of the Indies, and this is ample proof of it. Is there greater ignorance than to inculpate a people hitherto unknown to us, who lived without the knowledge of our existence, of the Catholic Faith, of the meaning of the words "conversion," "Christians"—except as experience taught them to mean a people uncouth, cruel, addicted to plundering and killing—and "communion of the faithful," especially when no Spaniard at that time knew anything of their language, nor they of ours? The members of the council may well say that Indians had been required many times to convert. Presupposing a knowledge of the rudiments of language, was this request by any chance as simple as stating that the sun is light and that two and two make four? Supposing also that they understood the meaning of the request, not just the words, is it right to require that they should adopt the Faith without further arguments, persuasions and deliberations? Did Christ, who is the principal dispenser of faith, order that Catholicism be imposed on a people by means of an injunction, threats and penalization, read over a thousand times or not?

Is there a single nation which would not think that the world is full of just such evil-doers as the Spaniards if their first experience with that outside world was with a people who entered territories by force, killed the people and despoiled them of their rights? Just because the Spaniards told them to obey the King of Castile, supposing they understood, what obligation did they have to obey since they already had their own kings? Or rather, if they had consented, would they not be judged as ridiculously stupid for doing so? If their natural kings turned themselves over to the Castilian King, the people would have a right to depose them; and if the people pledged allegiance to a foreign King without the consent of their own rulers, they would be traitors and would be punished as such with salt torture, as they do in Spain in such cases. Was trying to defend oneself from Spanish cruelties such a crime? Even beasts are allowed the right of self-defense. Was it not a most false argument to say that Indians tried to defend themselves from indoctrination? As if anyone had taken the trouble to explain to them what indoctrination meant! Yes, the legal ignorance of the members of the council is manifest indeed, to have lost such an opportunity in a matter so juridical, so important, so dangerous, so harmful and so beneficial if only their incompetence had not misguided the whole affair so irreparably.

Thus, God is sure to have imputed the injustice and irreparable harm to the members of the council; they simply had no legitimate reason to ignore such self-evident rights; they were paid to know the law, not to pose as gentlemen or as hidalgos, hidalgos though they were, for surely, there were other men around more capable than they of being both. So then, the jurists' fable about the law abiding in the hearts of princes is a mighty shaky and feeble thing, considering how intolerably the members of the council erred. It is also opportune to note how unjust these jurists were since they did not respect judicial procedure which they, not the King, were qualified to demand: they condemned those people without hearing a defense, solely on the strength of false testimony made by the capital enemies of the Indians, that is to say, the very Spaniards who worked toward nothing else but to oppress, capture and decimate the Indians, and in so doing, the members of the council did the King a grave disservice. No judgment more perverse and unjust ever existed on the whole face of the universe than the one I am recording here before God, who knows I am telling the truth, and as my *History* will prove. . . .

27

When the Indians saw Spanish men building houses and villages to settle on their land without asking permission, as if it belonged to them, and knowing how inopportune the Spanish were with their demands, as well as how they had forced other Indians to sail with them, they took the news of the settling very badly. The pilot Pedro de Ledesma charges them with reacting angrily to Spanish possession of land, and so does the admiral in the letter he wrote to the King from Jamaica. Everybody knows that no nation in the world, however uncivilized, would tolerate such a thing; indeed, all of them would resent it very much and resist mightily. The Spanish found discontent among the Indians and determined to add fuel to the fire and reward their hospitality by taking prisoner the cacique, his wife and children. Don Hernando speaks like a person ignorant of the Indians' rights when, not questioning his father's unjust policy (as I stated in Book I), he says he was warned by an interpreter of the fact that: "Quibia, the King of Veragua, intended to steal upon them, burn all their houses and kill all Christians out of his resentment at this colonization. Therefore, it seemed fitting that he should punish the King and set an example for the neighboring tribes by capturing him and his chieftains and sending them to Castile, while the tribe would remain to serve the Christians." These are don Hernando's actual words. Is there any greater insensitivity? What injury had the Indians caused the Spaniards, distressed as they were that these bearded, restless, fierce men had settled their lands, especially since they had already experienced the nature of their unholy, scandalous, unjust and evil exploits?

Was capturing the King, his family and his court, was the enslaving of his people to punish him while frightening the others the kind of medicine needed to palliate their grievances? Had they, by any chance, the obligation to feed and joyfully welcome the Spaniards? And who had made the admiral the judge, who gave him jurisdiction to punish them? What authority had he to enslave that whole tribe when, in a state of servitude, that tribe was equal, perhaps even superior, to the Spaniards as free men, except in matters of Faith and Christianity? On the contrary, didn't the Indians have more power and jurisdiction over the Spaniards? They were the natural lords there, and the Spaniards were offenders in their territory, violating the trust they should have had toward their hosts. Consequently, if they had plans to burn and kill, they were within their rights.

Moreover, the interpreter's message was not necessarily true, as the Adelantado had occasion to see later, when he captured the cacique. Supposing it had been true—and this is difficult to say because, having only sign language with which to communicate, perhaps they didn't understand each other correctly—the remedy should have been to placate the King and his subjects by doing them some good deed. But the safest and wisest way would have been to satisfy the Indians, go to Castile and inform the King, so that, if future traders and missionaries were to return, they would find a hearty welcome among peaceful and satisfied Indians. However, the Spaniards were not worthy of enlightenment; they sought only gold and the pursuit of their own interests; thus they fell into an intolerable error and ignored fundamental principles.

To continue don Hernando's story, he says that the Adelantado and his seventy-four men went to Veragua on March 30 for reasons of safety. The houses in Veragua were scattered like those in the Basque country and the cacique's dwellings were on a hill. When Quibia heard the Spaniards had come into the vicinity, he sent a messenger to warn them not to come nearer, but the Adelantado paid no attention. In order not to appear frightened, he decided to proceed with only five men, ordering the others to follow by two's and, at the sound of the gun, to fan out and surround the house, to prevent anyone's escape. This makes it quite clear that the Indians had no intention of killing them, since the Adelantado and his five men arrived there safely and then did what they did.

Near the chief's house, Quibia sent another message forbidding entrance to his house; he, although wounded, would come out to meet the Spaniards. They say Indians are exceedingly jealous and try to keep their women away from the eyes of strangers. Quibia came to the door, sat down and made a sign to the Adelantado to approach alone, which the Adelantado did, telling his men to attack the moment he would take Quibia's arm. He inquired about the cacique's health and other matters pertaining to the land, communicating by means of an Indian the Spaniards had taken a while back who seemed to understand something of the language. Pretending to examine Quibia's wound, the Adelantado seized the King's wrist, but the two men had such great strength that it took the four Spaniards to help the Adelantado while the fifth fired a shot and the ambushed men rushed to the house. There were some fifty persons inside, old and young, and most were taken captive, including a few of the chief's sons, wives, and principal men who offered as a ransom for him a treasure they possessed in the mountains.

And this is the kind of exploit the Adelantado performed. Before proclaiming the land his own, he hastened to dispatch the prisoners to the ships while he remained with most of his men to pursue those who had escaped their cruel hands. They discussed who would take the booty back to the ships and a pilot, reputed to be a conscientious man, offered his services. The chief, tied hand and foot, was entrusted to him; he was warned not to let his prisoner escape and he swore he would let his beard be shaved off if his vigilance failed and allowed such a thing. They started downstream. About half a league from the sea, the King began to complain of the crippling pain in his hands and the pilot, pitying him, untied him from the boat bench and kept the end of the rope in his hand. Suddenly, the cacique jumped in the water and because the pilot could not hold on to the rope without falling too, he let go of it and the chief escaped. It was dark; the men moved noisily about the boat and it was impossible to see or hear the direction taken by the cacique; thus they lost him, never to hear of him again. And to prevent other disasters, they determined not to stop until they had reached the ships, feeling very ashamed at having been tricked by the Indian chief.

The next day, March 31, the Adelantado gave up the arduous search in such a mountainous territory. He decided to return to the ships, happy with his loot of some 300 ducats' worth of mirrors and gold jewels from the King's house, tassels and beads they wear around their arms and ankles, and bands they use around their heads like crowns, all of which he gave to the admiral. They say the latter kept a fifth for the King and distributed the rest among the men who had taken part in the expedition, as if it had been won in a legitimate war against the Turks. To boot, don Hernando says that the Adelantado was given a crown for such a singular victory! Surely, the blindness of those people who first came here and treated the natives as if they were Africans was something to marvel at; first the admiral, then all who followed after him. Would to God that the blindness had stopped then and that the world weren't ravaged by it today. . . .

30

Since the holds of the ships were drawing water, the admiral ran aground safely away from the surf. The crew had orders to stay on board and the Indians, a gentle people (don Hernando, who was there, actually said this), came in canoes to exchange food and other objects for Castilian trinkets. To avoid inequities, disputes and grudges, Columbus placed two persons in charge of trading and distributing the goods equally among everyone, since all the food supplies were gone, either eaten, rotten or lost in the hustle of departure from the Belén river. Don Hernando says the Lord guided them to this island, then heavily populated and fertile, whose inhabitants flocked from all the villages in their eagerness to trade with the Spaniards.

For this reason, and to avoid Spanish misdemeanor on the island, the admiral decided to rest and recover at sea because, as don Hernando says, we are an uncouth lot of people and no manner of order or punishment could prevent our men from stealing and molesting women if they went ashore, and this would greatly endanger our friendly relations with the Indians. We would be forced to fight for food and would find ourselves in a scrape. This was avoided because all the men remained assigned to their posts and could not leave ship except by special permission, which pleased the Indians. They brought us essential things at a very low cost to us: we traded an end strip of brass for one or two *hutías*, a rabbit-like animal; a handful of green or yellow glass beads for cassava bread, made of grated edible roots; and a rattle bell for something of more value. Sometimes, kings and nobles would receive a small looking glass, a colorful cap or a pair of scissors; thus these gifts relieved their misery and left them in good spirits. The admiral bought ten canoes for the crews of the grounded ships. In this manner the Spaniards were very well provided for and the Indians communicated with them.

The admiral held councils with his officers to discuss how the ships would be put to sail and at least reach Hispaniola. They were deprived of all human help and all hope of a rescue ship except by miracle, since everything, especially qualified officers, was lacking to start that journey again. They weighed advantages and disadvantages, ways and means and dangers involved over and over again for many days and concluded, by resolution of the admiral, to inform the governor general as well as Columbus's manager on Hispaniola of their plight and ask that a ship be sent to Jamaica with all the necessary equipment and a food supply. For this difficult enterprise, he named two persons whose faithfulness, courage and common sense could be relied upon. It was indeed a dangerous matter to cross a gulf which measures twenty or twenty-five leagues between Jamaica and Hispaniola without counting the thirty-five leagues they had to navigate along the coast of Jamaica from its eastern point, all this in frail canoes that are nothing but hollowed-out tree trunks.

There is a large rock called Navasa in that gulf, eight leagues from Hispaniola. Crossing the gulf was an exploit demanding great prowess and courage. Canoes are so shallow they turn over like pumpkins. This presents no danger to the Indians because they can swim and empty their canoes with gourds and climb in again; canoes do not sink when they are overturned. Of the men Columbus named, I knew one personally, Diego Méndez de Segura, chief clerk of the fleet and a very prudent, honorable, well-spoken man he was; the other was Bartolomé de Flisco, a Genoese worthy of this mission. Each took a canoe, six Spaniards and ten Indian oarsmen. Diego Méndez was told to embark for Castile from Santo Domingo and present letters and an account of the voyage to the King; Bartolomé Flisco was told to return to Jamaica with news of Diego Méndez's progress. Two hundred full leagues separated the admiral's ships from Santo Domingo.

I have a copy of the long letter Columbus wrote to the monarchs, in which he relates the anguish and the many adversities of his voyage, the new lands he had discovered, the richness of the Veragua mines. He repeats the list of services he had rendered to the Spanish Crown by discovering the New World at the cost of much hardship, and he laments his fate and that of his brothers now made prisoners, their property confiscated, deprived of their honor and titles. Honor and titles he well deserved and well earned, for no services so famous were ever rendered to any other earthly King. The admiral did not write the last sentence; I am adding it because he is owed the praise.

Further in his letter, he asks for the restitution of his titles and satisfaction of his claims as well as for punishment of his accusers. He implores Heaven and earth to share his grief, saying: "Up to now I have cried alone; may Heaven take pity and may those on earth who are acquainted with charity, truth and justice cry with me!" and so on. He stresses his poverty, saying he has no roof of his own over his head, but instead must take to an inn when he needs to eat and sleep. After twenty years of extraordinary services, he and his brothers have acquired very little benefit. He misses the sacraments of the Church, especially since he is ill with the gout and fears death will overtake him in exile and isolation. He declares that he did not make this last voyage for personal fame and gains, as if to say he had these already, but sailed instead to serve the Crown with devotion and good intentions. Finally, he ends the letter by asking that, once back in Castile, he may be allowed to make a pilgrimage to Rome and other places, and entrusting the King to God, he signs his letter July 7, 1503, from Jamaica in the Indies.

Columbus also wrote a letter to the governor general of Hispaniola to notify him of his plight and recommend his two messengers for assistance in their mission, and not to forget the rescue ship. With these and other letters for Castile, Columbus dispatched Diego Méndez and Bartolomé Flisco with two canoes, with water, *ajes* and cassava bread for the Indians, and water, bread, and *hutías* or rabbits for the Spaniards which, though certainly not much, was all the canoes could hold. The ocean is always furiously rough near these islands; therefore, it was necessary to await the calming of the waves to enter the great gulf in such frail craft which, as I said, offer less danger to the Indians than our larger ships do to us. The admiral accompanied them to the tip of Jamaica, thirty leagues from where the ships had anchored, taking a few soldiers with him for the safety of his men in case of trouble with the Indians on the way. Then he returned slowly to his ships, visiting villages along his path and conversing joyfully with their inhabitants and leaving many friends behind.

. . .

36

A year later, the ship Diego Méndez had chartered arrived in Jamaica with a smaller caravel. Diego de Salcedo sailed it; he was Columbus's financial administrator I believe; and he brought with him a letter from the governor. Columbus complained a great deal about the governor's tardiness in sending help, accusing him of the deliberate intent to let him die there, since a whole year had passed without a sign of assistance. He said the governor finally relented only because people were talking in Santo Domingo and missionaries there were beginning to reprehend him in their sermons. Everyone, including Columbus, sailed from Jamaica on June 27, 1504. Unfavorable winds and currents made the navigation arduous but they arrived safely at the small island we call Beata, not far from Hispaniola, some twenty leagues from Yaquimo which the admiral used to call the port of Brasil. It is very difficult to cross from there to Santo Domingo Harbor; sometimes a ship has to wait eight months because of the strength of the currents. While Columbus was detained there, he decided to tell the governor that his return meant his intention to free himself from unfounded and frivolous suspicion. He sent the letter either by land with a sailor or by sea with the caravel, which, being light, could sail the currents. The letter reads:

Noble Lord: Diego de Salcedo has arrived with the ships you sent to my rescue, thus giving life to me and my men, for which we cannot repay you enough. I am so happy I have lost sleep over my happiness, not so much because I escaped death as because I bring victory to the King of Castile. Porras and his followers returned to Jamaica with an ultimatum: I was to deliver my command to them or we (myself, my brother, my son and my men) would pay dearly for it. I refused to comply and they tried to carry out the threat. There were deaths and many wounded but finally the Lord, who abhors arrogance and ungratefulness, delivered all of them into our hands. I forgave them and agreed to reinstate them in all their honors, but I am taking Captain Porras to Castile so the monarchs may learn the truth. I have done everything to stifle my suspicions, but Diego de Salcedo's heart is still heavy with doubts. The reasons for them I do not know, and I am astonished, for my intentions have been honest. I was as happy to see your signature as I would have been to see that of Diego or Fernando and I hope to see it again. The Lord keep you and your house. From Beata Island, where I am forced to wait for better winds, August 3. I remain at your service.

His signature was like this:

S.

S.A.S.

A.M.Y.

Xpo. ferens. (Christopher)

He says Diego de Salcedo's heart was heavy because Salcedo saw that he could not kill or rout the suspicions that still existed against his master, the admiral. What he means about being glad to see the governor's signature is that he was made aware for the first time that the governor had been named master of the Order of Alcántara.

Columbus arrived in Santo Domingo on August 13, 1504. The governor and the whole city came to welcome him with great respect and celebration. The governor made Columbus a guest in his house and gave him excellent service. But Columbus was unhappy with the governor because underneath the friendliness and benevolence, there was a will at work to humiliate him, which made him believe that the governor's kindness was false. For example, the governor sent for Francisco de Porras, whom Columbus kept imprisoned in the ship, unfettered him and freed him in the presence of Columbus. Also, the governor took it upon himself to punish those who had taken arms to defend the admiral, had participated in Porras's imprisonment, and had killed or wounded others, and he attempted to receive a full account from them of what had taken place in Jamaica. This right belonged only to the admiral since he was in general command of the fleet. Columbus gave advice and sentences that were not accepted or carried out because they said no one could understand him and all this I am told took place behind the admiral's back in mockery.

These vexations lasted until the ship they brought from Jamaica was repaired and they had equipped another for the return to Castile of Columbus, his brother, his son and his servants. The others stayed here and some went to San Juan to settle it or, rather, destroy it. They sailed September 12, 1504, losing a mast just as they came out of the river, which caused the admiral to proceed alone. They had good weather for one-third of their journey over the gulf, then a terrible storm broke out that greatly endangered them. On Saturday, the nineteenth of October, when the storm had ceased, the mast fell and broke into four pieces. But the admiral was a great sailor; despite an attack of gout, he repaired it by using the yard of a lateen sail, strengthening it in the middle with material from the forecastles undone for that purpose. Later, another storm broke the mizzenmast; indeed, it seemed the Fates were against the admiral, pursuing him relentlessly throughout his life with hardship and affliction. He navigated this way another 700 leagues until God willed he reach the port of San Lúcar de Barrameda, whence he went to Seville to rest a few days.

37

In Seville, the news that Queen Isabella had died filled Columbus with intense grief. To him, she represented protection and hope, and no amount of pain, hardship or loss (even loss of his own life) could afflict and sadden him more than such news. Just as that great lady, the Queen, had been his principal ally (as I show in Book I), so she had continued to favor, encourage, console, defend and support him, and she had received his services humbly and with gratitude. As for the Catholic King Ferdinand, I do not know why he was not only ungrateful in words and deeds but actually harmed Columbus whenever possible, although his words belied his actions. It was believed that if, in good conscience and without losing face, he could have violated all the articles of the privileges that he and the Queen had justly granted him for his services, he would indeed have done so. I have never been able to ascertain the reason for this dislike and unkingly conduct toward one whose unparalleled services no other monarch ever received. Perhaps he was unduly impressed by the arguments and false testimonies of the admiral's enemies and rivals, who were many; at least I came to understand some of this in conversations I had with people from the King's most intimate circle who opposed those arguments.

So then, after recuperating a few days in Seville, Columbus and his brother went to the court in Segovia in May 1505. The King received them graciously, although not as graciously as their long peregrinations, hardships and experience deserved. The admiral recounted his voyage—the new lands he had discovered, the wealth of Veragua province, the year he spent in isolation in Jamaica, the mutiny of Francisco Porras, in short, all the tribulations of that voyage.

A few days later he judged it timely to implore the King:

Most Excellent Monarch:
Our Lord God miraculously sent me here to serve Your Highness. I said miraculously because first I went to Portugal, whose King knows more about discovery than any other King, but God blinded and deafened him and dulled his senses, for in fourteen years I was unable to persuade him. I said miraculously also because three different princes showed interest in my plans and the Queen, may God save her soul, saw and read the letters to Dr. Villalón. Your Highness honored my request and conferred titles upon me, and now my work has opened the door to a world which means and always will mean what I proclaimed it to be.

Your Highness is a most Christian man; I, as well as all those who have heard of me in Spain and in all the world, will believe that if Your Highness honored me at a time when I had only words to offer, now that my work substantiates them, you will increase the signs of gratitude which you promised me verbally and by letter bearing your signature. If you would, be certain that I will devote these last years of my life to serving you. I feel, indeed I think I know for certain, that my future services will resound, by comparison to what I have done, a hundred times more significantly, etc.

The King answered that he was well aware Columbus had given him the Indies, and in order to fulfill his promise he asked him to name someone to represent his interests. The admiral left the choice to the King, although he added, "Who can represent me better than the Archbishop of Seville? He and the steward have been the instruments through which Your Highness received the Indies." He said this because the Archbishop, the Dominican Diego de Deza, tutor to Prince don Juan, had insisted very much with the Queen that she sponsor Columbus, and so did the steward Juan Cabrero, an Aragonese who was very influential with the King, as I said in Book I.

The King agreed and the Archbishop answered that lawyers should handle the admiral's estate but not his rights. I took this to mean that the admiral's rights were unquestionably clear. The King delayed and Columbus wrote again, reminding him of his services, the unjust seizure of his property, and of his disgrace from the high esteem in which he was once held at the court. Therefore, he begged the King for justice and the fulfillment of promises regarding his son, his position and dignity, taken from him without a hearing, without defense, without even having been incriminated or sentenced, thus depriving him of the procedures of law. Above all, he asked the King to remember recent promises made by royal letter before his last voyage, mainly: he, Columbus, could depart knowing for certain that his present privileges would be kept in their entirety and that new ones would be granted him, as appeared in the royal letter bearing the King's signature sent from Valencia de la Torre, which I transcribed word for word in Chapter 4 from the authorized copy in my possession.

Another day Columbus told the King in Segovia that he did not wish to take his grievances to court but that he left it to the King's discretion to allow him whatever he saw fit from among his privileges, because he wanted only to go and alleviate his weariness in some remote corner. Acknowledging his gift of the Indies, the King asked him not to leave: he would give him not only what had been promised but also additional grants from the estate of the Crown. The Archbishop of Toledo, Francisco Jiménez of the Franciscan Order, favored Columbus very much, as did several other grandees of the court. They transferred his case to the Council for Royal Matters of Conscience. It received two audiences but nothing came of them. Columbus hoped the procrastination was the result of the imminent succession of the King's daughter and her husband Philip; however, he continued to petition the King. I find the following paper, among others:

Most Serene and Excellent King:
My dossier contains the claims I made on what is owed to me. I have already said that the settlement rested with you at your discretion. I was unjustly deprived of my office and my property, which are the substance of my reputation. Our Lord God had not performed such a public miracle in a long time when He struck down the architect of my disgrace together with those who aided him. Out of thirty-four ships, the best one sank to the bottom in their very midst while still in the harbor and no one could tell why or how it sank. I humbly implore Your Highness to name my son my successor in office and dignity; as for the rest, I will be grateful for whatever you decide, for I believe that the delay of my case is what saddens and paralyzes me the most.

He was already quite paralyzed, bedridden with the gout. By the sinking of the ship, Columbus is referring to Governor Bobadilla, who had contrived the seizure of his rights, and to Francisco Roldán and all who had betrayed him.

He wrote a certain memorandum to account for income losses and damages accrued by the failure to honor his privileges in which he had large interests. I found this remark among others: "The Indians of Hispaniola were and are its very wealth, because they are the ones who till the land, provide the bread and other victuals for the Christians, dig the mines for gold, and do all the work which men and beasts usually do." He says he is aware that six out of seven Indians have died since he left the island because of maltreatment: butchered, beaten, starving and ill-treated, most died in the mountains and streams where they had fled, unable to bear their lot, and Spain was losing money this way. He adds that if he did send Indians to Castile who then were sold, it had been for the purpose of instructing them in our Faith, our customs, crafts and trades, after which he intended to reclaim them and return them to their lands so they could instruct others. All these are the admiral's words. His was a crafty ignorance, if indeed it was ignorance and not greed, and I am sure his troubles sprang from that. As for the rest, he speaks the truth: the natives died and were impaired in this fashion; but he was lamenting the loss of the tithe in gold and other temporal interests.

To return to the point, his oldest son Diego petitioned the King:

Most Excellent and Powerful King our Lord:
Diego Columbus, in the name of the Admiral, my father, humbly prays Your Highness to remember by how much toil my father earned your favors and those of our Lady the Queen (her soul be blessed). Remember also, how his services continue to benefit the Crown; I pray you to keep favoring him, as well as give him restitution of what was undeservedly taken from him, as you promised him in a letter you wrote when he left on his first voyage. Thus Your Highness will administer justice and ease your conscience and that of our Queen while at the same time doing the Admiral and me an outstanding favor. If you intend to reinstate my father in his governorship of the Indies, the Admiral begs you to consider me in his stead and I would go there with those persons designated by you, whose counsel and advice I would follow.

The more petitions were written, the more the King answered with words while delaying the action. The King sought a harmonious settlement whereby Columbus would renounce his privileges in exchange for a reward in Castile. It was my impression that they were beginning to mark off a certain estate in Carrión de los Condes for him. The idea displeased Columbus very much; he took it as a sign of ill will meaning that none of the promises would be kept; thus he complained to the Archbishop of Seville: "Since it appears that the King will not keep his and the Queen's promises, for me, who am essentially a plowman, to fight against him would be to whip the wind. It is better to leave my case in the hands of God my benefactor, for I have done all I can." Those are his words, entrusting himself to divine justice because he thought he had exhausted all the possibilities and certainly, I believe that God heard him. Between delays, his health and morale worsened every day and the King left Valladolid for Laredo to greet his son-in-law and daughter, Philip and Juana, who arrived a few days later from Flanders. Columbus rejoiced and his hopes for justice revived, but it saddened him that his illness prevented him and his son Diego from meeting the new monarchs in Laredo. He sent his brother, the Adelantado, with a letter to pay his respects and excuse his absence:

Most Serene, Noble and Powerful Lords:
I think Your Highnessess will believe that never before have I wished for good health as I did when I heard you were traveling by sea; my long experiences in matters of navigation would have served you well. But God willed it otherwise; therefore, I humbly beg Your Highnesses to consider me among your faithful servants as one who, even when grievously ill, can still offer you as yet unequaled services. These complicated times as well as other torments have unjustly put me in dire straits, so that neither my son nor myself have been able to greet you in person. Instead, I humbly submit my intentions and good will and hope in you to see that my honor be restored. May God bless Your Highnesses.

I believe that had the Admiral and King Philip lived longer, justice would have been done.

38

While his brother Bartolomé was at court to greet the new monarchs, the admiral's gout grew worse from the rigors of winter, aggravated by his mental state of desolation at finding himself and his exploits so unjustly forgotten, especially at a time when the reputation of the wealth of the Indies was spreading like wildfire and brought great quantities of gold to Castile. He devotedly received the holy sacraments, for he was a good Christian, and died in Valladolid, on the day of the Ascension, the twentieth of May, 1506, pronouncing his last words: "Into your hands, oh Lord, I deliver my soul." His bones were taken to the Carthusian monastery of Seville and later on buried in the cathedral of Santo Domingo. His will stipulated that the male line inherit his estate, first through his legitimate son Diego, then through his natural son Hernando, his brother Bartolomé, his other brother, and so on down to the nearest male kin; however, should they fail to produce a son, the daughter nearest him became heiress automatically. He also stipulated that his heir increase the value of his estate and use the income thereof to serve the King and for the propagation of the Christian religion, setting aside 10 per cent of it as charity for the poor.

Another clause reads:

I, by the grace of God, Our Lord, served the King and Queen by giving them the Indies as something that was mine, and I persisted in seeking their support for the discovery of lands as yet unknown, the way to which remained also unknown. I offered my knowledge and my person but Their Highnesses offered only a million *maravedís*, leaving me to supply the rest. Later, it pleased Their Highnesses to grant me a share of 3, 8 and 10 per cent on various things found in that land west of a line they traced from the Azores to Cape Verde and from Pole to Pole, as the official documents in my possession prove, etc.

These are his words. So he died impecunious and in a state of great misery, not even owning a roof under which to rest his weary head, as he himself said, and this was the man who had discovered a New World, infinitely bigger and richer than the old. He died dispossessed of the status and fame he had won at the cost of incredible pains, dispossessed ignominiously and unjustly imprisoned without due process, judged by people seemingly acting as if they lacked reason, as if they were mad, stupid and absurd and worse than barbaric brutes.

God's ways are subtle indeed: consider what this *History* has been telling you of the oppression Columbus imposed on Indian kings and nations in Hispaniola and Veragua; whether he actually did it himself or allowed it to be done, it was an absurd and unrighteous thing. It is not too bold to presume that his own anguish and misfortune were sent as divine punishment, for it is impossible to think of the Catholic King and Queen as being that ungrateful toward one whose service had been so unique—no other King in the world has ever received such a gift. How could they forsake their promises so often made orally and repeated and officially written down? Because God meant that Columbus should not enjoy this life; He moved the King not to reward him . . . and the same argument exonerates the King with re-spect to Comendador Bobadilla's ignorant or malicious action when he ordered that Columbus and his brothers be taken to Castile as prisoners. The punishment did not stop there since it is now being inflicted on the third generation of Columbus, a noteworthy circumstance to which we will refer again in the course of this *History*. . . .

40

At this time the governor general ruled with great care and inspired fear, love and reverence among the Spaniards of His-paniola. He had a way of keeping them in check by watching their movements and establishing a kind of information system whereby persons of other towns would report on their neighbors when they came here for business. If he knew someone was restless, or was a bad example, or had his eyes on a married woman and was causing gossip in town (even though reports only indicated that the man had occasionally been seen on her street) or misbehaved in any way, he would send for that person and graciously invite him to stay for dinner as if he intended to grant him new favors. He would inquire about his neighbors, their plantations and business and social relations, in short, about all sorts of things in which he pretended to take an interest. The person would then think that the governor held him in higher esteem than his neighbors and he would give all the information required of him hoping to receive a larger allotment of Indians. And because the governor always managed to send for these people when ships were readying to sail, he would say: "X, which of those ships would you choose to go on to Castile?" and X would turn many colors saying, "But Sir, why?" Then the governor: "Well, you will get ready," and X: "Sir, I haven't the means, I couldn't afford the lowest fare." And the governor would say, "Don't let that stop you; I will see that you do," and so it would happen.

After a few cases of this sort, he had the island residents living in peace and harmony and none of them, among whom there were many noblemen, dared move for fear of provoking him. I knew of two high-ranking gentlemen who started a fight one evening and settled their dispute on the spot with mutual forgiving just to avoid the governor's suspicions. They endured this either not to be sent back to Castile or to be given more Indians, in both cases not to be interrupted in their quest for gold. So then, good conduct, peace and harmony reigned as a result of fear and temporal interests; the Indians got the brunt of it. It is well to note here that to be exiled to Castile meant more than death or any other injury; it meant returning a poor man and losing all hopes of acquiring wealth, and many an esteemed man here would have chosen death rather than such exile. The situation had turned a full circle: before, next to death, exile to these parts was the worst criminal punishment, as I have shown in Book I, while now the worst that could befall a man was to be sent to Castile. In the meantime, this fired their eagerness for gold, which had always been the principal reason for their being here; consequently, the death rate among Indians increased.

The Indians were satisfied with little, and with a minimum of cultivation, this fertile land gave them abundant sustenance. In addition, being of a delicate constitution, they could not last long in a life which abruptly plunged them into harsh labor. Up to a third died after each six or eight months' work in the mines, which was the time required of a crew to dig enough gold for melting. Who could recount their starvation, affliction and the cruel treatment these unfortunate people received not only in the mines but wherever they were put to work? Cases of illness were taken for laziness and cunning; but if fever was apparent, the sick were given a little bread and *ajes*, a truffle-like root, and were told to go home ten to fifty leagues away and take care of themselves. Surely, they did not even treat their sick mares that way.

In order to leave such a wretched existence, these people poisoned themselves by drinking the juice of the cassava root, which is poisonous when uncooked, but otherwise tastes like vinegar and is quite good. There were many deaths on this island also because pregnant women took certain herbs to produce abortion. There were cases when a married man would whip his Indian diggers if he didn't find them in a sweat, saying: "Why aren't you sweating, dogs?" And his wife would do the same with Indian women grating cassava roots, and use the same words. And it would happen sometimes that the Lord would punish these people by having a whole family drown at sea: husband, wife, lovely children, brothers and sisters and in-laws, all would perish with the gold they had hoped would give them leisure and pleasure in Castile. I have seen quite a few of these divine punishments; I shall relate some of them later on.

More than one man was needed to administer justice on the island. The governor sent for an attorney to help Alonso Maldonado. A learned and serious man called Lucás Vázquez de Ayllón, from Toledo, came as mayor of Concepción and the neighboring towns of Villa de Santiago, Puerto de Plata, Puerto Real and Lares de Guahaba. Later, Ayllón returned to Castile, finished his law studies and was appointed auditor of this Audiencia. Since Indians were the principal currency, the governor paid him some 500 of them, most of whom Ayllón drove to death in his mines and other profitable ventures.

41

From 1504 to 1507 Castile was without a King. After Queen Isabella's death in 1504, King Philip and doña Juana reigned in 1505, but after Philip's death that same year and because of doña Juana's illness and unfitness to govern, no one sat on the Castilian throne until the arrival of don Hernando from Naples. Don Hernando was present when Queen Isabella died and he assumed the regency, but, because Philip and Juana were expected to arrive shortly and diverse matters occupied his mind, he hadn't full notice of the disorders caused by the allocation of Indians [to Spaniards]. The admiral had given him an account of it but either he did not believe him or had other important things to attend to; the fact is that he paid no attention. He went to Naples after Philip's arrival; then Philip died and don Hernando did not return until 1507.

These turmoils and changes of government allowed the free blossoming and firm establishment of the allocation system and no one thought about the damage this system caused the Indians because everyone's mind was on gold. As the inventor of the allocation system, the comendador mayor should have thought about Indian mortality as well as about remedying it; but this was part of his general insensitivity and he did not notice it or he simply did not care. When the King came from Naples the only subject of conversation was gold—and it was plentiful then; no mention was made of the Indian lives involved in the extraction of gold and, what was even more painful, of the fact that they were dying without the sacraments. People talked about how one could get gold if one had an allotment of Indians and about how many unpaid servants of the Crown had followed the King to Spain. It occurred to some, perhaps to many, to request Indians as payment for their services, and the King agreed to get them off his back, unaware of what he was giving away. He gave orders to the governor to allow 200 Indians to each claimant, as was customary; but the governor could not always comply because many of the claimants remained in Castile, especially the more important people, and Indians could be of no use to them. Whether the governor allocated Indians to the newcomers or not, whoever received them killed them off.

In those days the comendador mayor sent a pilot named Andrés de Morales, already mentioned above, to record in detail all rivers, sierras, mountains and valleys of this island. I haven't seen the description, although I could have seen it many years ago by asking Morales for it; I think the Sevillian cosmographer Alonso de Santa Cruz has it; he has quite a few of these things. Also, in 1508, the comendador decided to explore the length of Cuba and determine whether it was an island or part of the mainland and whether it was dry land, for he had not seen the description of Cuba the admiral had written when he discovered it in 1494 and thought it was flooded all the time.

A former servant of Queen Isabella, a Gallician hidalgo named Sebastián de Campo who had come with the admiral on the second voyage, was made captain of two ships and left with sailors to explore the Cuban coast. He sailed around it and, because the ship needed careening, which means cleaning and caulking the underwater part of a ship, entered what we now call Havana but was named at that time Puerto de Carenas after this operation. It is an excellent harbor capable of accommodating many ships; I saw it when it was discovered. Campo sailed westward to the tip of the island which, I do not know for what reason, is called San Antonio and is approximately fifty leagues from Havana; then, sailing last, he anchored in Xagua, one of the best and largest harbors in the world. He enjoyed his stay and the natives served him an abundance of partridge and mullet fish which thrive there, the water being so still that the Indians build sea corrals for them and catch them as easily as if they were in an aquarium. These corrals are made of woven reeds stuck in the mud bed of the harbor and can be built of many sizes, though most of them are a good stone's throw in length.

After some eight months, if I am not mistaken, he brought back the news that Cuba was an island. I'm sure that if the comendador had had more authority, knowing the island was dry and good, he would have settled Cuba. At that time they found copper in a sierra near Puerto Real which was said to contain a large proportion of gold detectable from the outside. The comendador sent an expert who certified it and so overrated it that the comendador wrote to the King to recommend extensive development of this resource. The King hoped this would bring Spain an affluence of wealth and, since the comendador had asked for officials and costly instruments, they began to dig sierras and strip mountains under the direction of that expert. But the expenses, labor and pain suffered by the Indians came to so little copper it barely covered the cost and the comendador was greatly embarrassed, given his customary prudence and authoritativeness, to have to inform the King and risk his displeasure.

We have already said, toward the end of Book I, that 300 Spaniards were living a very easy life on the island when the comendador mayor came to rule it; and, among other privileges, they enjoyed Indian mistresses whom they took freely or by force, calling them servants, yet living in sin with them. The families of these women believed them to be legitimate wives and as such they were given to the Spaniards and respected. There were a few good Franciscan fathers on the island at that time who disapproved of this sort of concubinage and tried to convince the comendador mayor to ban it or to enforce marriage, which he did, especially at the insistence of Fray Antonio de los Mártires, I believe. The Spaniards reacted angrily. Many of them were up-starts of low breeding and lower caste who had achieved an appearance of status; others were hidalgos; and both, with the same presumptuous madness and detestable arrogance, held in contempt a people with whom they could have lived most honor-ably since many were the natural kings and noblemen of this land. They had come in rags in a state of starvation from Castile, but next to death they thought marriage the worst torment, the greatest dishonor and affront.

However, they complied in order to inherit an estate from their "wives"—I understand that these marriages were the only right the Spaniards had to receive any favors or rewards from the Indians—and the comendador, for all his wisdom, committed a grave and foolish injustice by transferring Indians of one wife's clan to other clans. Is there greater blindness and irrationality than this? They say he acted to prevent Spanish conceit in case a man should feel too powerful as the head of a clan. They give this and other ill-founded reasons and thus he added insult to injury by depriving those ladies and, consequently, their husbands, of their estates and vassals; by depriving, too, those Indian vassals of the chance of better treatment from their Queen even when the husband was low and mean; and finally he deprived the children of their union of the natural, universal and God-given rights of inheritance; and I saw them dispossessed of their mothers' vassals, with no memory or trace of their real identity, unremembered and unnoticed. And this was another reason why the sooner those poor Indians died, the better off they would be.

42

When the comendador mayor, then comendador of Lares, came to govern this island, he brought four officials of the royal treasury: the treasurer Villacorta from Olmedo I believe; the auditor Cris-tóbal de Cuéllar from Cuéllar, who had served Prince don Juan; the *veedor* [overseer] Diego Marque of Seville; and I don't re-member the name of the commissioner. A silversmith named

Rodrigo de Alcázar came to mint and mark the gold and he was a very capable man suited to master cities as well as silver. He received 1 per cent of the gold minted, a privilege granted him because the mines were not famous then, and not much gold had been extracted, and, seeing Castile not flooded with wealth overnight, the Indies had become a venture of dubious interests, since no one valued the spiritual wealth God had placed in our hands. Had Rodrigo de Alcázar held this privilege, he could have bought a mighty estate in Castile. But the Spaniards worked the mines and their Indians at such a speed that gold began to flow in abundance and Alcázar's benefits were so exorbitant that the King was notified and, the Queen being dead, he revoked Alcázar's privilege himself.

At the beginning they established four gold foundries in four years: two in the town of Buenaventura, eight leagues from Santo Domingo on the Hayna shore for the gold of old and new mines; and two in the town of Vega for the gold of the Cibao and numerous neighboring mines. In Buenaventura a mint produced from 110,000 to 118,000 gold pesos, but did not exceed 120,000 at a time. In Vega, the usual yield was 125,000 to 130,000, but never reached 140,000 gold pesos. The Vega mints, then, were richer than those of Buenaventura by about 15,000 or 20,000 castellanos and the total yield of gold per year for this island was between 450,000 and 460,000 gold pesos, bringing Alcázar a yearly income of 4,500 gold pesos. And in those days this was such an outstanding sum that his privilege was revoked. The minting slowed down considerably as the Indians who extracted gold at the cost of sweat, hunger and a desperate way of life perished. This should have stimulated the comendador mayor and the rest of the gold exploiters to slow the work and feed the men properly to derive more profit; but they were not moved by compassion, and blindness kept them from caring. God gave another more obscure warning sign to those who, stealing and doing evil, worked for wealth; namely, that nobody was thriving despite the flow of gold. No one could walk out of the mint with as much as 1 gold peso from the 500 or 1,000 he had brought for minting. Rather, many were imprisoned for debts incurred by excessive spending on dress and other such items or by trading in one another's estates, so that, after deduction of the King's 20 per cent, the balance went to creditors and they were left empty-handed, death, affliction and cruelty weighing their spirits down.

Once, a man named Juan de Villoria left the mint playing with two or three gold ingots shining in his hands and everyone marveled at this, attributing it to the fact that he was a pious man who treated his Indians with some humanity because, having brought some means from Castile, he could afford humanity. But even he received divine punishment, as I will show later, if God wills. In short, no matter how much gold they found and how many Indians they killed in the process, they simply could not get rich. And another generality holds true also: the people who used Indians in other types of work fared much better as a result of driving those innocent people at a slower pace.

To return to the story of the King's officials, the treasurer Villacorta died shortly after arrival. He had brought with him a bright young clerk named Santa Clara of Salamanca, very clever and witty and gifted in accounting, for which the comendador mayor liked his company and favored him. After the treasurer's death, the comendador turned the office over to him until the King made a new appointment and in that post he remained for a few years. At that time they did not yet use three padlocks to lock up the King's monies but instead the chests had one single key for the treasurer alone and the auditor only recorded the amount of gold the treasurer declared. This way Santa Clara had occasion to help himself at will to the King's money, and he bought many large estates on this island, gave banquets in honor of the comendador mayor and spent so much beyond his means that he had to use the King's money. He gave a lavish reception, I think it was on Corpus Christi Day, for the comendador and all the high officials of Santo Domingo, and as an example of one of his extravagances, they filled the salt cellars with tiny grains of gold of the kind they find in Cibao.

The King's revenue suffered great gaps this way and it is surprising that the comendador mayor, being so wise, failed to stop such open embezzlement in time, which must be imputed to him anyway, since he gave the post to Santa Clara. But the King's officials notified the King, especially the auditor Cristóbal de Cuéllar, who was a man of courage and a long-time royal servant, and who, moreover, was on bad terms with the comendador because he had not been given the Indians he wanted. The King then sent an auditor to examine the books of Santa Clara rigorously, which were found to be 80,000 gold pesos short. After confiscating his estate, the comendador ordered an auction and he managed it so well that the property was sold well above its value. Holding a pineapple in one hand—the pineapple is a delicious fruit just being cultivated on this island—and when items were called at 500 or 1,000 pesos, like teams of mares or such things of value, he would say: "I will give this pineapple to the bidder of 1,500," and it was a fight as to who would cry first, "I take the pineapple. Sir"—not for the pineapple or the item itself, which often was not worth half the bid, but because they knew they were buying the comendador's favor and hoped to gain more Indians and more privileges from him. Santa Clara's estate was liquidated in this manner for 92,000 gold pesos, which left an excess of 12,000. But the total amount was collected for the King to settle sundry debts owed him by absent or defunct debtors and when, years later, Santa Clara's son requested compensation, he received nothing because it was impossible to estimate the amount owed him. Santa Clara was a long-time honored resident of Santo Domingo.

Among those who complained about the mishandling of royal funds was the wise and influential silversmith Rodrigo de Alcázar who, judging the treasurer's office to be one that required great qualities of wisdom and loyalty, recommended the Castilian Antonio de Fonseca for the position. This Fonseca was a gentleman of high rank, wise and respected and adviser to the Catholic kings; he was the King's secretary of finance, which is the highest office in court, and a brother of Bishop Juan de Fonseca, who was for a long time in charge of the Indies, as I often indicated before and will again, if God wills. The Catholic King understood the importance of the office and appointed his trusted Aragonese servant Miguel de Pasamonte, a very honest and experienced man who had the reputation of having lived in chastity all his life. Pasamonte arrived here in November of 1508 with such honor that he was called officially treasurer general of all the Indies, in charge of all the treasurers on the mainland and other islands; I do not know whether this was by express order of the King or the King's secretaries. He was such a person that, contrary to the Castilian practice, his office was higher than that of the auditor. The King trusted him to the degree of acting upon his recommendations in all matters concerning the Indies.

When this treasurer arrived in 1508, there were 60,000 people living on this island, including the Indians; so that from 1494 . . . to 1508, over three million people had perished from war, slavery and the mines. Who in future generations will believe this? I myself writing it as a knowledgeable eyewitness can hardly believe it, but it is a fact born of our sins, and it will be well that in time to come we lament it.

43

When the Spaniards saw how fast they were killing Indians in the mines, plantations and other endeavors, caring only to squeeze the last effort out of them, it occurred to them to replenish the supply by importing people from other islands and they deceived King Hernando with a crafty argument. They notified him either by letter or by a special court representative, presumably with the comendador's consent, that the Lucayo or Yucayo Islands close to Cuba and Hispaniola were full of an idle people who had learned nothing and could not be Christianized there. Therefore, they asked permission to send two ships to bring them to Hispaniola where they could be converted and would work in the mines, thus being of service to the King.

The King agreed, on the blind and culpable recommendation of the council, acting as if rational beings were timber cut from trees and used for buildings or a herd of sheep or any other animals and nothing much would be lost if they died at sea. Who would not blame an error so great: natives taken by force to new lands 100 and 150 leagues away, however good or evil the reason may have been, much less to dig gold in mines where they would surely die, for a King and foreigners they had never offended? Perhaps they sought justification by deceiving the King with a falsehood, that is, that the Lucayo Indians would be instructed in the Faith: which, even if it were true was not right—and it wasn't true, for they never intended anything of the kind nor did anything in that direction. God did not want Christianity at that cost; God takes no pleasure in a good deed, no matter its magnitude, if sin against one's fellow man is the price of it, no matter how minuscule that sin may be; and this is a fact all sinners, especially in the Indies, deceive themselves into ignoring. In total condemnation of this lie, let it be remembered that the Apostles never expatriated anyone by force in order to convert them elsewhere, nor has the universal Church ever used this method, considered pernicious and detestable. Therefore, the King's council was very blind and, consequently, because its members are scholars, it is guilty before God, since ignorance cannot be adduced.

The King's permission arrived and ten or twelve residents from Concepción and Santiago gathered 10,000 or 12,000 gold pesos, bought two or three ships and fifty to sixty salaried men, and raided the Indians who lived in the Lucayos in peace and security. Those are the Lucayo Indians I spoke of at length in Book I and in my *Apologetical History*, so blessed among all Indians in gentleness, simplicity, humility and other natural virtues, it seems Adam's sin left them untouched. I haven't found any comparable nation in the world in ancient history, except perhaps the Seres of Asia, who are a peace-loving and gentle people (Solinus, Ch. 63), who love justice (Pomponius Mela, III, 6), and who know not how to kill or fornicate, have no prostitutes, adulterers, thieves or homicides and adore no idols (Eusebius, *Praeparatione Evangelica*, VI, 8). To this kind of people the Spaniards did the following. They say that the first harvesters of Lucayo Indians, fully aware of their simplicity and gentle manners (they knew this from the report of Christopher Columbus), anchored their ships and were received as they always are before our deeds prove the contrary, that is, as angels from Heaven. The Spaniards said they came from Hispaniola, where the souls of their beloved ones were resting in joy, and that their ships would take them there if they wanted to see them, for it is a fact that all Indian nations believe in the immortality of the soul. After death, the body joins the soul in certain delightful places of pleasure and comfort; some nations even believe that the souls of sinners first undergo torment. So then, with those wicked arguments, the Spaniards deceived the Indians into climbing on board ship, and men and women left their homes with their scant belongings.

On Hispaniola, they found neither father, mother nor loved ones but iron tools and instruments and gold mines instead, where they perished in no time; some, from despair at seeing themselves deceived, took poison; others died of starvation and hard labor, for they are a delicate people who had never imagined such type of work even existed. Later, the Spaniards used every possible wile and force to trick them into ships. At the landing sites, usually Puerto de Plata and Puerto Real on the north shore facing the Lucayos, men, women, children and old people were thrown helter-skelter into lots; the old with the young, the sick with the healthy —they often fell ill in the ships, and many died of anguish, thirst and hunger in the hottest and stuffiest holds—without any concern for keeping man and wife, father and son together, handled like the basest animals. Thus the innocent, *sicut pecora occisionis*, were divided into groups and those who had contributed their share in the raiding expedition drew lots. When someone drew an old or sick one he protested, "Give that old man to the devil, why should I take him? To feed and bury him? And why give me that sick dog? To cure him?"

Sometimes, it happened that Indians died on the spot either from hunger, debilitation, sickness or the pain of a father seeing his son or a husband seeing his wife bought and taken away. How could anyone with a human heart and human entrails witness such inhuman cruelty? Where was the principle of charity, "Thou shalt love thy neighbor as thyself," in the minds of those who, forgetting that they were Christians or human beings, performed such "humanity" upon human beings? Finally, to cover the cost and pay the salaried men, they agreed to allow the sale of allotted Indians at not more than 4 gold pesos per piece—they referred to them as pieces as if they were heads of cattle. And they thought selling and transferring so cheaply was an honorable thing to do, while in truth, had the price been higher, the Indians would have received better treatment as valuable items and would have lasted longer.

44

As I said, the Spaniards used many ways to draw the Lucayos from their homeland where they lived as in the Golden Age, a life of which poets and historians have sung such praise. Sometimes, especially at first, they won their trust because the Indians did not suspect them and, living off guard, received them like angels. Sometimes they raided by night and other times in the open, *aperto Marte* as they say, knifing those who, having more experience of Spaniards, defended themselves with bow and arrow, a weapon ordinarily used for fishing and not for war. They brought more than 40,000 people here in a period of four or five years, men and women, children and adults, as Pedro Martyr mentions in Chapter 1 of the seventh *Decada*. . . .

He also mentions the fact that some killed themselves from despair, while others, who were stronger, hoped to escape and return to their land and thus endured their hopeless lives, hiding in the northern mountains closer to home and hoping to find a way to cross over. Once—and Pedro Martyr records this in the same chapter—one of these Indians built a raft from a very large tree trunk called *yauruma* in the vernacular (the penultimate syllable is long), which is a light and hollow wood, tied logs to it with *liana*, which is a type of extremely strong ropelike root, placed some corn from his harvest in the hollow of the logs and filled gourds with fresh water; then, closing both ends with leaves, he took off with another Indian and a few women of his family, all great swimmers like all the Lucayos. Fifty leagues from the coast, they unfortunately met a ship coming full speed from their place of destination; they were captured and returned to Hispaniola in tears and lamentations and perished there like the rest.

We do not know, but it is believable that others made the same attempt, and if so, it was to no avail, since the Spaniards were continually raiding those islands until not one single Indian remained. They chose the rockiest and most inaccessible island to corral all the Indians taken from the neighboring islands; and there they left them in charge of a Spanish guard, after breaking their canoes to prevent escape until the ship returned for another load. Once they had 7,000 Indians and seven Spaniards guarding them like shepherds and, the ships being delayed, they ran out of cassava, which is all the food they ever gave Indians. As two ships laden with provisions neared the coast, a terrible gale storm sank them all and the islanders died of starvation; I do not remember what I heard about the fate of those shipwrecked. Nobody thought to attribute these disasters to divine punishment for sins committed here; rather, they attributed them to chance, as if there were no Rector in Heaven to see and register such cruel injustice.

I could have found out, and I could consequently now relate, the particulars of many more cruelties inflicted upon this innocent flock, if in those days of my residence in Hispaniola I had cared to question the men who performed such things. But I want to tell what one of them told me in Cuba. He had come to Cuba in an Indian canoe, perhaps as a runaway from his captain or to escape danger or again from a sense of guilt and a desire to leave such reprobate ways. He told me they used to stuff shipholds with hundreds of Indians of both sexes and all ages, pack them like sardines and close all the hatchways to prevent escape, thus shutting off air and light. And, since ships carried food and water only for the Spanish crew, the Indians died and were thrown into the sea, and the floating corpses were so numerous that a ship could find its course by them alone, without need of a compass, charts or the art of navigation. Those were his words. This is certain: no ship ever raided the Lucayos that did not for the above reasons have to throw overboard one-third or one-fourth of its human cargo, and this inhumanity went on sometimes more and sometimes less but it is a fact that it went on. This arrangement, if such a thing can bear that name, brought to Hispaniola over a million souls over a period of ten years—men, women, children and elderly; a few shipments were made to Cuba also, and they all perished in the mines from overwork, anguish and exhaustion.

Pedro Martyr declares that according to his information there were 406 Lucayo Islands, from which the Spaniards enslaved 40,000 Indians to work the mines, and, from all the island they had a total of 1,200,000. . . . He adds that the Lucayo Indians sometimes killed Spaniards. This happened when a small group of

Spaniards were caught off guard because, when they realized the Spaniards meant to destroy them, the Indians used bows and arrows invented for fishing to kill their killers. But it was all in vain since they never succeeded in killing more than a handful. As to what Martyr says about the number of Lucayo Islands, he is including those called Jardín de la Reina and Jardín del Rey, which is a string of small islands south and north of the Cuban coast. The Indians there shared the natural goodness of the Lucayos. However, by Lucayos we refer only to the larger islands that go from Hispaniola to Florida away from Cuba, and these number between forty and fifty, large and small. Pedro Martyr also adds that he kept his information constantly up to date, and this was possible because at that time he was a member of the council of the Indies which he joined in 1518 and I was there when he presented his credentials to the council. The Emperor gave him this post in Saragossa almost immediately after the coronation ceremonies.

45

The Lucayos were dying from hard labor and destitution in the mines and other occupations; still, the enemy of human nature invented another type of greed among the Spaniards which was to put an end to all the Lucayos: they discovered pearls in the sea around Cubagua Island, which is near Margarita on the mainland side called Cumaná (the stress is on the last syllable), just as the mines there were slackening production. The Spaniards decided to use the swimming skills of the Lucayos to collect pearls, since it is necessary to dive great depths to find oysters. For this reason, the Lucayo Indians were sold almost publicly, not at 4 pesos as in the beginning, but for as much as 150 gold pesos each. The profits were such and pearl fishing was so infernally dangerous that in a short time finding a single Lucayo alive was almost a miracle. From here to Cubagua it is necessary to circle various islands and this makes a voyage of 300 good leagues; all the remaining Lucayos were sent there to be exterminated in that harsh and pernicious exercise, more cruel than that of extracting gold in the mines; and thus a multitude of people were extinguished, who had lived on so many islands, which we call Lucayos or Yucayos.

There lived at that time in Santo Domingo an honorable God-fearing merchant named Pedro de Isla who, to appease his conscience, had given up his business a good while back and was living on his income. This virtuous man knew the devastation and acts of cruelty performed on the simple Lucayo Indians; he knew also that the Lucayo Islands were thought to be depopulated since no one bothered to sail ships there any longer. Moved by God's zeal and compassion for so many lost lives, he thought a few Indians might have succeeded in escaping from this infernal fire and deadly pestilence; therefore, he went to those who ruled Hispaniola and requested permission to equip a brig at his own expense and search the islands for them. His plan was to bring them to Hispaniola, organize a township with them, instruct them in the Faith and keep them out of reach of raiders who would use them. This Christian project was heard and agreed to by the rulers of Hispaniola. Pedro de Isla bought a brig, which is a small caravel, equipped it with eight or ten men and ample food supplies to last a long time, and sent them to search all those islands for Indians. They were to console and reassure the Indians as much as possible that no harm would come to them: they would not be enslaved like their families and neighbors had been, nor would they be sent to the mines, but instead would live as free men in the way they saw fit. In short, they were to try to make the Indians lose their fears of past calamities, console their sadness and soothe their bitterness.

They left and carried out the recommendations of this good employer and good man, Pedro de Isla, scrupulously combing the Lucayo Islands as much as they could. After three years they found only eleven persons whom I saw with my own eyes because they disembarked at Puerto de Plata where I lived at the time. They were men and women and children; I do not remember how many there were of each but I do remember an old man among them, probably over sixty years old, who like the others was stark naked and looked as calm and gentle as a lamb. I stood there staring at them, especially at the old man, who was tall and venerable and had a long face, dignified and authoritative. To me he looked like our father Adam before the Fall, and thinking how many like him there were all over these islands, and how in so short a time and almost under my eyes they had been destroyed without offending us in the least, nothing was left for us to do but lift our eyes to Heaven and tremble at divine judgment. That was what Pedro de Isla gleaned after the harvesters had passed. Later, Our Lord repayed Pedro de Isla's zeal and virtue by accepting him into the Franciscan Order, where he lived a holy life. He was ordained as deacon but from humility he asked to be excused from saying Mass, feeling unworthy of it as he remembered the life of his patron St. Francis; thus, after long years God recalled him to his side and I believe he is enjoying the sight of God forever.

To return to the Lucayos, as we said in our other *History*, they were a most blessed people. We believe that as a people they were more prepared than any other in the whole of mankind to know and serve God. I confessed and administered the sacraments of communion and extreme unction to a few who had received Catholic instruction and baptism, and I say I pray to God I should feel such contrition for my sins when my time comes as I seem to have found in them. And with this I bring the story of the Lucayos to an end, who were so unfortunate as to fall into the hands of those who destroyed them without shame, reason or right, although I have no doubt we the tormentors are less fortunate than they who suffered our torments. . . .

57

The order of our *History* requires that we return to the two governors who first went to the continent: Alonso de Hojeda and Diego de Nicuesa, whom we mentioned in Chapter 52. And since Hojeda was the first to leave this harbor, it is well to begin with his story.

Four or five days later he anchored in the harbor of Cartagena, where the Indians are always in a state of upheaval and always ready to resist the Spaniards because, as we said in Book I, Chapter 172, they had been savagely treated in the past by Cristóbal Guerra and other traders and, as we said in Book II, Chapter 19, for this reason had killed some of our men with their fierce and deadly poison. When news of this reached the King, who had been kept ignorant of the insults and the violent and evil acts of Christians, no one was at court to defend the Indians and tell how disquieting our reputation was among them. For this reason, the King gave permission to declare an all-out war against them and capture them as slaves, and this was done thanks to the blindness and culpability of the members of the council, as we already proved. Hojeda was to use this license himself. A certain Cristóbal de la Tovilla mentions it in a history he calls *La Barbárica*, and he knew that territory for many years, although not at the time of these events but much later. He heard what happened from those who had gone with Hojeda or from his immediate successors. At the beginning of Chapter I he says:

Here in Cartagena [Hojeda] anchored at the King's order to make war against the Indians who had mistreated the traders. Since the continent remained so long unsettled by Christians, those who lived on the islands came to trade with the natives here and received great quantities of gold and many chickens in exchange for beads, knives and other similar objects from Spain and thus they returned laden with riches and lived in leisure. But when this commerce began to dwindle and greed increased, they used trading as a pretext to come fully armed and capture a large number of Indians whom they sold on Hispaniola and other islands without any right. Therefore, the Indians were hurt and they retaliated by killing the Spaniards they found off guard, whether they had come in war or peace, and this was the reason why the King don Hernando declared war, it being nonetheless true that, had he known the truth, he would not have declared it.

These are Tovilla's own words and it is no small proof of what we said in Chapter 19 as well as here, because he, like Oviedo, praised Spanish exploits and degraded the Indians and he died in this state of blindness, but truth spoke louder and he could not keep it silent.

To return to the point, Hojeda decided to attack Calamar and capture Indians to sell on Hispaniola and thus settle his many debts. His captain, Juan de la Cosa, a great pilot, remembering what had happened on their previous trading expedition there and knowing the courage of those Indians as well as the poison of their weapons (for they used a deadly herb), prudently advised Hojeda: "Sir, it seems to me it would be better to settle the Gulf of Urabá first, where the natives are less fierce and use a less dangerous herb; then after winning there, we might try it here to better advantage." But Hojeda had always been foolhardy, trusting in the fact that he had escaped from innumerable scrapes in Castile and in the Indies without a scratch, so at dawn he cried "Santiago!" and charged upon the village, knifing, killing and capturing right and left. Eight Indians, unable to escape, entered a straw hut and fought so fiercely with their poisoned arrows that not a Spaniard dared approach the hut. Hojeda chided them: "What? Aren't you ashamed? So many and the kind of men you are, afraid to go near eight naked men who are making fun of you!" Ashamed, a Spaniard ran through a shower of arrows with great impetus and arrived at the door, but an arrow hit him in the chest and he fell instantly dead. This exasperated Hojeda even more, so he ordered his men to set fire to the hut from both sides and in a wink burned all eight Indians alive; he captured sixty persons and sent them as prisoners to the ships.

Then they agreed to capitalize on their victory and pursue those who had fled to the hills, pushing on toward a larger town named Turbaco. But the Indians had been forewarned and, taking their women, children and belongings to safety, went into hiding; and when Hojeda arrived in the morning he found the place deserted. Since they were careless and unaware that the Indians were men— a fact which vexation and nature itself were to teach them—they were led by their contempt and their blindness, caused by greed and sinful ways, to disperse in the woods in search of what each could plunder. But the Indians had spies, and when they found out the Spaniards were dispersed, they attacked with a clamor that reached the sky and a shower of arrows that darkened the air. The Spaniards, confident that nobody would dare disturb them, were taken by surprise and panicked like a herd of trapped deer, stunned and unable to escape; if they ran one way, the Indians were waiting for them; if another, Indians were fighting toward them, snatching arrows from fallen bodies as they approached and shooting and killing again, Juan de la Cosa and his group managed to back up against the entrance to a certain enclosure where Hojeda and his men were fighting for their lives. Hojeda kept ducking behind his shield to avoid arrows, for he was short and extremely agile and could protect his whole body that way. When he saw that most of his men had fallen and that Juan de la Cosa's reinforcement was being shattered too, trusting in his agility, which, as we said in Book I, was truly extraordinary, he leaped among the Indians and escaped so fast he seemed to be flying into the darkest part of the forest in the direction of his ships. For his part, Juan de la Cosa found a roofless hut (perhaps they had destroyed the straw roof to avoid being burned alive) and fought until he saw all his men dead on the ground; then he fell, dizzy from the poison of the many arrows that still stuck to his body, and, seeing a man still alive and fighting, said to him: "Well, brother, since God has kept you alive until now, take courage and run to safety and tell Hojeda how you found me at my death."

We think that he and Hojeda were the only survivors of the more than one hundred Spaniards engaged in that encounter, but others report seventy deaths. As for the men on the ships, when they saw no sign of their governor Hojeda, they began to suspect disaster and put the small boats out to sea to row up and down the coast in a diligent search for news. They reached a mangrove swamp—mangroves are trees with large entangled roots that grow in sea water and do not rot—and found Hojeda hidden there, sword in hand and a shield on his back on which they counted more than 300 arrow marks. He was almost paralyzed and faint from lack of food and was unable to speak. They built a fire to warm him and they fed him until he came to himself; then, as all listened with sadness and pain to Hojeda's story, they saw Nicuesa's fleet nearing the harbor and Hojeda, anguished at the thought that Nicuesa might seek revenge for the quarrels they had had with one another only a few days and even a few hours earlier in this city, asked his people to leave him hidden there and return to the ships as long as Nicuesa was there.

58

Hojeda's men went out to meet Nicuesa in the harbor of Cartagena; they told him with pain and great sadness how Hojeda and

Juan de la Cosa had destroyed Calamar, had made many slaves and had gone inland only to find nobody there. They strongly suspected the worst; therefore, their duty was to go and search for Hojeda whom they promised to bring back, should they find him, only if Nicuesa promised, as a caballero, to forget the past. These words angered Diego de Nicuesa because he was a gentleman and he promised that if they brought Hojeda back, he not only would not harm him but would treat him like a brother. So, they brought Hojeda back and Nicuesa's first gesture was to embrace him and say: "Gentlemen have to distinguish between a fair fight and the obligation to help a man in need; to fight now would not only be foul and weak-spirited but heap afflictions on an anguish-ridden man. Therefore, Señor Hojeda, let us forget the bad words we exchanged on Hispaniola, that they may not stand between us. You give orders and I shall follow you until Juan de la Cosa and his fallen men are avenged, and I shall have no other intention but to help you."

Hojeda felt a great consolation and thanked Nicuesa for his goodness and his help. They each took a horse and, with 400 men under the strictest orders not to spare a single Indian life, left in the evening for Turbaco and, nearing town, separated into two groups. There are large colorful parrots there called *guacamayas*, which screech and make loud noises, and when they heard the people they flew and screeched wildly. The Indians interpreted this as a sign of people approaching, but believing most of the Spaniards dead, were not alarmed. Suddenly the Spaniards were upon them and they panicked, trying to escape and, leaving their huts with or without arms, ran straight into the Spaniards who disemboweled them and cut them to pieces. If they fled to their huts, the Spaniards burned them alive. The horror and torment of fire drove out the women carrying their babies, but the sight of horses, which they had never seen, gave them such a fright that they ran back into the flames, preferring to be burned than to be swallowed by those beasts. The Spaniards committed incredible slaughter there, sparing neither women nor children, old nor young. And then they plundered: it is said that Nicuesa's share came to 7,000 castellanos. In their search for things to steal, they came upon the body of Juan de la Cosa tied to a tree and covered with arrows as a porcupine is with quills; and because the poison had swelled him monstrously, his body was deformed; the Spaniards were so shocked no one dared remain there for the night. The confederation Hojeda-Nicuesa went to the harbor where they separated again and Hojeda sailed toward the Gulf of Urabá, which was his final destination and the place where he intended to enjoy the benefits of his stolen goods.

Just so that we do not pass over things as animals do, it would be well to consider what injury the people of Calamar had done to Hojeda and Juan de la Cosa. Did they usurp their estates, kill their families, bear false testimony or commit culpable acts whatsoever toward a people at peace on their own territory? Are the people of Turbaco to blame for killing Juan de la Cosa and the others and doing to them what Spaniards had done in Calamar? Are they guilty because they wanted to avenge the people of Calamar? Is there a reasonable nation in the world that would not do the same on the strength of natural law? All the nations in the world are made up of human beings and a single definition applies to all: all have intelligence and will, five exterior and four interior senses that motivate them; all praise the good and feel pleasure in the pleasurable and the happy, and all abhor evil and feel pain in the unpleasant and harmful.

In Book I of *De legibus* Cicero asks which nation does not love and praise gentleness, benignity, gracious and good deeds? Which does not abhor or dislike proud, cruel and evil people? That is Cicero, and I would add, did Nicuesa deserve a reward from God for helping Hojeda to avenge the death of Juan de la Cosa or did he enjoy special privileges that would force him to vengeance or excuse him from it? Rather, was not their friendship like that of Herod and the unfair judge Pilate? I ask also: were Hojeda and Nicuesa preparing the way for the preaching of Christ's gentle law, a law that even certain sinners wise in the ways of the world dare teach in their writings? Solely by virtue of what Hojeda and Nicuesa performed there—they were the first to assault the continent and kill, plunder and enslave—the natives of that land acquired the right forever until the Day of Judgment to declare legitimate war against the Spaniards, as they acquired also a likely reason to resist the Christian Faith for a long time, as long in fact

as they believed the Spaniards to profess and keep the law of
Christ. Surely, these men were a sad case, as God proved by the
ensuing turn of events.

59

Hojeda was on his way to the Gulf of Urabá but was forced by
contrary winds to stop thirty-five leagues away from Cartagena on
a small island called Isla Fuerte; and there he enslaved and
plundered to amend the perversity of what he had done earlier
and to dispose God in his favor for the future. In the Gulf of
Urabá he looked for the Darién river, famous among the Indians
for its wealth and warriors. But, unable to find it, he settled a town
on a hill and named it San Sebastián, believing that the patron
saint would intercede against the poison of arrows which God
knows were abundant there. However, since God and his Saints
aren't wont to favor injustice and iniquity, even St. Sebastian
disappointed Hojeda, as we shall see. This was the second Spanish
town on the continent—the first was Veragua, as we stated in
Chapter 26, begun by Christopher Columbus who discovered
these Indies—and God surely would not take offense if it remained uninhabited; on the contrary, since it would prevent many
sins.

As they were trying to find the best place to build the town, a
big crocodile came out of the river—they called it alligator by
mistake—caught a mare by its leg, dragged it into the water and
dined handsomely on the corpse. This was at the beginning of
1510, and Hojeda had not enough people for his wretched town.
Since he feared the wrath of the natives for his daily raids there,
he sent one of his ships to Hispaniola with a cargo of gold and
slaves and ordered it to bring back known thieves, arms and other
necessities. San Sebastián became a village of straw huts with a
fort built of thick wood. When the roof of a fort is made of slates
or long planks of palm trees, it is as formidable to the Indians as
Salsas is to the French. Hojeda, like all Spaniards who were to
come to the Indies, was obsessed with gold, and he learned from
some of his captives that the nearby King Tirufi was a King of

enormous wealth and numerous people. He decided to leave enough men to guard San Sebastián and take the rest to go and capture Tirufi. But the reputation of the Christians had spread over the land and when Hojeda arrived, he was greeted by a thick rain of poisoned arrows which killed many Spaniards. Leaving the Indians unscathed, Hojeda ordered a retreat back to the fort.

A few days passed, provisions became scarce, and rather than wait until they were all gone, Hojeda decided to search for food among the Indian villages—and we can believe that if they found gold on their way they did not disdain it. However, no sooner did they arrive at a village than the Indians attacked with their usual weapons, and the danger became so pressing that Hojeda ran back to the fort with Indians hard on his heels. Inside, the Spaniards were kept busy tending the sick and burying the dead, for few escaped the poison. Some days later they ran out of food and fear prevented them from leaving their walls. Their hunger reached such a peak that they ate whatever herbs and roots they found, not knowing whether or not they were edible. This affected the humors and caused great illness from which many died, as, for instance, the sentinel who fell dead at his post one night; or again, the many who would suddenly drop to the ground without feeling pain, dying from sheer starvation. Death came to be seen as a desirable state, a rest from all this anguish.

In the midst of their misery God chose not to abandon them. A resident of Yaquimo named Bernardino de Talavera was deeply in debt, like so many Spaniards who worked their Indians to death yet could not prosper. He decided to leave the island and not pay his debts and he had a choice of the two places we are describing in these pages. Perhaps he had made a deal with Hojeda or perhaps he had heard about Hojeda's need for recruits; at any rate, he assembled a group of seventy characters in rags for debts and other unpunished crimes and together they stole a ship that had anchored at Tiburón Point and belonged to Genoese merchants trading in cassava and bacon from island to island. One fine day they arrived where Hojeda and his men were starving; one can imagine the pleasure they received from this resurrection! Hojeda took the bread and the meat and paid for them in gold or slaves to those who later came to claim the ship, but he once more lived up to his reputation as an unfair distributor and many continued to starve. Those who had been slighted began to form intrigues, devising ways to leave on brigs or ships; but Hojeda kept them there with the hope of imminent rescue by Anciso.

Meanwhile, the Indians renewed their attacks and tried to kill Hojeda by trapping him, for they knew his agility: always first in battle, he wounded but never received a wound himself. Four archers hid behind some bushes with bows and arrows ready, while others attacked from the opposite direction. Hojeda heard the war cry and darted outside, but when he faced the spot where the four Indians were hiding, an arrow hit him in the thigh and pierced it through and through. Hojeda limped back and thought he would die from his rage at being wounded for the first time in his life and he thought, too, that he would not recover and this fear made him send for a surgeon and two white-hot irons. The surgeon refused to apply them, saying they would burn him to the quick and Hojeda, who knew that the herbs worked their poison in a cold medium, solemnly swore to God that if the surgeon insisted, he would have him hanged, and so the surgeon complied to avoid hanging. He took both irons with pincers and held them against Hojeda's thigh so that the heat not only neutralized the effect of the poison but invaded his body to such a degree that they had to use a whole cask of vinegar to soak the sheets wrapped around his body to lower his temperature. Hojeda suffered this voluntarily, refusing to be tied down or held, which is a sign of his great courage. Thus he was cured, the heat of the fire consuming the cold poison of the herbs.

60

They [the Spaniards] finished the provisions Bernardino de Talavera had brought and again found themselves in a state of hunger and misery. Anciso was not coming and boredom and despair drove them to criticize Hojeda and plot ways to return to Hispaniola. Hojeda understood the situation and proposed a plan they found agreeable: he would go to Hispaniola himself and, if he had not returned after fifty days, they could consider themselves free from duty and go wherever they pleased. He appointed Captain Francisco Pizarro—the same Pizarro who was to become a marquis in Perú—to take his place until the arrival of the *alcalde mayor*, Anciso. The seventy men who had come with Talavera chose to risk returning to Hispaniola rather than share the hardships of those who remained there. So, Hojeda embarked with Talavera and his crew on the stolen ship and sailed to the Harbor of Xagua in Cuba, which we mentioned in Chapter 41 and which the Spaniards had not yet settled at the time. They disembarked and started a march eastward in the direction of Hispaniola but somewhere along the way, for reasons I did not bother to find out then, Hojeda and Talavera quarreled. Hojeda's men, seeking revenge for past grievances, took sides with Talavera and together they apprehended Hojeda, though he was not chained because, in the many encounters they had with the Indians, Hojeda fought better alone than half of them together. He was their prisoner, yet his ability and courage were such that he shamed and challenged them saying: "Rascals, traitors! Just come to me by two's and I will fight you all to death," but nobody dared approach him.

Many Indians from Hispaniola had sought refuge in Cuba and they knew by experience what to expect from Spaniards; they also knew of the slaughter performed on the Lucayos; therefore, they came out to stop them from entering their villages and kill them if they could, but Indians are by nature a peaceful people who have no greater weapons than bows and arrows, and they did not harm the Spaniards as much as they could have, considering their great numbers. For their part, the Spaniards were wan and weary and followed the coast whenever possible to avoid fighting. They had walked more than 100 leagues when the seashore turned into a swamp. They marched on, knee-deep in mud, for two or three days, unwilling to retrace their steps and hoping they were closer to the end of the swamp than to the beginning. But the swamp widened and deepened and for eight days they trekked on in mud and water up to their waist, enduring fatigue, thirst and hunger, sleeping in the mangrove roots for a few bitter and restless hours. They drank salt water and ate cassava, *axi* (the pepper of the Indians), raw *ajes* (a carrot-like root) and potatoes and a bit of cheese if they chanced to have some in their bags. Sometimes the putrid water was so deep it reached their armpits and at times came above their heads so that those who could not swim had to drown. Their food bags were wet from floating on the water and wet cassava is as useless as wet wafers. Hojeda carried an image of Our Lady with him that had been painted in Flanders and had been given him by his good friend the Bishop Juan de Fonseca, and he worshipped this image as a devout servant of the Mother of God. He often placed it on a mangrove and prayed to it while those who lagged behind were catching up; then he would exhort them to join him in prayer. To retrace their steps and trek back in anguish was unthinkable; they could only hope to see an end to this or die, as so many had died already, from drowning, thirst and starvation.

The swamp was thirty leagues long, took thirty days to cross and cost endless misery and the lives of half the men. Surely the pains and suffering the Spaniards chose to endure in their quest for gold are among the harshest which men endured anywhere and Hojeda's trials here stand among the worst. God willed that the strongest should survive and reach the end of this calamity by finding a straight path leading to an Indian village called Cueyba (the y is stressed) where they collapsed. Astonished, the Indians were told by sign language or by an interpreter that many were still in the swamps and the Spaniards found as much pity and compassion among the Indians as they would have from their own families: they were given baths, recreation and the food that grows so abundantly in Cuba, and the chief sent his people to help those who had been left behind in the swamps, which they did extremely well, treating the survivors as they would angels, as is their custom when we do not exasperate them, although in that state they could easily have killed one or ten thousand of them.

Hojeda had vowed that, should he come out alive, he would leave his image of Our Lady in the first village; so he gave it to the Indian chief and built a shrine for it, explaining the meaning of the image. The Indians' devotion to it was admirable: they kept the shrine sparkling clean and adorned it with colorful cotton strips; they composed songs to it which they sang while dancing. And when, God willing, we come to Book III, we shall speak in detail of the Indians' devotion to this shrine.

61

The Spaniards remained there as long as they wished and the Indians served them like brothers; then when they had recovered, they thanked God and the Indians and took their leave, accompanied by guides and carriers provided by the cacique. They passed through uninhabited lowlands—so low that those of us who passed later mistook them for the ocean—and arrived at a village called Macaca (the middle syllable is long) where they received the traditional welcome. Isolated as they were, they could not reach Hispaniola and, remembering the Spaniards on Jamaica, twenty leagues away, they discussed the possibility of reaching it by canoe. A certain Pedro de Ordás volunteered to go (I do not remember if other Spaniards went with him); they asked the cacique to man a canoe for Ordás, and the cacique complied readily, stocking the canoe as well with all things necessary for the crossing to Jamaica.

They arrived and notified the admiral's lieutenant, Juan de Esquivel, who had just got there a few days earlier, as we said in Chapter 52. Esquivel sent for Hojeda in a caravel in charge of Captain Pánfilo de Narváez, of whom we will have much to say later, especially of his disastrous end. The caravel arrived in the harbor of Macaca to the rejoicing of the Spaniards; Hojeda asked for a canoe to go meet it and when Narváez saw him he said humorously, "Hojeda, Sir, come this way and we shall take you," to which Hojeda replied, "Sir, this oar of mine is not for rowing," by which he meant that he too had been aggrieved by Talavera. Narváez, who was a gentleman and knew Hojeda's reputation well, received him with all the respect he deserved, then picked up the others and sailed back to Jamaica. Juan de Esquivel was also a gentleman but he had seen himself at the height of prosperity and the bottom of destitution, having, as he told us on many occasions, followed for many years the dizzying movements of fortune; he did not remember that in Santo Domingo Hojeda had threatened to cut his throat if ever they met in Jamaica, and he received Hojeda graciously, made him a guest in his own house, and treated him like himself.

After a few days spent resting from his past tribulations, during which Esquivel and Hojeda sealed their friendship, Hojeda returned to Hispaniola. However, his crew dared not accompany him, afraid of being punished for stealing the ship, as well as for misconduct toward Hojeda; but the admiral's court found out where they were and sent for them in Jamaica, especially Bernardino de Talavera who was among the most guilty. They sentenced Talavera to be hanged and justice was done; if I have not forgotten, I believe they hanged others too for the same crime, and I do not think Hojeda's men were punished for their misconduct, Hojeda being the kind of man who would not accuse them.

Hojeda stayed in Santo Domingo over a year I believe, and I saw him. One night some of his old crew tried to kill him on his way back from visiting his friends but he chased them in his usual way down a street with a knife. Shortly thereafter it pleased God to end his days and he died of illness in this city, so poor he had not a penny for his burial from all his loot and bargaining and slaves, pearls and gold. He asked to be buried at the entrance to the Franciscan monastery in a spot near the door; thus, those who say that Hojeda died of the wound he had received in Urabá are mistaken, because, as I said, I saw him quite healthy in the streets of Santo Domingo, and later, after I had left, I heard that he had died. And that was the end of Alonso de Hojeda who had caused so much damage to the Indians, as we said in Book I: he was the first to commit injustice on this island by using authority he did not possess and cutting off the ears of a cacique who had more right than he to mistreat him. And this was true of all those who had come, including the admiral, as unjust and violent tyrants, invaders of foreign kingdoms and territories. He was also responsible for the crafty apprehension of King Caonabo, who drowned chained in a ship that was to take him prisoner to Castile and died unjustly and without reason. Likewise, he plagued the continent and other islands that had never offended him and captured a great number of Indians whom he sold in Castile as slaves, as we said in Book I. Finally, for what he did and caused Nicuesa to do in the Gulf of Urabá (together with other insults I could relate if I had cared to ask him and others who had gone with him), for the fact that he committed no less injury in his days than any other Spaniard (later, the Spaniards were to exceed these first settlers 100 per cent), for all this he should have had a more catastrophic death. But I attribute it to his devotion to the Mother of God that God allowed him to die peacefully in his bed and gave him time to repent for his sins in this city of Santo Domingo. I hope God gave him the knowledge, before he died, that what he had done to the Indians was sinful. . . .

63

Anciso left Cartagena for Urabá, together with Francisco Pizarro and the men who had suffered such hardships with him. The helmsman was careless and caused the brig to run into shallows where it splintered, tossed as it was by high surf and by a strong undertow. The men scrambled ashore as best they could, almost naked and with a few arms, a little flour, biscuit and cheese, while horses, mares and sows were left to drown, which is to be interpreted as a warning sign from God. Hunger drove them to eat the fruit of certain palm trees but God took pity on them and showed them herds of native pigs on which they fed. When all supplies were exhausted, they decided to steal and he who exposes himself to danger that way is not excused before God for his crimes. Anciso and 100 men, determined to use violence to get food, set out in search of Indians to plunder and were risking their lives for it, unmindful of their souls. They met not 100 nor 1,000 Indians, but only three naked ones who attacked with such ferocity they seemed to be outnumbering the Spaniards. These Indians were so swift with their poisonous arrows that, before the Spaniards realized what was happening, quite a few men were already fatally wounded, and when they had emptied their quivers, the Indians took to their heels like the wind.

Anciso and the survivors turned back, demoralized. They met again to deliberate the advisability of leaving a territory that had proved so ill-fated for them; it is likely that Francisco Pizarro and his men cursed Anciso for having dragged them there. The Indians had burned Hojeda's fort as well as the thirty houses the Spaniards had built, and this was a good argument in favor of leaving. They say Anciso tried to desert but was later cleared of the charge under oath. In the midst of their despair, not knowing what to do, each and every one awaiting his death, Vasco Núñez de Balboa suddenly said that he remembered how, "in the past, when I came to explore with Rodrigo de Bastidas, we entered this gulf. It seems to me that we landed on the west side, the right-hand side, and we saw a large town beyond a big river where it is cool, where they have lots of food, and the Indians do not poison their arrows." They believed Núñez on the spot and decided to look for that river, which was the Darién, reputed to resemble the Nile in Egypt. They went back to the brigs and found out that Núñez's memory had served him well; but the Indians, who had seen the ships and had heard about Spanish ways, evacuated the people unfit for battle, gathered 500 warriors on a hilltop and waited. The Spaniards saw them and, fearing the poison of arrows, sank to their knees and with much devotion, which they thought they had, prayed to God, making a vow to Our Lady—as they say in Seville—of Antigua to dedicate their first church and their first town to her if they came out victorious from that encounter. They even promised to send a pilgrim to Seville—Santa María del Antigua is very popular there—to offer her a present of gold and silver in their names.

Anciso made everyone promise under oath that there would be no turning back and no desertions, and they charged upon the Indians. Since those Indians did not use poison, as Núñez had said, their arrows caused no serious wounds and each Spaniard was able to dispatch twenty Indians with his lance in a trice. The Spaniards entered the town and found it full of food. The next day, they scoured the neighborhood, finding houses empty of people but full of household vases and jugs, cotton things like short women's skirts of interwoven cotton and hair, and a lot of what their hearts desired most, that is to say, fine gold jewels of various shapes worth up to 10,000 pesos.

I just found another account in my notes, told to me by some people who I think took part in that expedition. It says that the cacique Cemaco, lord of that territory, made a truce with the Spaniards and gave them 8,000 or 10,000 gold pesos of his own accord. The Spaniards asked where it came from; he answered:

"From Heaven." They forced him to tell the truth, and he said the larger pieces came from a place twenty-five leagues away and the smaller pieces from the nearby river. They told him to lead them there; he answered he would gladly do so but that he had to see some of his Indians first. He notified his Indians of the Spaniards' request. They advised him not to reveal the place because once they knew it, the Spaniards would never leave, and Cemaco did not return but went into hiding in the territory of one of his vassals. The Spaniards went after him and caught him. They asked him where the gold came from, and he answered as before: "From Heaven." They tortured him until he revealed the truth. They let him go. He gathered his people and attacked the Spaniards and it is then that Anciso and his holy company prayed and made the above-mentioned vows.

After this great triumph, Anciso sent for the men who had been left behind for lack of space in the brigs, and when they heard the news of such riches in food and gold, they were overcome with joy. Vasco Núñez became a hero; he won many friends and acquired a bloated sense of pride. I would like to place a few Christian considerations here, in the manner of pagan historians, very wisely and to the point. To think of such blindness! The licenciate Anciso, for all his knowledge of the law, could not even see the incongruity of praying to God and Our Lady of Antigua for help and intercession in a matter so odious to God as is the perpetration of crime against a people who lived in innocence and peace in their own territories without offending anyone. What else was he doing but asking God and the Virgin to be his criminal accomplices, his fellow participants in homicide and all his other crimes? He was attributing to God and to His Holy Mother the very works of the devil himself. As St. Chrysostom says in his commentary of St. Matthew . . . those who (like Anciso and company) are busy doing the devil's work and defaming the Faith of Christ need not the help of God but of the devil. Indeed, they live with the devil and, however much they may seek God's help, they will never find it, as in the case of a thief bent on robbing or a man bent on fornication. God's justice is incapable of lending a hand to crime and injustice. Let the Christian reader ponder St. Chrysostom's words and see whether they apply to Anciso and company. Let

him consider, too, if naming a church Santa María del Antigua
and sending a present of jewels to her shrine in Seville is a sacrifice
acceptable to God and to His Holy Mother. Anciso should have
remembered the words of Ecclesiastes, which surely he must have
read in the *Decrees*, assuming he professed them, about *Immo-
lantes ex iniquo oblatio est maculata. Dona iniquorum non probat
Altissimus, nec respicit in oblationibus iniquorum*, etc.

God allowed Anciso to conquer those poor innocent Indians,
but that is not a reason for Anciso and his people to think of
themselves as recipients of divine favor for their devotion and
holiness. God is bound to reap glory for Himself from our wrong-
doings, otherwise He would never allow them. In this case, the
benefit He received from such infernal work must have been the
reaping of a soul He had predestined as an Elect, even if it was
only one, and it does not follow that He approves of the work of
those who fail to serve him by flaunting His law and His commandments so implacably. It is fitting to recall the history of
Alexander the Great, who dealt with the world in much the same
criminal way as Spaniards deal with the Indies, killing and mistreating people who were in no way indebted to him and usurping
their kingdoms. When this idolatrous pagan and infernal enemy
of the human race arrived in the Caspian Mountains where the
ten tribes of Israel had been exiled and taken in captivity by the
Assyrian kings Tiglathpileser and Shalmaneser—2 Kings 15, 17—
he received a request from them. Since the edict made public by
the Assyrian kings prohibited them from leaving, and since Alexander the Great had conquered the world, they beseeched him to
give them permission to return to their land, the Promised Land
of Jerusalem.

Alexander inquired about the reason for their exile; he was told
they were apostates, for they had abandoned the God of Israel to
worship and make sacrifice to the Golden Calf, as Jeroboam had
persuaded them to do, a sin for which the prophets had predicted
perpetual exile. Alexander answered that they should be more
confined than they were and he ordered his soldiers to shut off the
mountain pass through which they had been led. But Alexander
himself knew this to be a superhuman task; he prayed to the God
of Israel to bring it about, and the mountains closed so tightly that

passage is now altogether impossible. It is clear that God did not will any of the ten tribes to leave; the ten tribes will leave their exile toward the end of the world and will cause great damage among the peoples, as the Master says in *Scholastics* while commenting on the Book of Esther, Chapter 5. . . . Josephus also relates that when Alexander marched against Darius, the Pamphylian Sea opened to give him passage, the will of God being that Persia should be destroyed by Alexander—that infidel and bloody victimizer of the human race—yet He did not spare him from going to Hell. Anciso should not presume, then, that the victory God gave them was a sign of His approval of actions so loathsome to Him. Therefore, unless they repented on their deathbeds in a way satisfactory to Him, I am afraid they found themselves in a bind not worse, I hope, than that of Alexander, since the sins of Christians are much graver than the sins of infidels. And everyone who misbehaves in the Indies would do well to have the same fear for himself.

Book Three

1

We have written about events worthy of making history in the eighteen years that passed between the discovery of the Indies in 1492 and the year 1510. As we promised in the Prologue, Book III will refer to the years 1511 to 1520 and record what deserves perpetual memory. The writing of this diffuse and general history, with its numerous interpolations, was interrupted many times over a long period of years by the immense and continuous occupations that kept me absorbed in and out of my cell. Consequently, it is likely that I have altered the order of things, recording events in the first two books that pertain to this decade, and vice versa; but I trust in the benevolence of my readers to blame my memory and to continue reading nonetheless. They will discover the truth, which has been the guideline of this *History*, more than a concern for style or for filling up pages with superficial material.

Let us begin this third book, then, with the spiritual measures of the Pope in this year of 1511, one of which was to erect the first cathedrals and another to select the first bishops in the Indies. It must be said that when Queen Isabella was alive—I think around the year 1503 at the beginning of the pontificate of Julius II—she and King Ferdinand petitioned the Pope to erect cathedrals to serve the seventeen Spanish towns on the island of Hispaniola, despite the fact that greed kept the Spaniards from realizing that at the present rate of exploitation, Indians were bound to disappear altogether, reducing those Spanish townships to nothing. As it turned out, a Spanish town lasted only as long as its Indian population, and the Spaniards abandoned it the minute they saw an open door, such as going to San Juan, Jamaica, Cuba or the continent to wage cruel wars against the Indians and cast them in mine pits, only to start again elsewhere after exhausting both gold and captives. So then, the Catholic King believed in the steady growth of those towns—he had not been apprised of the high Indian mortality rate—and the King and Queen asked Pope Julius II to create churches and bishops to help convert the Indians. The Pope created a metropolitan church, the archbishopric Hiagutensis, the location of which I was not able to ascertain but it must have been in the province of Xaraguá, whose prosperity made it a kind of court. The second cathedral was called the bishopric Vainensis, located, I believe, in the province of Vaynoa to the north, in the town of Lares de Guahama; and the third was called Maguensis, probably in La Vega—Maguá, with stress on the last syllable, in the Indian tongue—in the town of Concepción. My conjectures are based on the Indian root words of these names, but of course they referred only to the Spanish settlements there. Hiagutensis could refer either to Yaguana, in the Yaraquá province, or to the province of Higuey, on the easternmost side of the island coming from Castile.

The Pope elected three persons reputed for their religiosity and virtue: the Archbishop of Hiagutensis was a Dominican doctor of canon law, I believe, and his name was Pedro de Deza, a nephew of Diego de Deza, Archbishop of Seville; the Bishop of the Vainensis cathedral was a Franciscan friar called García de Padilla, from what province or family I do not know; the third was the theologian Alonso Manso, the canon of Salamanca, and I knew him well; he was very religious, fair-minded, but not much of an expert in things of this world. My acquaintance with Pedro de Deza was superficial but he was thought of as a religious man.

After these nominations were made, the bulls expediting them were delayed. Perhaps the King wished to take more time because something had transpired concerning the decimation of the Indians. Meanwhile, the Queen died and the kingdom remained with Ferdinand, regent for his daughter Juana, who was unfit to rule, and the news of what was happening to the Indians was spreading more and more. The King discovered that in those three townships selected as bishoprics no one was left to be preached to except the birds and the trees, and he notified the Pope of this ineptitude by saying that the disposition of the land and the difficulties of supplying those townships with necessary maintenance rendered them inadequate. The papal bull refers to it in those terms, and the King would have done better to inform the Pope that, because the natives had been killed, those townships were now deserted. The truth is that large cities and cathedrals could be erected anywhere on this island [Hispaniola]; in itself the land is most fertile and abundant in natural goodness if only our Spaniards had known how to use it and its inhabitants.

The King then beseeched the Pope to eliminate the metropolitan church and transfer the sites of two bishoprics, in addition to another for the island of San Juan, all subject to the metropolitan cathedral of Seville until His Holiness should dispose otherwise. The new sites were to be Concepción and Santo Domingo on Hispaniola and the principal township of San Juan on San Juan Island. The Pope acceded to the request, canceling the first arrangements with the express consent of the three parties involved, and renamed the three designated townships, granting them city charters and city privileges. The diocese of Santo Domingo comprised the towns of Buena Ventura, Açua, Salvaleón, San Juan de la Maguana, Vera Paz or Xaraguá, and the newly established Yaquimo. The diocese of Concepción comprised Santiago, Puerto de Plata, Puerto Real, Lares de Guahaba, Salvatierra de la Çabana, Santa Cruz, and they forgot Bonao, which was as important as any other. The diocese of San Juan was the whole island. Fray García de Padilla was made Bishop of Santo Domingo but he died in Castile before he could come; I think he had not yet been consecrated. Dr. Deza came as the consecrated Bishop of Concepción and died within a few years of his arrival. Alonso Manso also came as a consecrated Bishop and lived many years in San Juan while still retaining his canonship of Salamanca. The Pope granted them the customary tithe and privileges, spiritual and temporal authority and jurisdiction, rights and pre-eminence over all things except gold, silver and other metals, as well as pearls and precious stones. . . .

3

The Dominican friars had already pondered on the sad life and harsh captivity suffered by the natives on the island and had noticed the Spanish lack of concern for their fate except as a business loss which brought about no softening of their oppression. There were two kinds of Spaniards, one very cruel and pitiless, whose goal was to squeeze the last drop of Indian blood in order to get rich, and one less cruel, who must have felt sorry for the Indians; but in each case they placed their own interests above the health and salvation of those poor people. Of all those who used Indians, I knew only one man, Pedro de Rentería—of whom there will be much to say later, if God so wills—who was pious toward them. The friars, then, weighed these matters as well as the innocence, the inestimable patience and the gentleness of Indians, and deliberated on the following points among themselves. Weren't these people human beings? Wasn't justice and charity owed them? Had they no right to their own territory, their own kingdoms? Have they offended us? Aren't we under obligation to preach to them the Christian religion and work diligently toward their conversion? How is it that in fifteen or sixteen years their number has so decreased, since they tell us how crowded it was when they first came here?

Moreover, a Spaniard who had participated in the slaughters had knifed his wife to death on the suspicion of adultery and his wife belonged to an important family of Concepción. To escape the law, he hid some four years in the mountains and when the Dominican Order arrived on Hispaniola, he heard about their holy life and went to the friars' straw house to make confession, begging with great persistence and importunity to be accepted as a lay brother to serve God the rest of his life. They accepted him, for he was indeed very contrite, doing penance to such a degree that he died a martyr, which shows God's mercy and miraculous nature; we will speak of his martyrdom toward the end of this book. This man, whose name was Juan Garcés and whom I knew well, gave the friars a detailed eyewitness account of the loathsome atrocities which he and others had committed in war and in peace. The friars were horrified and strengthened in their conviction thoroughly to fight this new and dreadful tyranny. And, full of compassion toward the Indians and zeal to defend the sullied honor of God, they prayed, fasted and kept vigils in order to receive enlightenment as to the best way to fight for a cause that had no other defendants. They knew how new and scandalous it would be to awaken people from such an abysmal slumber, and after mature reflection they decided to preach from the pulpit and in public that to oppress Indians was to go straight to Hell.

The most scholarly among them composed the first sermon on the subject by order of their superior, fray Pedro de Córdoba, and they all signed it to show that it represented common sentiment and not that of the preacher alone. They gave it to their most important preacher, fray Antón Montesino, who was the second of three preachers the Order had sent here. Fray Antón Montesino's talent lay in a certain sternness when reproaching faults and a certain way of reading sermons both choleric and efficient, which was thought to reap great results. So then, as a very animated speaker, they gave him that first sermon on such a new theme; the novelty consisting in saying that killing a man is more serious than killing a beetle. They set aside the fourth week of Advent for the sermon, since the Gospel according to St. John that week is "The Pharisees asked St. John the Baptist who he was and he said: *Ego vox clamantis in deserto.*" The whole city of Santo Domingo was to be there, including the admiral Diego Columbus, and all the jurists and royal officials, who had been notified each and every one individually to come and hear a sermon of great importance. They accepted readily, some out of respect for the virtue of the friars; others, out of curiosity to hear what was to be said that concerned them so much, though had they known, they would have refused to come and would have censured the sermon as well.

4

At the appointed time fray Antón Montesino went to the pulpit and announced the theme of the sermon: *Ego vox clamantis in deserto.* After the introductory words on Advent, he compared the sterility of the desert to the conscience of the Spaniards who lived on Hispaniola in a state of blindness, a danger of damnation, sunk deep in the waters of insensitivity and drowning without being aware of it. Then he said: "I have come here in order to declare it unto you, I the voice of Christ in the desert of this island. Open your hearts and your senses, all of you, for this voice will speak new things harshly, and will be frightening." For a good while the voice spoke in such punitive terms that the congregation trembled as if facing Judgment Day. "This voice," he continued, "says that you are living in deadly sin for the atrocities you tyrannically impose on these innocent people. Tell me, what right have you to enslave them? What authority did you use to make war against them who lived at peace on their territories, killing them cruelly with methods never before heard of? How can you oppress them and not care to feed or cure them, and work them to death to satisfy your greed? And why don't you look after their spiritual health, so that they should come to know God, that they should be baptized, and that they should hear Mass and keep the holy days? Aren't they human beings? Have they no rational soul? Aren't you obliged to love them as you love yourselves? Don't you understand? How can you live in such a lethargical dream? You may rest assured that you are in no better state of salvation than the Moors or the Turks who reject the Christian Faith." The voice had astounded them all; some reacted as if they had lost their senses, some were petrified and others showed signs of repentance, but not one was really convinced. After his sermon, he descended from the pulpit holding his head straight, as if unafraid—he wasn't the kind of man to show fear—for much was at stake in displeasing the audience by speaking what had to be said, and he went on to his thin cabbage soup and the straw house of his Order accompanied by a friend.

When he had left, the congregation began such whispering that I believe they could not finish the Mass. You can imagine they didn't sit around reading *Menosprecio del mundo* after dinner that day, and they can't have enjoyed the meal either since presently they all met at the admiral's house, that is, Diego Columbus, the discoverer's son. They decided to reprehend and frighten the preacher and his companions, to punish him as a scandalmaker and originator of a new doctrine that condemned them against the King's authority by stating they could not use the Indians the King had given them, which was a most serious and unpardonable matter. They called at the friars' house, the porter opened the door, they asked for the superior, and the venerable father fray

Pedro de Córdoba came alone to meet them. Imperiously they demanded to see the preacher; he answered prudently saying that as a prelate he could speak for all his friars. They insisted but he evaded the issue by using grave and modest words, as he was wont to do, with an air of prudence and authority. Finally, the reverence of his person prevailed upon the admiral and other royal officials to change their tone; they softened and begged him to please bring the friar to them because they wanted to question him about the basis of a sermon that had preached such new and prejudicial things in disservice of the King and damage to the residents of the island.

When the holy man saw that they showed a better disposition, he called fray Antón Montesino, who came with a great deal of fright. After all were seated, the admiral exposed their grievance, asking how he had dared say they couldn't use the Indians given them by the King and acquired at the cost of so much difficulty in wars against the infidel. And because the sermon had caused such scandal, they demanded a revocation; otherwise they intended to resort to the necessary measures. Fray Antón Montesino answered that what he had preached was the result of mature deliberation and the common opinion of all: the need to save the souls of both Spaniards and Indians on the island had to be pointed out as gospel truth because they had noticed the extinction of the Indians, as well as the fact that they were left as uncared for as beasts in the fields. Therefore, as professed Christians and preachers of the Truth, their duty was to serve the King faithfully who had sent them to Santo Domingo to preach whatever was necessary for the salvation of souls; moreover, they were certain that once the King was informed of these happenings, he would thank them for the service. This justification of the sermon spoken to placate their anger fell on dead ears: to prohibit the tyrannization of Indians was hardly the way they could satiate their thirst for gold, since without Indians, they were defrauded of all their desires.

They decided then, each one for his own reasons, to demand a retraction on the following Sunday, and blindness drove them to the point of threatening to send the friars back to Spain if they should not comply. The superior answered that, "Surely, this could be easily done," and this was true, for, besides their habits of coarse frieze, they owned nothing but a rough blanket for the night. They slept on straw pads held up by X-shaped supports; as for the articles of Mass and their scant library, that would easily fit in two trunks. When they realized that threats brought no results; they softened again and asked them to consider another sermon which in some way would satisfy a scandalized town. The friars, in order to put an end to their frivolous importunities and get rid of them, conceded that the same fray Montesino would preach the following Sunday and do his best to satisfy them and elucidate things, and once this was agreed upon, they went home happily.

5

The news of the friar's recantation to be made the following Sunday spread so rapidly that, come Sunday, no invitation was needed to draw the whole town to church. Fray Antón Montesino went to the pulpit and read a theme from Job 36: "From the beginning I shall repeat my knowledge and my truth and I will show my words of last Sunday, that so embittered you, to be true." They were quick to sense the tenor of the sermon and sat there itching to restrain him. The friar backed up his sermon with supporting authorities and gave more reasons to condemn the tyranny of Spanish oppression as illegal, while stressing the point that in no way could a Spaniard save his soul if he persisted in that state. He asked them to mend their ways and said that his Order would refuse to confess anyone except those who moved from place to place. They could publicize this; they could write to anyone they pleased in Castile; for their part, the friars knew for certain this was the only way to serve both God and the King. After he left, they grumbled in indignation, frustrated in their hopes that the friar would deny what he had said, as if a disavowal could change the law of God which they violated by oppressing Indians.

It is a dangerous and sad thing when people improved their lot at the expense of others, for the fact is that it is harder to give up what one has acquired than to jump down a ravine and I might add that it is impossible unless God performs a miracle. For this reason, to hear reprimands from the pulpit is held as an abomination: silence induces people to think that God is not looking and that the divine law is revoked simply because the preachers do not mention it. We have innumerable examples of this insensitivity, danger, obstinacy and evil design among our Spaniards in these our Indies, as well as many more examples of it than anywhere else in the world in any other nation whatever.

To return to the subject: they left the church in a state of rage and again salted their meal that day with bitterness. Not bothering with the friars, since conversation with them had proved useless, they decided to tell the King on the first occasion that the Dominicans had scandalized the world by spreading a new doctrine that condemned them all to Hell because they used Indians in the mines, a doctrine that went against the orders of His Highness and aimed at nothing else but to deprive him of both power and a source of income. The King required an interview with the Castilian provincial of the Order—the friars of Hispaniola had not yet been granted a charter—and complained to him about his choice of friars, who had done him a great disservice by preaching against the state and causing disturbances all over the world. The King ordered him to correct this by threatening to take action. You see how easy it is to deceive a King, how ruinous to a kingdom it is to heed misinformation, and how oppression thrives where truth is not allowed a voice. The most influential letters were those of the treasurer Miguel de Pasamonte, who enjoyed great favor with the King, and his secretary Lope Conchillos, also an Aragonese; and the fact that the King was old and weary did not help the cause of Truth. In addition to the letters, they contrived another way to combat the friars, a way inspired by the devil so that Hell might reign over Christ and Truth in the disguise of goodness, thus making it more difficult to recognize and destroy.

I have already said that in 1502 some Franciscan monks had come to Hispaniola under the leadership of the venerable father fray Alonso del Espinal. He was a most virtuous and zealous religious man but his knowledge was limited to the *Summa* and other general topics, and this is the man the grandees of the city asked to represent them in Castile. He was to inform the King that the Dominicans had caused great disturbances, unsettling consciences all over the island: they preached a change in the system that would deprive the King of an income as well as of the means to support the land. For this reason, this friar was to request the King to take measures necessary to maintain Spanish tyranny, and in the end, they were playing friar against friar to confuse issues. This good friar accepted the embassy in all ignorance, unaware that they were sending him to further the cause of servitude and captivity in which millions of innocent people died and not one was saved from extinction, as I will show later; unaware, too, that the Spaniards were committing the greatest mortal sin and were under strict obligation, *in solidum,* to make amends for the damage they had done.

I do not know if ignorance exempts this friar from the crime of participation; I dare not affirm that the following reason weighed in the balance when he accepted, and that is, the Franciscan monastery received its share of Indians in Concepción de la Vega, though not in Santo Domingo and Xaraguá, where, in Xaraguá at least, the Franciscans had only a handful of friars. Indians were not allotted directly to the friars (in whose hands they would have received better treatment); they were given instead to a Spanish resident in charge of providing them with food, who also sent the six or eight friars there cassava bread, potatoes, some pork meat and that was all; as for wheat bread and wine, they barely had enough to celebrate the Mass and not a whiff of it otherwise. Besides the mines, this same citizen used the same Indians to work his plantations and was reputed to collect some 5,000 gold pesos worth from the mines alone. For this reason, the Indians allotted to the friars worked just as hard as any other and died the same death. These religious men were of course good men but blind as bats not to recognize the danger they incurred by owning Indians who, though they brought very little to them, were dying from hard labor while officially belonging to them. This is why I question the motives of the good and simple father Alonso del Espinal when he accepted a mission against the interests of the Indians and the Dominicans, but I believe that his simplicity and ignorance are to blame and I do not for one instant doubt his goodness, for we knew each other quite well.

When the time came for the journey, I can assure you that he had no need to go begging for assistance. They equipped him like a King, matching their generosity with their expectations. They wrote to recommend him as if he were a canonized saint, telling His Highness that he was an utterly reliable person who had had long experience with the Dominicans and adding all kinds of non-sense about things of which they knew nothing. They believed that the success of their cause depended solely on accrediting fray Alonso del Espinal while discrediting the Dominicans who had preached against their sins. They addressed the letters of recommendation to the real rulers of Castile, Juan de Fonseca, the Bishop of Burgos, and Lope Conchillos, the King's secretary. But they wrote also to the steward Juan Cabrero of the King's inner circle and other powerful figures of the royal council meeting on Indian affairs since at that time the council of the Indies had not yet been constituted as a separate body. . . .

8

I believe that Francisco de Garay, an old-time resident of His-paniola of whom there is much more to· say later, was at court then, and so were Juan Ponce de León, the merchant Pero García de Carrión (a man of authority in his way), and other people who had owned and enslaved Indians and had exterminated them by their greed. Some were there on private business, others belonged to a delegation that was negotiating to acquire perpetual rights to Indians for three generations. I understand that these men were among the first to defame the Indians at court by saying that they needed tutors since they were incapable of self-government, and the rumor grew into a heresy that denied the Indians the ability to receive the Faith and equated them with animals. As if they had needed our tutoring in the thousands of years nature requires to build cities and establish kingdoms in which men multiply *in immenso* and live in peace and harmony, abundance and prosperity! I wish to God they had never known our tutelage, and that we had never made such unjust use of it. The Indians would not have perished so profusely in body and soul and we would not have been punished, nor would we be punished so fiercely later on.

Our great arrogance and inhumanity, as well as their gentle and docile nature, are the reasons behind the infamy of a people who, by comparison with us, know no guilt, a people always at hand to serve us, regardless of the difficulty of the task. So then, some of those Spaniards introduced that notion at court and informed the members of the junta. It is likely that these in turn informed the King, either as a matter of duty or because, as it proved later, they themselves, though living at court, needed to own Indians to keep gold flowing into their pockets. Since gold was always the object of Spanish actions here—at least from about 1500, as I showed in Book II, Chapter 1, to today, 1559—these men established the Indian reputation so that to accuse the Indians of all imaginable defects, such as being lazy animals unfit for self-government, became the pretext with which to hold them in a state of hellish servitude under the guise of serving God and the King by providing supervision and teaching them work habits. The first two volumes of my *History* well show the kind of supervision they imposed and the kind of benefits God and the King received from it. The very men who destroyed the Indians spoke of it themselves, and it is quite clear that the Indians were better equipped to supervise the Spaniards and give them a way of life superior to what the Spaniards had in Castile.

The learned council met to discuss the government of Hispaniola—the only territory subject to discussion then, since Spanish settlements did not exist elsewhere, except in San Juan and Jamaica. They had all the false secular testimonies as well as the single true testimony of fray Antón Montesino [sent by the Dominicans to counteract the influence of the Franciscan Alonso del Espinal], which was, simply, that the infidel must be brought freely to the Faith through love and gifts, not harshness, slavery and torture such as was exercised upon the Indians, as can be read in St. Sylvester, who converted Gentiles with his presents, and in Ezekiel, Chapter 34 (*Vae, pastoribus Israel, qui pascebant semetipsos*), where the King is threatened lest he abolish slavery. After long deliberation, the theologians and jurists of the council composed seven propositions which, although contaminated by prejudice, could not deny Indians the condition of free men, at least in the first two. As for the rest of the propositions, they smack of the tyranny the informers were striving to maintain:

Most mighty Lord:
Your Highness requested that we study the reports of certain Franciscan and Dominican friars. After hearing both sides, as well as additional information from people who had been to the Indies and were familiar with the land and the Indians, we present the following recommendations. One: that Indians be treated as free men, as Your Highness and our Queen (may she rest in peace) decreed some time ago. Two: that they be given Catholic instruction diligently, according to the papal bull and the decrees Your Highness issued on the matter. Three: it is lawful that Your Highness employ Indian labor provided that said labor does not prevent indoctrination into the Faith and that it benefit Indians, the Republic, and Your Highness, since such service is owed you in exchange for maintaining Faith and Justice among them. Four: said labor must be tolerable to the Indians and should include recreation periods daily and throughout the year when convenient. Five: Indians must be allowed to live in their own houses and time must be given them to cultivate their land as they please, which land shall be delineated by the governors of the Indies. Six: communication between Indians and Spaniards is mandatory in order to facilitate and hasten instruction in our holy Catholic Faith. Seven: Indians must be paid for their labor, not in money but in clothing and other household goods.
Johannes, episcopus Palentinus, comes.—Licenciatus Santiago.—El Doctor Palacios Rubios.—Licentiatus de Sosa.—Frater Thomas Durán, magister.—Frater Petrus de Covarrubias, magister.—Frater Mathias de Paz, magister.—Gregorius, Licenciatus.

The seven propositions show the good intentions of those learned men and how they departed from the infamous recommendation that Indians be held in perpetual servitude. However, propositions 3, 4, 5 and 7 assume that Indians are allotted to Spaniards and live under their power, even though the propositions limit the power. Those scholars lacked information which even fray Antón Montesino could not give (since at that time he had lived but a short while in Hispaniola) about the multitude of peaceful Indian kingdoms, well organized and wisely governed, which is proof that it is possible to live in peace and harmony, abundance and prosperity, without knowledge of the true God and the Faith. They also lacked information about the impossibility of having Indians survive under the Spanish *encomienda* system. They did not know it required despotic slavery instead of hiring the service of free men. And after he had examined the question more carefully, in a matter of two weeks, fray Matías de Paz wrote a treatise in Latin to impugn the despotic way in which the Spaniards used Indians and to prove that they ought to be treated as free men. . . . The first corollary of the third conclusion condemns the *encomienda* system as the despotic slavery it actually is, and determines that the Spaniards are obliged to make restitution to the Indians they used. I ask the question: even with the King's power behind him, who could ever make up for the damages suffered by the Indians, inasmuch as they died of the inhuman and bitter treatment they received in the mines and from other pestilential practices because of Spanish greed? . . .

57

The King gave instructions to Governor Pedrarias [Dávila] regarding his conduct in the New World and included an injunction requiring the allegiance of the Indians to the King of Castile, the text of which was later used throughout the Indies. The King's council once more showed grave and harmful ignorance in this, for whatever is founded on injustice is doomed to fall apart at the seams and cause a thousand ills that will corrupt and unnerve the moral and political edifice of a nation, replacing it with consummate malice.

The injunction reads:

In the name of King Ferdinand and Juana, his daughter, Queen of Castile and León, etc., conquerors of barbarian nations, we notify you as best we can that our Lord God Eternal created Heaven and earth and a man and woman from whom we all descend for all times and all over the world. In the 5,000 years since creation the multitude of these generations caused men to divide and establish kingdoms in various parts of the world, among whom God chose St. Peter as leader of mankind, regardless of their law, sect or belief. He seated St. Peter in Rome as the best place from which to rule the world but he allowed him to establish his seat in all parts of the world and rule all people, whether Christians, Moors, Jews, Gentiles or any other sect. He was named Pope, which means admirable and greatest father, governor of all men. Those who lived at that time obeyed St. Peter as Lord and superior King of the universe, and so did their decendants obey his successors and so on to the end of time.

The late Pope gave these islands and mainland of the ocean and the contents thereof to the above-mentioned King and Queen, as is certified in writing and you may see the documents if you should so desire. Therefore, Their Highnesses are lords and masters of this land; they were acknowledged as such when this notice was posted, and were and are being served willingly and without resistance; then, their religious envoys were acknowledged and obeyed without delay, and all subjects unconditionally and of their own free will became Christians and thus they remain. Their Highnesses received their allegiance with joy and benignity and decreed that they be treated in this spirit like good and loyal vassals and you are under the obligation to do the same.

Therefore, we request that you understand this text, deliberate on its contents within a reasonable time, and recognize the Church and its highest priest, the Pope, as rulers of the universe, and in their name the King and Queen of Spain as rulers of this land, allowing the religious fathers to preach our holy Faith to you. You owe compliance as a duty to the King and we in his name will receive you with love and charity, respecting your freedom and that of your wives and sons and your rights of possession, and we shall not compel you to baptism unless you, informed of the Truth, wish to convert to our holy Catholic Faith as almost all your neighbors have done in other islands, in exchange for which Their Highnesses bestow many privileges and exemptions upon you. Should you fail to comply, or delay maliciously in so doing, we assure you that with the help of God we shall use force against you, declaring war upon you from all sides and with all possible means, and we shall bind you to the yoke of the Church and of Their Highnesses; we shall enslave your persons, wives and sons, sell you or dispose of you as the King sees fit; we shall seize your possessions and harm you as much as we can as disobedient and resisting vassals. And we declare you guilty of resulting deaths and injuries, exempting Their Highnesses of such guilt as well as ourselves and the gentlemen who accompany us. We hereby request that legal signatures be affixed to this text and pray those present to bear witness for us, etc.

If I remember well, my good friend the honorable Dr. Palacios Rubios told me he had drawn up the injunction but aside from this, he was in favor of the Indian cause and had much compassion for their misery. The text smacks of a mode of thinking founded on the errors of Hostiensis, whose disciple he was, as I said at length in my first book, *De unico vocationis modo omnium gentium ad veram religionem*, written in Latin.

58

Let us briefly examine the substance of this injunction. First, the wise reader will consider, supposing the Indians understood our language, what they must have felt when they heard that one God created Heaven, earth and men, believing as they did that the Sun God and other deities had created them. What reasons, proofs or miracles proved to them that the god of the Spaniards was more God or more Creator than their own? If Moors or Turks had come with the same injunction, declaring Mohammed the ruler of the world, were they to believe it? Did Spaniards show better proof than the Moors would have with Mohammed? Also, what reasons did they use to prove the God of the Spaniards more powerful than theirs, a God who elected one man called St. Peter as supreme lord over the world when they had their own rulers and believed themselves alone in the world? Thus, how could they—especially if they were rulers—love and revere the God of the Spaniards when they heard that St. Peter and his successor the Pope disposed of their territory by giving it to the Castilian King? They believed themselves the true owners of their land by the age-old law of inheritance, and here they were asked to acknowledge a ruler they had never seen or heard of, not knowing whether he was good or bad, whether he intended to govern or steal and destroy, a confusion made the greater by the fierce look of his bearded messengers armed to the teeth with terrible weapons! What could they have expected? Allegiance was demanded, without previous agreement stating the duties of both parties, to a new King who was to rule on ancient territory and who showed no regard for its laws.

The cacique of the Cenú province must have known this.

According to what Anciso says in his pamphlet *Suma de geografía*, when this cacique received the injunction, he answered that the Pope was out of his mind to give his land to the King of Castile and that, by accepting it, the King had not only lost his mind, but was at fault for sending his men to usurp territories so distant from his own. I would not dare write this here if Anciso had not written it first, and in more shameful terms too, as we shall see below, God willing. I would like to ask the authors of this injunction what credit should a people who lived at peace in its territory without harming anyone be expected to give to such a bill of sale? Even if presented with bulls bearing the papal seal, should they be excommunicated if they disobeyed them and would this be sinful? Or rather, would all this not seem like delirium and the summum of foolishness and nonsense, especially when told they were under obligation to subject themselves to the Church.

Let us see: to understand what the Church and what such obligations are, does it not presuppose that we know and believe the teachings of our Christian Faith? Why do we believe in the Church and Pope if it isn't because we believe in the Holy Trinity, Father, Son and Holy Ghost, and we confess the fourteen Articles of Faith? Well then, not having this Faith in the Holy Trinity, Christ or his Church, how can anyone believe in the Church or the Pope, great and admirable father though he may be? If one cannot and should not believe in the existence of the Church and the Pope and has no knowledge of Christ as the true Son of God and founder of the Church, by what law, human, natural or divine, is one bound to believe in them? Therefore, if there is no obligation, nonbelieving is not a sin, and there were no reasons to believe that the Pope had the power to give away territories and kingdoms owned for generations by a people who lived so far from our Old World and were ignorant of its existence. If they did not believe in the Pope's power to subject them to the King of the Spaniards, why should they obey him and, as free men, discredit their estate by acknowledging a King they had never seen or heard of, a foreign ruler of a fierce people, bearded and armed, who, *prima facie*, look horrible and frightening?

Let us see: if kings wished to submit to the Castilian King without the consent of their people, would these people not be justified by right to disobey, depose and even kill them? Likewise, if the people wished the same without the consent of their rulers, would this not be called treason? Therefore, if neither kings nor subjects, together or separately, are under obligation to obey a foreign King, no matter how many injunctions they receive, it is made clear beyond all proof that the threat of an all-out war and captivity of men, women and children intended for slavery is based on neither law nor justice. And if these reasons have led and are leading to war, what law, right or reason justifies it? Hence such wars against such infidels as Indians were, are, and always will be unjust and detestable and condemned by law.

By the same token, any war waged by such infidels against Spaniards or Christians who so treat them is justified, and this has always been the case ever since we discovered the Indies. Indians possess this right forever because their wrongs have never been righted. The ignorance of the King's council is then manifest; I pray to God it is remissible—how unjust, impious, scandalous, irrational and absurd this injunction was! I will not speak of the infamy it caused the Christian religion; I don't know whether to laugh or cry at the absurdity of the council, who believed these people to be under more obligation to acknowledge the King as their Lord than Christ as God and Creator, since one cannot be constrained to receive the Faith, and yet, to obey the King, the council used force. There were other falsehoods in the document, such as stating that Indians in other islands had willingly and without resistance acknowledged the King of Castile. In those days there were no notices, proclamations, information or injunctions, and Indians never served the King willingly but were forced to it violently and tyrannically by cruel wars and hard slavery, and God is witness to how they perished there. They would, however, serve the King willingly and readily if they had been converted by the Christian means of peace and love.

Finally, the wise reader may infer that if they had understood our language, they could have answered the injunction and proved it insane. But what excuse do the authors and executors of the injunction have, who were addressing people who understood not a word of it, as if it had been Latin or gibberish? Those who study law know very well the value of an injunction written in a language other than that of the people to whom it is addressed, whether these people are subject to the obligation of fulfillment or not. . . .

60

Pedrarias Dávila anchored about one-half league from the town and, before allowing anyone to leave ship, sent a servant ahead in order to notify Vasco Núñez of his arrival. Vasco Núñez had some 450 men with him in Darién at the time but hard work had toughened them and they were stronger than the 1,200 or 1,500 men Pedrarias had with him. The messenger asked for Vasco Núñez. "There he is," someone said, pointing to a man dressed in a cotton blouse over a linen shirt and wearing hemp sandals and coarse breeches, who was looking on and helping his slaves at thatching a house. The man stared, for he could not believe that was the Vasco Núñez, whose exploits and riches were so famous in Castile that he had expected to see him seated on a majestic throne. He told him that Pedrarias had come to govern here, and Núñez answered with a welcome (God knows the truth), that he and the others in the King's service were ready to receive and serve him.

The news that a large and well-armed fleet had arrived spread excitement and speculations about, among other things, how best to receive Pedrarias, whether armed as when at war with the Indians or as a township, unarmed. Opinions were divided, but Núñez followed the safest course by walking to the shore unarmed and casually dressed. Pedrarias had taken his precautions, for he was experienced and had posted his men in case Núñez and his group opposed him. He stood holding the hand of doña Isabel de Bobadilla, and Núñez came up to him, bowed ceremoniously, and offered himself and his men to the governor. Then they all walked to town showing exterior signs of gladness (but God knows how cheerful they felt inside) and the 1,200 men of Pedrarias were assigned to the straw houses of the 400 residents. They exchanged corn and cassava bread, native roots and fruit, fresh water and slave service gotten with the injustice we described earlier, for Castilian things from the King's provisions, such as rations of bacon, salted fish and meat, biscuits, etc.

The next day Pedrarias began his inquiry into the truth of what Núñez had written to the King about the wealth in pearls and gold of the Southern seas and all was verified except for the notion that gold came up by the netful. Not Núñez, but Colmenares or someone else had publicized this and the greed and vanity of Castile had believed it. The people, on the other hand, did not bother to inquire the wheres and hows of gathering gold. Rather, I believe they immediately lost courage when they noticed the absence of nets and other fishing gear as well as the silence surrounding this; instead, they heard of the pains the men had endured and of the many rich mines that produced gold stolen from the Indians not by fishing but by digging strenuously, and they felt they had been deceived and lost their enthusiasm. Pedrarias then proclaimed an investigation into Vasco Núñez's conduct; Espinosa carried it out. Núñez was fined a few thousand castellanos for the damage he had caused to Anciso and others, but he was acquitted of the death of poor Nicuesa and other crimes because of his good service to the Crown. The charges made no mention of the robberies, slaughters, captures and other scandalous crimes he committed against individual Indians of high rank and common people as well, and nobody accused him because to kill and rob Indians was never considered a crime in the Indies. The most powerful reason for this is none other than the great insensitivity in most of us which God allowed for the sins of Spain, secretly reserving total punishment for the sins so inhumanly committed against the peoples of these Indies. Because Núñez had written to the King that to exploit the Southern seas it was necessary to settle Spanish towns in the kingdoms of the caciques Comogre, Pocorosa and Tubanamá, Pedrarias, consulting Núñez, immediately made arrangements to settle those three areas.

61

While preparations were being made, the food brought from Castile disappeared rapidly and rations were cut back and this meant hunger for the many who depended on the King's provisions for their sustenance. For this and other reasons—such as the dampness of the marsh region and the quality of the air which for the most part was healthier than the Spanish climate but nevertheless was different—many of the people Pedrarias had brought with him were dying. He too was afflicted with a grave illness even though he had more ample provisions, and had to leave Darién for the nearby Corobarí river (the last syllable is long) because his doctors had recommended a change. Pedrarias's illness postponed the settlement of the said three regions though not the death by starvation and disease of many of his men, especially when the King's rations drew to an end and illness compounded malnutrition. Hunger became so acute that many gentlemen, who had mortgaged their inheritance in Castile, were dying with the cry "Give me bread," while others exchanged garments of crimson silk for a pound of corn bread, Castilian biscuits or cassava. There was even a nobleman, once one of Pedrarias's most prominent persons, who fell dead in front of the whole town after clamoring in the street that he was starving to death.

Nothing of the kind had ever been seen before: people richly dressed in silk and brocade worth a tidy sum of money falling dead of pure hunger, others grazing in the fields like cattle on the most tender grass and roots, while those who were stronger shamelessly dragged firewood from the mountains for a piece of whatever sort of bread was given in return. The death toll was such that many were buried in the same grave and sometimes they would not close a grave because they knew that in a matter of hours others would die and be buried there. Many were left one or two days without burial because the healthier ones had not the strength to dig the grave and in all cases rites and shrouds were neglected. Everyone saw quite clearly then how gold came up by the netful!

In the midst of this anguish, which did not spare Pedrarias and his household, Pedrarias gave permission to a few important noblemen to return to Spain. A boatful of them went by way of Cuba where we killed their hunger, for we were in a land of plenty and they were coming from bare land, not because the land was barren—in its day it too had been most fertile—but because the Spaniards had depopulated it by killing its inhabitants or engaging in slave trade or by causing the remaining Indians to run far away.

Those provinces were devastated but it is a fact that, had the Spaniards acted like Christians toward the Indian chiefs, noblemen and common people, they and more than they would have lived in abundance; but they were not worthy of this because they had not fulfilled God's aim since they had left Spain. So then, such were the effects of believing that gold grew on trees and of their coming with such rapaciousness.

When Pedrarias had somewhat recovered from his illness, he was informed that the mines in Darién were rich and numerous. And, ignoring the unhealthy atmosphere of the region—which, given what was happening there, he should have taken seriously— he sent Luis Carrillo with sixty men to build a town seven leagues from Darién near the river called, since the days of Núñez, I do not know for what reason, the Río de las Anades, and I do not know either what he provided by way of sustenance since everyone was so starved and there was not a trace of Indians anywhere except for the few slaves he was taking with him, which is why that township lasted such a short time.

About that time also, Vasco Núñez began to feel the pinch of having to take orders when he was used to giving them, and he contrived a way to go where he would rule alone. He secretly sent Andrés Garavito to Cuba to find men to build towns and settle on the Mar del Sur. I have no idea on what he based his authority; I believe he had not the title of Adelantado then but perhaps he had certain royal privileges. At any rate, even as Adelantado he could not have ruled without being subject to Pedrarias. Perhaps that was the beginning of Pedrarias's suspicion which, in the end, caused Núñez's downfall.

62

With Luis Carrillo away to settle the Anades river region, Pedrarias hurried to dispatch his captain Juan de Ayora with the 400 ablest men from among his group and that of Vasco Núñez to steal all the gold they could find in the area, breaking all pacts of friendship and confederation which Núñez himself had previously established, although sometimes through plunder and tyrannical force. Perhaps Pedrarias spared the confederates in his instructions but his captain did not in carrying out orders; at any rate, I believe Pedrarias had decided to send his wife back to Spain and she was not to return empty-handed. His orders were to establish three townships, with the usual fort, in the lands of Pocorosa, Comogre and Tubanamá. Juan de Ayora and his fleet of one ship and three or four caravels anchored in a harbor of Comogre's territory, twenty-five or thirty leagues west of Darién, and sent Francisco Becerra with 150 men to the South Sea to find a good place for the establishment of a town; and Becerra took an already known short-cut which reduced the distance to twenty-six leagues from coast to coast. Juan de Ayora then ordered Garci-Alvarez to wait for him with the ships and the sick in the harbor of Pocorosa's territory further west, while he and 200 men went inland to see what they could steal.

They arrived in Ponca's territory. . . . Ponca, feeling secure, came in peace to meet Juan de Ayora, but Ayora laughed and said friends helped one another while helping himself to Ponca's gold and searching his house against Ponca's will. From there Ayora went on to the domain of Comogre who had given such a welcome to Núñez and had been the first to notify the Spaniards of the other sea. Comogre's spies had forewarned him of Ayora's coming and of the latter's search for gold; so, he came out to meet him with a sizable gift of gold, jewels and food, took him to his house and feasted him. But his past good deeds toward him and Vasco Núñez, as well as Núñez's promise that Spaniards would never harm him, failed to prevail upon Ayora's good will and this wretched tyrant took Comogre's women by force.

Someone has written that Ayora did the same to Pocorosa. He stole what he could and Pocorosa, informed of his coming, fled to the woods not daring to wait for him. The worst of it was that the unfortunate Pocorosa, King of those lands, thought he could placate Ayora by carrying in person a load of all the gold he had been able to gather and offering it to him in exchange for the women, people and things Ayora had taken. But it was in vain; Ayora captured him and took him prisoner to the land of Tubanamá in order to frighten the other chiefs and ransom him for gold. He found Tubanamá's territory at peace, as had been promised to Vasco Núñez, and he was received with signs of joy. Tubanamá fed him and his men and gave him a sizable present of gold, but Ayora was not satisfied with these good works on the part of someone who owed him nothing, and repaid his services by taking as many slaves and things as he could.

Tubanamá escaped and rallied his people and neighbors and furiously attacked Ayora from the other side of the river, shooting clouds of arrows, fighting like lions, naked though they were. Surely, had they possessed better weapons they would have done us more harm than ever before, for they were a courageous people and braved death to defend their own land, as we experienced many times. Ayora defended himself but I do not know if many were killed on both sides; I do know, however, that Ayora's men felt pressed and afraid enough to build fortifications with earth and branches in anticipation of another attack at dawn. But the Indians did not return, thinking it unlikely to win, which argues that they had been hurt either by the swords or the dogs.

Ayora left Hernán Pérez de Meneses with sixty men in that flimsy fort as rear guard to ensure his retreat and goings back and forth between Becerra's force and himself, and he went back to Garci-Alvarez who was waiting in the harbor of a river they named Santa Cruz, in Pocorosa's territory. He drew up the town of Santa Cruz there, naming mayor and aldermen according to Pedrarias's instructions, and this was in May of 1515. After the town of Santa Cruz was established with settlers less than holy, Juan de Ayora was told of a cacique rich in gold and people who dwelled further west and whose name was Secativa (the penultimate syllable is long). He dispatched a certain Gamarra with boats and men with orders to capture and plunder under the disguise of seeking allegiance to the monarchs of Castile; but the news of the Spaniards' horrible deeds had spread all over the land and all Indian villages were on the alert. They had spy networks (Indians are experts at this), fearing that the Spanish plague would fall upon them any day, and the cacique Secativa was informed that Spaniards were approaching from the sea. He put all the women and children in safety and the men went hiding behind the bushes; the Spaniards landed and were nearing the town when Indians darted from all sides and, with frightening war cries, attacked them with fire-hardened rods as sharp as javelins and probably arrows too, leaving the captain and his men wounded and beating a retreat.

When Juan de Ayora saw his men defeated, he was filled with

poisonous anger which he decided to spill in Pocorosa's land. He gave orders to raze all the territory surrounding the wicked town he had just established, seize Pocorosa and make him yield more gold; but a Spaniard named Eslava notified his Indian friend and when Ayora found this out, he tried to hang Eslava. After completing his work of evangelization and propagation of love for the Christian Faith in this way, Ayora thought about returning to Castile by way of Darién to pick up the gold barrels he had left there. And so he did, stealing a ship that had remained in port, and they say Pedrarias knew and approved because he was a good friend of his brother, Gonzalo de Ayora. It could be that Ayora paid the King's tribute of one-fifth part as well as Pedrarias's share from the gold he had stolen, and rumors have it that he brought more gold than he declared to Castile. This wicked tyrant was an esteemed hidalgo from Córdoba whose greed for gold was insatiable, as his deeds proclaim. Pedro Martyr describes him as such in Chapter 10 of the third *Decada*. . . .

As for Garci-Alvarez and his settlers of Santa Cruz, they chose not to remain idle but raided the neighborhood for women and Indian slaves. For his part, Pocorosa, who had been so injured by the ungrateful Spaniards, gathered his people and his injured neighbors and at dawn one day came upon Santa Cruz, found it asleep and wounded everyone before they could take arms. When arrows are not poisoned, they leave no greater wound than a Spanish snake's bite; thus the wounded Spaniards got up and took their weapons and killed with their swords as many as the Indians killed with their clubs. The Indians fought so vigorously that, although they suffered many deaths, by the first light of day they had dispatched all but five Spaniards who escaped by hiding and fleeing night and day to Darién, where they told the news. And thus the good township of Santa Cruz came to an end six months after having been created. . . .

77

We left out a few things in order not to interrupt the story of Vasco Núñez. For instance, after Espinosa's quest for the gold recovered from Badajoz by Cutara, King of Pariba (also called

Paris [*sic*]), the commissioner Juan de Tavira requested permission to lead the holy conquest of the Dabayba temple. Pedrarias granted it and he [Juan de Tavira] spent a lot of money, earned by trading slaves, to equip three boats and to buy many canoes from his Spanish neighbors so that he might go up the river Grande where gold, his idol, was reputed to be. He not only spent all his ill-acquired capital—the good money he possessed was money he had brought from Castile—but much of the King's money as well. Strong currents made sailing upstream difficult for his three boats, his canoes, 160 Spaniards and an infinite number of Indians enslaved by the kind of justice already described, all of them in chains to row the boats and serve the Spaniards' every need.

The people of Dabayba had been informed of their coming; they placed three large canoes across the river and caught the Spaniards by surprise, killing one and wounding many, while the Spanish canoes sought shelter behind the boats. It was decided that a contingent of men would go on foot by land while the rest would proceed upstream; but soon they found the river swollen with heavy forest rains that covered the trees completely. The commissioner's canoe ran into a tree and turned over in such a way that both Tavira and the inspector Juan de Virués drowned; only those who could swim were saved. Finding themselves without a captain, they elected Francisco Pizarro to guide them back to Darién; and thus they returned, having lost both commissioner and inspector, as well as the money spent on the expedition. Pedrarias lamented the disaster and tried to encourage the survivors by promising another expedition under Pizarro, this time to Abrayme, reputed also for its gold. About fifty men went with Pizarro; the rest chose to remain there, for many were wounded and others quite beaten down.

They traveled by land to the territory of Abrayme, whose inhabitants had been so mistreated during the previous encounters that, this time, the Spaniards not only found not a soul to capture (capture being second to gold in the aims of the Spaniards), but they found no food either and had to kill and eat seven horses in order to survive and return to Darién, where they arrived in a state of weakness, disillusion and angry frustration. A few days later, Diego Albítez returned with a great quantity of gold and many slaves taken to a coast they call Nombre de Dios and from the provinces of Chagre and Veragua, which they left full of bitterness and calamities, killing everyone who resisted them. During one of those encounters, I do not remember under whom, the Spaniards got to the mountains and tortured Indians to find out where the others were hiding—they had fled, of course, from the Spanish pestilence and horrendous cruelties. They attacked one hiding place and took away about eighty women, the wives and young daughters of Indians who had died in battle or were hiding elsewhere.

The next day, the Indians, enraged at seeing their wives and daughters taken in slavery, assembled and attacked the Spaniards from the rear as they were marching, apparently confident that the Indians would not attack them. The Indians gave their terrible war cry and wounded many Spaniards, and the Spaniards, seeing themselves in a bind and unable to enjoy the women, killed them all by ripping open their bellies with the sword. The Indians recoiled in horror and frustrated pain shouting, "Oh Christians, evil, cruel men, killers of *iras.*" *Ira* means "woman" in that region, which shows that they hold the killing of women as a sign of bestial conduct, abominable and cruel.

Even when Indian chiefs brought gold of their own accord, the Spaniards were not satisfied, and they would catch a few Indians, torturing them horribly and inhumanly to find out where they hid their gold. Once, a chief brought 9,000 gold pesos, prompted either by fear or a desire to please. But the Spaniards were not satisfied. They seized the chief and tied him to a pole in a seated position, legs and feet extended. They burned his feet while asking for more gold. He ordered his Indians to bring 3,000 pesos more. The torture continued even though he screamed that he had not one peso left and they stopped the torment only when the marrow oozed from his feet and the poor man died. It happened that some of those delicate Spaniards had wounds on their legs and it seems that the devil, whose will they followed, inspired them to think that human fat was good medicine and so they decided to kill the fattest Indians they had captured to melt their fat and smear it on their wounds, saying that a healthy Spaniard was worth more than any one of those devil-loving dogs. And this is how the Indians paid for their innocence!

78

Let us leave aside the history of the continent in order to bring the happenings on the islands up to date (1514). We have already spoken of Alburquerque's distribution of Indians and his lack of concern, like everyone else, for the poor oppressed Indians, as well as his refusal to stop their decimation in the mines and other types of work. It was the same story on all the other islands, where not one had the sensitivity to pity them. During all this time the treasurer Pasamonte, the judges and other officials of the Santo Domingo Audiencia used Pasamonte's favor with the King to persecute Admiral Diego Columbus by writing to the King, to his secretary Lope Conchillos and to the Bishop of Burgos, Juan Fonseca, who had never been on good terms with either of the admirals, father or son. I have always believed they tried to depose the admiral in order to assume full government themselves because they were the kind of men who resent having a superior. They succeeded in persuading the King to order don Diego back to Castile, I know not under what pretext because at that time I neglected to find out. Don Diego started from Santo Domingo at the end of 1514 or early 1515, and left his highly respected wife, doña María de Toledo, with their two daughters on the island. Meanwhile, the judges and officials ruled as they pleased and they did not fail to harass the admiral's household, without respect for the personal dignity and lineage of the said Señora doña María de Toledo.

In those days all eyes and hopes were on Cuban wealth and the pacific nature of the Cuban natives; and Diego Velázquez had already been there for two years. As for the continent, Pedrarias was exploring it, nobody knew with what results, and no reports were coming from anywhere else.

To return to the story of Cuba—begun in Chapter 32—we explained how, as lieutenant governor, Diego Velázquez had marked out five townships, including Barocoa, for Spanish residence. The

Indians of each region were allotted to the Spanish residents; and every Spaniard, according to the degree of his thirst for gold and the laxness of his conscience, not considering that Indians were people of flesh and blood, heaped them in the mines, where their untimely and massive extermination is proof enough of the kind of inhuman treatment they received. The perdition of these people was more vehement and accelerated here than elsewhere because the Spaniards were engaged in pacification—as they call it—and they were accompanied by a multitude of Indians taken in the villages to serve them. Thus, they consumed the island resources and did not bother to reseed them, and the whole island was quickly left unattended and unproductive, since when the Indians were not caught or killed, they deserted their villages to find a hiding place away from the Spaniards.

As I said, then, greed kept the Spaniards from cultivating the land while they marched on to harvest the gold they had done nothing to produce. The price of scant nourishment was endless scavenging; thus they forced men and women, with a diet well below sustenance level, to the most arduous labor. And it is true, as I already mentioned, that in my presence someone told us, as if recounting an exploit, that he had made his Indians dig and form thousands of cassava mounds by sending them out into the hills every third day for a bellyful of fruit that was to last them two whole days of hard labor, during which they had not a bite to eat. Digging cassava mounds a whole day is much more toilsome than hoeing vineyards in our country since it consists of digging enough earth to form a heap 3 or 4 feet square and deep, not with hoes but with cudgel-shaped sticks.

So then, death made speedier ravages among Indians here than in other places, starvation and hard labor helping. Since all able-bodied men and women were away at the mines, only the old and sick stayed in town with no one to look after them. So they died of illness, anguish and starvation. I was traveling the Cuban roads then and it happened that entering a town I sometimes heard crying in the houses. I would inquire and was greeted with the words "Hungry, hungry." Anyone strong enough to stand on his feet was sent to work, including nursing mothers whose milk dried up in their breasts from lack of food and excessive labor, which caused infant mortality at the rate of 7,000 in three months, as someone who investigated the situation informed King Ferdinand. Once too, 300 Indians allotted to an official of the King were reduced by nine-tenths in three months because they were driven relentlessly.

79

Greed increased every day and every day Indians perished in greater numbers and the clergyman Bartolomé de las Casas, whom we mentioned earlier, went about his concerns like the others, sending his share of Indians to work fields and gold mines, taking advantage of them as much as he could. He always tried to maintain them well, treat them mildly and pity their misery but, like everyone else, he neglected the fact that they were infidels in need of indoctrination into the Christian fold. One day, Diego Velázquez left Xagua with his Spaniards in order to establish the town of Santo Espíritu, and only one priest remained in Baracoa besides the said Bartolomé de las Casas. So, at Pentecost time he decided to leave his estate on the Arimao river, one league from Xagua, in order to say Mass and preach in town. As he studied his past sermons, he began to consider passages of the Scriptures, especially, if I remember correctly, Ecclesiastes, Chapter 34. . . .

As I said, he began to consider the suffering and servitude of these people and he remembered having heard that the Dominican friars of Santo Domingo could not own Indians with a clear conscience and would neither confess nor absolve Indian owners, which the said clergyman disapproved. He remembered how one day on Hispaniola, where he had owned Indians with the same carelessness and blindness as in Cuba, a Dominican friar had refused him confession. He asked why, was given the reason, and proceeded to refute the friar, giving frivolous arguments and vain solutions that had a semblance of truth, but the friar interrupted him with, "Enough, Father, truth has many disguises but so do lies." The clergyman conceded to the venerable person of the friar and to his great learning, but as far as giving up his Indians, he paid no attention. Thus, this memory helped him understand his own ignorance and the danger of his soul, owning Indians like everybody else, unscrupulously confessing Indian owners, a few in Cuba and many on Hispaniola.

He spent a few days in meditation on the matter until by dint of applying his readings to this and that case he was convinced Indians were being treated unjustly and tyrannically all over the Indies. He read everything in this new light and found his opinion supported; as he used to say, from the day the darkness lifted from his eyes, he never read any book in Latin or a vulgar tongue—and he read an infinite number in forty-four years—which did not in some way provide the proof of Indian rights and Spanish injustice. Finally, he decided to preach this, but having Indians on his property and the written reprobation thereof in his hand, he could not freely condemn the *encomienda* system as tyrannical unless he officially renounced his Indians to Governor Diego Velázquez. He knew Indians were better off with him because he treated them with more compassion and would even show more consideration in the future. He knew that they would be redistributed to a master who would oppress them to death, which is what happened; but, even if he treated them as a father treats his sons, he could not preach the subject of his sermons with a clear conscience. Someone would inevitably blame him with, "In the last analysis, you too own Indians; why don't you renounce them since you accuse us of tyranny?" He decided then to relinquish them entirely. To understand this well, let us recall the clergyman's friendship with Pedro de Rentería, a wise man and a good Christian. They were not only good friends but partners who had combined their allocation of Indians.

Pedro de Rentería had chartered a caravel for 2,000 castellanos and was in Jamaica visiting his brother and buying pigs to raise, corn to plant and other things that were lacking in Cuba when the clergyman decided to give up his Indians and preach against ignorance. Casas paid a call on Governor Valázquez one day to tell him how he felt about himself and those who held Indians. He said he could not absolve Indian holders, and in order to rescue himself, as well as to preach what he had to preach, he had determined to renounce his Indians who from that moment were to be considered unowned and at the governor's disposal. He asked the governor to keep it a secret and not to reallot the Indians before Rentería's return from Jamaica, since the estate and the Indians were owned by them jointly and Rentería would suffer from any transaction carried out in his absence.

The governor heard this novel and monstrous news with astonishment, first, because as a clergyman involved in worldly affairs like everybody else, Casas joined ranks with the Dominicans and dared make his opinion public; secondly, because of the clergyman's contempt for worldly benefits apparently strong enough to make him renounce a prosperous estate, especially when he was beginning to have a reputation as a greedy man and was managing his mines and plantations with great diligence. The governor, thinking of the material aspect of this rather than of the danger of his soul as the head of the tyranny perpetrated against Indians, said: "Father, think twice before you act and have occasion to regret your decision. By God, I would like to see you rich and prosperous! I do not accept the remission of Indians; instead, I will give you two weeks to think it over, at the end of which you may come and tell me your decision."

The clergyman answered: "Sir, I thank you for your good wishes and signs of appreciation, but please pretend that the two weeks are already past. If I should regret my decision and in two weeks come to you with tears of blood for the restitution of my Indians, and for the love of me you should listen, I pray God to punish you rigorously for this and never to pardon your sin. I only ask you to keep this secret and not to reallot the Indians before Rentería's return so his estate will not be hurt." The governor promised and kept his word, and from then on held the clergyman in higher esteem, improving his government with good works toward the Indians, and improving himself personally as well, for he believed the clergyman as if he had seen him perform miracles. The people of the island also changed their minds about him when they learned that he had given up his Indians, which was about the greatest proof of sanctity a man could show in these parts, such was and still is their blindness!

The matter was made public in the following manner. On Assumption Day, the clergyman was giving a sermon on the subject of the day: the contemplative and the active life. Speaking of spiritual and temporal works of charity, he pointed out to his listeners their obligation to act charitably toward the Indians whom they exploited cruelly and chided them for their carelessness. He felt it appropriate to reveal his secret and, turning to the governor, said, "Sir, I now permit you to divulge our secret to anyone you please and I hereby announce it to all present." Then he denounced the blindness, injustice, tyranny and cruelty committed against an innocent and gentle people. He said owners of Indians could not win salvation but should feel it a duty to liberate them and that he, knowing the dangerous state of his soul, had relinquished his, and so on. Everyone was surprised, even astonished, to hear this and some walked away remorseful while others thought they had been dreaming—the idea of sinning because one used Indians was as incredible as saying man could not use domestic animals. . . .

88

The first duty of the Hieronymite fathers in charge of reforming the Indies was to call a meeting of all the principal old-time Christian settlers and inform them of their purpose: clamorous protests had arisen against the settlers, especially against the *encomienda* as a system leading to the mistreatment of Indians, nonsensical killing, abuse of wives and daughters, women and children, overwork and malnutrition, abortions, unnursed children and other acts of violence. The protests were written down in memorandum form and presented to the Cardinal and many instructions ensued.

Their Highnesses, the Cardinal and the Ambassador wish to know the truth of what is happening in order to prevent the total loss of the Indies. They hereby order the fathers to investigate the situation by requesting information, under oath if necessary, from the settlers and other sources. The fathers will study the means by which to preserve the natives and the land; means found agreeable to God and Their Highnesses will be taken into account. Therefore, let there be meetings between the fathers and all the principal settlers and let the matter be discussed frequently. Let there be meetings between

Spaniards and Indian caciques in which the fathers will explain their presence as an order from Their Highnesses to stop oppression, punish wrongdoers, and see to it that from now on Indians are treated as the Christian free men they are in reality. Therefore, the caciques must inform their people and hold councils about what should be done to remedy their situation, and solutions found amenable to both Indians and Spaniards will be taken into account. Above all, the fathers will stress that their sole reason for being there at all is to enforce the freedom of the Indians. When the fathers report their findings to the Indian population, they must be accompanied by religious men known to those Indians as trustworthy people in order to win their confidence and interpret their language.

It is well to note here that the clergyman had known for a long time how deeply rooted Spanish tyranny was in these islands and on the continent, and he knew how Indians perished under it; however, he had never dared open his mouth as much as to hint that Indians were free men, as if he tried to avoid saying something absurd or blasphemous. Until one day, as he was discussing Spanish oppression with the Cardinal, he asked what reason could possibly justify this servitude and the Cardinal answered with short temper: "None, of course. Why should there be a reason? Aren't the Indians free men and does anyone doubt this?" From that day on, the clergyman made no bones about declaring that Indians are free and he based his criticism of Spanish actions on that principle. It seems, then, that the Cardinal knew very well what had caused the servitude of Indians since this document underlines that Indians are indeed free men.

The fathers took with them the following statutes:

First, the fathers will visit each island in person and take a census of the Indian population, counting the number of caciques, the number of Indians each one possesses and the total number of Indians on each island.

They will require a written account of the treatment given to Indians from settlers, *encomenderos*, governors, judges and other officials.

They will survey the land surrounding gold mines in order to determine the best location for Indian townships—near rivers and on good soil—so that the Indians may live near their places of work and may engage in their own occupations such as fishing and tilling their land. This survey must begin with Hispaniola, then Jamaica, San Juan and Cuba, in that order.

Townships will comprise about 300 inhabitants and will have houses large enough to accommodate growing families—by the grace of God, we hope they will multiply. A beautiful church, streets and plazas will make it a proper town. The cacique will live in a house near the plaza and it must be bigger and better than other houses, since it is to serve as a meeting place for all.

Caciques and Indians will choose the location of their towns whenever possible to spare them the sorrows of moving. It must be thoroughly explained to them that these measures are taken to promote better treatment and are intended for their well-being. Indians living away from the mines will have their towns and cultivate cotton, raise cattle, make bread and other things from which they will pay the King a tribute equivalent to that paid by other Indians. Regions lacking gold will be settled in this manner, since moving Indians to the mines is harmful and detrimental. La Çabana will remain permanently settled because of its proximity to the harbor and the facilities of commerce between Cuba and the continent.

Town limits must be ample enough to accommodate population growth, and the territory must be divided among the Indians in such a way as to give each one a parcel of the best land where he may plant trees and other things, the size of which tract will depend on the quality of the individual. The rest will be used for pasture, farming and the raising of cattle. The cacique is to have a tract four times larger than that of everyone else.

To promote good will, the Indians nearest the town site will have priority over the others and the cacique will try to allure his people to it without using force. He will also have charge of his people, ruling over them in the manner described below.

Should one cacique alone fail to bring enough people to form a township he will join forces with the nearest chiefs and their people, each one maintaining his rights over his own tribe yet subject to the most powerful cacique who, together with a friar or a priest and an administrator, will rule the town.

Should a Castilian or a Spaniard wish to marry an Indian female chief or an Indian chief's daughter or heiress, he may do so with the priest's and the administrator's consent. The Spaniard will then become the town cacique and enjoy the same rights and privileges as other caciques. This way, it is hoped that all caciques will soon be Spaniards and our expenditures will be substantially cut down.

Each township will have its own jurisdiction: Indian chiefs will punish delinquency among Indians provided punishment does not exceed beating, the execution of which must be subject to prior consultation with the priest. Other crimes fall under ordinary penal laws, as do the caciques themselves if they commit a crime.

The chief cacique, the priest and the administrator will nominate candidates for the posts of regidor, alguazil, etc.; should disagreement arise, a two-vote majority will elect the candidate.

Order will be maintained better if one person supervises the administration of two or three townships. This administrator will live in a stone house outside the town limits to prevent friction with the Indians. He must be a man of clean conscience, have experience of Indian ways, show that he treated his Indians well and be fit as a ruler of people.

He will visit the towns assigned to him and meet with the caciques, especially the chief one, and see that Indians live a well-organized life, that each family remains together and works in the mines or is engaged in the raising of crops and cattle and other occupations described below. He will also see that Indians are not molested or forced to work overtime. Any offense will be charged against his conscience, for which reason he will be sworn into office under oath to fulfill the charges of that office well, and he will become subject to royal penalty in case of default.

He will choose three or four Castilians or other Spaniards to assist him in office, bearing weapons if necessary to enforce the law, and will not allow any Indians, not even the cacique, to carry arms unless it be for hunting. Should he think it necessary to have more than four assistants, he may hire them provided he pays them a fair salary, and the priest will always witness the transaction. Should Indians choose to live with him, they may, but in no case should he take more than six and only if the six choose it of their own free will. These Indians must not be made to work in the mines; they can only be used for housework, and if at any time they become discontent, they must be free to return to their homes.

This administrator will cooperate with the priest to see that Indians dress properly, sleep in beds, take care of their tools and are satisfied with their wives. A husband should not abandon his wife and the wife must be chaste. Should a wife commit adultery and should the husband complain about it, the priest and the administrator must be consulted before the cacique punishes both the wife and her lover, since punishment for this does not exceed beating. Indians may not be allowed to exchange, sell or gamble their belongings—except food and charity contributions—without permission from the priest or the administrator, and they must not be allowed to eat on the ground. The administrator will receive payment according to the degree of his responsibilities, half from the King's treasury, half from the towns of his administration. Unless he is known as a reliable citizen, the administrator must be married to avoid the inconveniences resulting from being single.

He will keep a house-to-house written account of the Indian population in order to keep track of missing people as well as of people who stop performing their duty.

Each town will have a religious man to instruct the Indians in the Catholic Faith, administer the sacraments, preach on Sundays and holidays, explain the tithe owed to God, the Church and its ministers, act as confessor, bury the dead and pray for their souls. Indians must be made to attend Mass and to sit in order, men and women separately.

The priest will say Mass on holidays and whenever he wishes on weekdays, and he must ascertain that Mass be said on the plantations as well. Normally, holiday masses are to be said in the town church. He will receive his share of the tithe in addition to alms. He will encourage charity among the people, each individual giving cassava or *ajes* according to his ability, and he may not accept special payment for hearing confession, administering sacraments, marrying people or burying souls. On holiday afternoons a bell will call the people for Catholic instruction; those who refuse to come will receive a mild punishment in public in order to serve as an example for all.

The sexton may be an Indian provided he be found capable of assisting in the Mass, teaching children—especially those of important families—up to nine years of age to read, write and speak the Castilian tongue, and on the whole also teaching all adults to speak Castilian.

A hospital must be built in the center of town for the sick, the elderly and orphaned children. Enough land will be cleared around if for 50,000 cassava hills, and the hospital will house a caretaker and his wife who will collect alms for his and the patients' maintenance. Since butchers will have communal shops—as we shall describe below— they will give the hospital a pound of meat per person and this must be done in front of the cacique or the priest to avoid fraudulence.

Men between the ages of 20 and 50 will be forced to work in the mines in three shifts, rotating every two months or whatever period of time the cacique shall establish. When an individual is sick or kept away from work, he will be replaced by another from another shift. They will leave for work at about sunrise, take three hours for mealtime at home, and will return to work until sunset. No woman shall be forced to go to the mines unless she so wishes, in which case she is to be counted as a man in the making up of a shift.

The cacique will send his Indians divided in groups, headed by Indian supervisors since experience has proved that it is not advisable for the supervisor to be a Castilian.

When not working in the mines, Indians will work their own land within sight of the priest or the administrator.

Because of his superiority over other Indians, the cacique will require all resident workers to work two weeks per year for him since his estate is larger; he is not to feed or pay them in any way. Women, children and the elderly will weed his land for him whenever necessary.

Indians must work their land when not on their shifts and be helped in this by women and children.

His Highness must permit the confiscation, from the royal domain, of farm and plantation land necessary and most convenient for the founding of towns, which lands will be appraised at their fair value and paid for out of the Indians' share of the first minting. Crops will be divided among the residents according to individual needs, while other tracts are being developed in the land assigned to each one. And as for cattle, the chief cacique will control them so that Indians may be supplied in the manner required.

If possible, every town of 300 residents will maintain 10 or 12 mares, 50 cows, 500 pigs for slaughter and 100 sows. The work involved in raising them will be communal until Indians learn to handle cattle properly.

Each town will have a butcher who will supply the cacique with 2 *arreldes* of meat and each household with half an *arrelde*, provided the husband is home and not working the mine. When the husband is away, his wife will receive a pound of meat, unless the size of her family requires a larger ration, in which case the family itself will raise its own supply as well as provide its victuals during the days when eating meat is prohibited. The wives of men working in the mines will make bread from their individual harvests and the communal mares will be used to transport it, as well as corn, *ajes* and other necessary items.

There will also be a butcher near the mines to distribute from 1½ to 2 pounds of meat to each worker. A meat dispensation for Lent and other meatless days is advisable to compensate for the scarcity of fish. To ensure the meat supply, part of the common cattle will graze on the mine site; and if more meat is needed, it will be sold at the fair market value and paid for out of the first minting.

The gold will be brought every evening to the Indian supervisor who will keep it until time for minting, every two months or so, according to the decision of the officials. To avoid cheating, this supervisor, the cacique and the administrator will take the gold to the mint together. Minted gold will be divided in three parts: one for the King, one for the cacique, one for the Indians.

Farming costs, cattle, and all common expenses will be paid for out of the cacique's and the Indians' shares; the balance will be divided equally among each household; the cacique will receive six times an individual share and the supervisors two times.

Each household share will be used for buying tools and other equipment necessary for the digging of gold, which will belong to the individual and must be written down and accounted for. Out of what remains, the cacique, the priest and the administrator will buy for each household clothes and shirts, twelve chickens, one rooster and whatever else they think necessary, also to be itemized in writing and accounted for. If any amount is left over, it will be entrusted to a good person who will account for it on demand and will keep a record of its provenance.

Twelve Spanish gold prospectors paid jointly and in equal parts by the King and the Indians will mark out gold sites and proceed ahead to prospect the land, leaving Indians in the newly discovered sites to dig the gold. No Spaniard may be allowed to remain behind, for fear of stealing gold or harming Indians. The gold those twelve men might find while prospecting must be divided between the King and the Indians, and this shall be strictly enforced.

To the Spaniards in the Indies.—Spanish settlers will earn a livelihood in various ways: as owners of farms bought for them in the manner described above, as town administrators, salaried gold miners, gold diggers—in which case married men living with their wives will be taxed one-tenth of their proceeds, others will be taxed one-seventh —as owners of a handful of slaves, half male and half female so they may multiply; and as for Indian owners, they will receive benefits as compensation for losing their Indians.

It would be profitable if His Highness supplied the Spanish settlers with caravels and provisions for raids against the Caribs who eat human flesh and are a tough people. The Caribs are slaves and must be used as such because they refuse to welcome our preachers, and harass the Christians and converted Indians by trying to kill and eat them. However, it is forbidden to raid other territories under the pretext of hunting for Caribs without incurring the death penalty and confiscation of property.

Spanish islanders will be rewarded for going to the continent, since as experienced settlers they are more capable and less likely to court danger than the ones newly arrived from Spain.

And because many Spaniards have unpaid debts which will remain unpaid from the loss of their Indian allotments, it is better not to imprison or otherwise punish them if they wish to move on to other islands or to the continent. Indians will be taught trades for the smooth functioning of the Republic: they will become stone cutters, blacksmiths, sawyers, tailors, etc.

This is what appears must be done to help the Indians and it will remain so until experience proves the usefulness of these statutes, the execution of which requires a powerful administrator, since to take away Indians from people used to them will be an arduous task. The fathers will see how this must be done; they are entitled to make all necessary adjustments. The Old Christians who mistreat Indians are to be punished under royal justice; Indian testimony will be heard and believed at the discretion of the judge. . . .

90

After Cardinal Francisco Ximénez had given specific orders to the Hieronymite fathers concerning the welfare of Indians, he made arrangements with the monarchs so that Clergyman Casas would accompany the fathers, instructing and counseling them on Indian matters. The royal certificate reads:

The Queen and King.—Clergyman Bartolomé de las Casas of Seville, resident of Cuba in the Indies.—We are told that you have a long experience of Indian affairs, especially those concerning the welfare of Indians, that you have dealt with Indians, and that you are a devoted servant of God. We hope that you will carry out our orders with care and diligence, seeing to the salvation of the souls and persons of both Spaniards and Indians, our orders being that you go to the Indies

—Hispaniola, Cuba, San Juan, Jamaica and the continent—to counsel the Hieronymite fathers whom we are sending to reform the Indies. You will also advise other people in charge of the same task about the freedom, good treatment and the spiritual and physical health of the Indians. You will report all progress to us, and to facilitate your mission we hereby grant you full powers, including contingencies, dependencies, emergencies, annexations and associations attendant thereon. We are instructing our admiral and our legal officers in the Indies to honor your title, ordering each one not to restrict it in any way lest they incur our displeasure and a fine of 10,000 *maravedís*. Madrid, September 17, 1516.

Signed F. Cardinalis, Adrianus Ambasiator. George de Baracaldo, in the name of the Queen, the King, their son and our governors.

In addition, the Cardinal and Adrianus made Clergyman Casas procurator and universal protector of all Indians in the Indies, with a salary of 100 gold pesos per year, a tidy sum then, considering the fact that the hellish Peruvian wealth was yet undiscovered which was to bring poverty and destruction to Spain. Licenciate Zuazo was named judge in charge of investigations and Dr. Palacios Rubios ordered that his powers be definite and extended to include all judges in the Indies, especially those of Hispaniola. Licenciate Zapata and Dr. Carabajal thought it an exorbitant power for any one person to hold. It was believed that Zapata knew a lot about what was happening in the Indies and he, together with Carabajal, were trying to protect the interests of many personal friends, judges and other officials, and Zapata must have had his own reasons. Also he was very influential with the Bishop of Burgos in deciding Indian policies, and since this new order went against their own, the licenciate and the Bishop tried to stop it by refusing to sign Zuazo's contract. They delayed so much that Zuazo began to tire of it and prepared to return to his college. He notified Clergyman Casas that if his case was not settled while he was making preparations, no one could drag him away from his college in Valladolid again.

The clergyman went to the Cardinal, who was a man of no nonsense and who summoned Zapata and Carabajal, asking them to produce the documents and sign them on the spot, which they did, making their signatures in such a way as to be able to prove to the King that they had done this against their will. Thus Zuazo's power became legal, much to the sorrow of those who had private interests in the Indies.

Taking leave of the Cardinal, the clergyman decided to speak his mind about the Hieronymite fathers and held the following discourse with him:

"Sir, I would not wish to leave with my conscience over-burdened with scruples and I find myself obliged to advise you on matters that are still amendable. Your Reverence must know that the Hieronymite fathers, in whose hands you have placed the lives of an infinite number of Indians, have already shown disturbing signs by taking sides with the secular men who destroyed the Indians. They believe what these men tell them and disguise their tyranny with false arguments; annihilating and defaming the Indians, they intend to carry out your orders in their own way to favor secular power. Dr. Palacios Rubios can testify to a conversation he had with the fathers in which they defended the secular to such a degree that he was horrified and said: 'Upon my word, fathers, I am beginning to think you have little charity for spiritual business of such importance.'

"Despite his gout, the doctor came to see you twice to warn you against entrusting such a venture to them and to ask you to replace them with a more trustworthy lot. However, Your Reverence was ill and the doctor left, concerned and worried." The Cardinal was astonished and after a pause said, "Well, whom can we trust then? Why don't you go and arrange everything?" Clergyman Casas left with the Cardinal's blessings and started for Seville, since the friars had already rejoined their monasteries. They were two friars of the Mejorada monastery; its prior, the intelligent fray Luis de Figueroa, and fray Bernadino Manzanedo; the Seville representative was a fray Alonso de . . . [sic], prior of the Burgos monastery called San Juan de Ortega. They also took along an older friar for company, although the first three alone were authorized to carry out the mission. Fray Luis de Figueroa went as their superior. The Cardinal arranged their passage and provided them with wine, flour and other things not found here. At the King's expense, he also supplied Clergyman Casas with passage and an abundance of necessary items for the trip.

91

The Sevillian officials of trade with the Indies hastened the departure of the clergyman and the Hieronymite fathers; Judge Zuazo was made to wait another three months before embarking, for it took that long to put his papers in order. The clergyman tried to convince the Hieronymites that they all should board the same ship and fill the long hours of the voyage conversing about the Indies, since it had become his duty to instruct them. But try as he would, they refused, giving all sorts of pretexts, such as the discomfort of their ship and the luxury of his cabin on another ship, a pretext designed less for the clergyman's comfort than for the safeguard of their own freedom in planning what they were to accomplish in the Indies.

So then the clergyman boarded the larger ship, although he would gladly have traded his comfort for the unpleasantness of the other, at least it would have given him a chance to influence the course of action and prevent the disastrous end of that enterprise. The fleet sailed on November 11, 1516, from San Lúcar and arrived in San Juan without any mishap, delaying four or five days in the harbor of Puerto Rico. The clergyman's ship was scheduled to delay another two weeks or so to unload a cargo of merchandise; therefore, the clergyman asked permission to change ships in order that he might arrive in Santo Domingo at the same time as the Hieronymites. But permission was refused and the fathers got to Santo Domingo a full thirteen days before him. The fathers had had ample opportunity to surmise what the Spaniards were up to in the Indies, for they had witnessed two events in San Juan. One concerned a Basque named Joan Bono—a misnomer if I ever heard one—who had just arrived in Puerto Rico Harbor after a raid in the island of Trinidad.

The natives of Trinidad were a good people whose enemies were the man-eating Caribs. Joan Bono went to Trinidad with fifty or sixty Spaniards well trained in offering similar sacrifices to God. The Indians came to meet them carrying their bows and arrows and asked who the newcomers were. Joan Bono answered that they had come to live peacefully among them. Indians are simple folk, much too credulous and not sufficiently cautious, considering that they knew of past Spanish cruelties from the days when the admiral had discovered Trinidad as well as more recent cruelties performed on them by the Spaniards. They believed Joan Bono and welcomed him, saying that if indeed the Spaniards wished to live among them, they would be pleased to start building houses for them. But Joan Bono had no use for houses, so he asked them to build a single large one instead, which they did, making it bell-shaped as usual and large enough to hold about 100 people. The scaffolding was completed in a few days, and now only the straw remained to be laid upon it from the outside; and surely they use marvelous straw there, beautiful to look at, sweet-smelling and sturdy. In the meantime, the Spaniards were served most generously and given everything they asked for. Joan-the-Bad spurred them on, for he was anxious to see the house finished, and the Indians complied willingly. When the straw had reached two *estados* from the ground and was high enough to keep the workers from seeing what was going on inside, Joan Bono invited the village people to come inside and watch the construction. Some 400 Indians entered the house with signs of great pleasure, while a handful of Spaniards surrounded it on the outside and were drawing their swords. Then Joan Bono stood at the door with his men and sword in hand commanded the Indians not to move.

The Indians feared death less than captivity, so they charged toward the entrance, thrusting their naked bodies against the blades in a vain attempt to get out. The Spaniards slaughtered them—bowels, arms and legs were torn apart; terrible wounds were inflicted. Those Indians who had remained behind were petrified at the sight of so much blood and they started to yell in expectation of the same treatment, but all they received were handcuffs and a slave's destiny, which is what Joan Bono had intended all along. I think 185 Indians were taken to the ship that day. Those who had managed to escape joined others in a village house and armed themselves against another attack. Joan Bono went to them and promised that if they came out he would not kill them, but the Indians knew better and defended the entrance with arrows.

Bono realized that he could not capture them; therefore, in order to repay their hospitality, he set the straw on fire and burned them all alive. He sold some of his slaves in San Juan, keeping the rest for Hispaniola where he arrived just before the Hieronymites and he himself is the one who described to me what I am now describing in writing. The clergyman then told the fathers about this and showed much grief, but the fathers were unmoved. They did not reprimand Joan Bono nor did they try to prevent future happenings of this sort. I could cry when I think that the Clergyman Casas had to reproach Bono, whom he had known well. Bono himself used to say that he had found his only true mother and father among the people of Trinidad, who had showed him such love. The clergyman reproached him for ungratefulness, saying, "Damn you, man, how could you be so cruel toward your father and mother?" And Joan Bono answered, "My word, Father, I had orders to destroy them. I mean, I was told that if I could not catch them by peaceful means, I was to use war." He called his raiding instructions "destruction," and he had received those instructions from the auditors of the Audiencia in Santo Domingo. This, then, was the kind of fair government the chancellery meant to execute for the welfare and the well-being of Indians; it became the pattern for all the chancelleries in the Indies and it destroyed them most unjustly.

The Hieronymite fathers had another example of deadly Spanish tyranny in San Juan. We said in Book II that every Spanish settlement had a visitador, usually the highest-ranking resident, who was to supervise grievances but turned out to be the worst victimizer of Indians. So, a Spaniard came to him with complaints about one of his Indians who either did not serve him well or was shying away from work as cattle shy away from the slaughterhouse. The visitador tied the Indian to a post and whipped him so cruelly he almost killed him. The clergyman chanced to be passing by; he heard the blows and went straight to the scene where, overcome by compassion, he vehemently reproved the man for such injustice. The visitador was silent from embarrassment but, if I remember well, no sooner had the clergyman left than the man resumed his beating. The fathers knew all this and it should have sufficed to guard them against believing the capital enemies of the Indians, especially since they, like the rest of the world, were well aware that the Indies were being destroyed in just such ways as these. . . .

114

Grijalva hurried back to Santiago and Diego Velázquez in order to man a fleet and bring people to establish settlements on the land he and Francisco Hernández had discovered and called Isla Rica (Yucatán), down the coast as far as Tabasco, which has a river named after Grijalva. He appeared before Diego Velázquez but was shown little gratitude for his work and the gold he and Alvarado had brought him. Velázquez was angry and verbally insulted him, for such was his temperament, because Grijalva had followed his instructions by refusing to claim the land when his men demanded it. This reprimand deserved a greater one still in return for Velázquez's insulting a faithful and obedient servant who chose not to deviate an inch from Velázquez's orders, especially since deviating would have been so profitable for him, both in wealth and status, as well as for Velázquez's supporting the indignation of Grijalva's men. Grijalva himself told me this when he came to Santo Domingo in 1523, a needy and beaten man. After he left me, he went to that part of the continent being misruled by Pedrarias and was sent to Nicaragua, where he and other Spaniards were killed by the Indians they were trying to subdue in the valley of Ulanche. And thus Grijalva paid for the damage he had caused Indians there, in Cuba, and other explorations, although with respect to the Indians, I knew him as a moderate and pious man.

After Alvarado and Grijalva had brought samples and descriptions of great wealth from the new land, Diego Velázquez speedily armed a fleet of nine brigs and ships. And in order to give his project a more solid foundation, he dispatched Juan de Saucedo to Santo Domingo to obtain settlement permission from the Hieronymite fathers, thinking they were empowered to rule, as was not the case, since they had come to free the Indians, as we already mentioned. In addition, Velázquez sent the priest Benito Martín to the court of King Charles in Barcelona with certain impressive gold pieces and the news of the discovery, and Martín asked to be given the bishopric of a land that turned out to be nothing less than the whole of New Spain, as will appear later.

To return to the fleet: Velázquez spent many thousands of those gold pesos, ill-earned from Indian sweat and anguish, and since he had to give it [the fleet] a captain, he thought of the hidalgo Baltasar Bermúdez who, like him, I believe came from Cuéllar. To honor him, for he liked him well—I know, for I often saw him treat Bermúdez very well—he asked Bermúdez who, being ambitious and overconfident, put such conditions upon it that Velázquez, impulsive by nature, blew up and dismissed Bermúdez, perhaps with verbal abuse, as was his custom. Thinking the situation over, he set his mind (they say he had been induced to it) on Hernando Cortés, who had served him as secretary and had given him cause to hang him, as we said in Chapter 27. He knew Cortés was an astute and clever man, and he had given him many Indians, named him mayor of the city of Santiago, and on the whole had bestowed many favors upon him, trusting that gratitude would keep him in check. At that time the royal accountant was a most clever person named Amador de Lares who, they say, had spent twenty-two years in Italy serving the Gran Capitán, which proves his cleverness for he was a short man and knew neither how to read nor write; his astuteness and prudence made up for these deficiencies. I used to warn Diego Velázquez to beware of a man who had spent twenty-two years in Italy. At any rate Cortés ingratiated himself with Lares, for he was every bit as clever. They say both men reached such a degree of understanding that they connived to share equal parts of the loot; and since Velázquez consulted with the official accountant, Lares, about these matters, it is believed that Lares persuaded Velázquez to name Cortés captain of the expedition.

Velázquez had suspicions about Cortés, but Heaven help the man who receives counsel from people who carry some weight and with it seek their own interests, because they manipulate things for their own good as surely as an arrow hits its mark. Velázquez did make Cortés captain of the fleet, and Cortés, who was a proud *bon vivant* as well as an expert in human affairs—the mayorship had taught him much about people—contrived to content every gold-thirsty individual who signed up for the expedition, which was voluntary. He used the 2,000 pesos Velázquez had given him to adorn himself and provide the necessities of the voyage, behaving as captain of 500 men whose purpose was to fill their pockets with wealth.

In his *History*, Gómara falsifies the story of Cortés's assignment and speaks as a man who did not witness events but rather heard them from Cortés himself, orally and in writing, when, back in Spain, he served the present Marquis Cortés as chaplain. Gómara says that Velázquez proposed to share the cost of the expedition with Cortés because he and the merchant Andrés del Duero had 2,000 pesos at their disposal, and that he begged Cortés to accept the captainship, etc. As if 2,000 pesos meant anything to someone who was spending over 20,000 on that expedition! Besides, Velázquez was not humble or generous enough to beg Cortés to captain the fleet when so many people here would have considered themselves honored and greatly favored to be given that position.

Assuming someone lent Velázquez money, he was not the kind of person to humble himself and form partnerships since he was lord and master of it all and as governor he had the power to do as he pleased. Gómara adds that Velázquez changed his mind after Grijalva's return, and that he tried to stop the expedition which Cortés was preparing because he wanted everything for himself. This and other obvious falsifications of the truth are inventions of Gómara's patron, that is, Cortés himself. Consider: who had the power to prevent Velázquez from disposing of the fleet and its captain as he so wished? Particularly not Cortés, who dared not breathe before Velázquez and, in appearance at least, always strained to please him. What Gómara adds is also false: "That Diego Velázquez asked Lares to persuade Cortés to abandon his project against full reimbursement of funds, but that Cortés refused, if only not to lose face, because he had guessed Velázquez's intentions." This is a most absurd statement which no one can believe who knew both Velázquez and Cortés; besides, the outcome of the project proves him wrong, as will be made clear later.

Gómara adds another insolent and arrogant lie, namely, that Velázquez held his tongue and did not prevent Cortés from sailing for fear of riots and ensuing deaths. This is nothing but arrogance on the part of Cortés and cleverness on the part of those who have deceived the world until now, as well as of those historians who recorded Cortés's exploits in the Spanish tongue, all of whom had only one goal: to become rich on the blood of the poor, humble and peaceful Indians. These men were insensitive to the evil they praised, and wrote only to excuse the tyranny and abominations of Cortés and the rest of them, as well as to undermine and condemn the defenseless Indians. You can well imagine whether Velázquez, who was governor and administrator of justice on the island, who was worshipped and obeyed by all for his power to do good or evil, to give or take away Indian allotments, to make one rich or poor, and who enjoyed the protection of the King or of those who ruled Castile at that time, you can well imagine, I say, whether such a person could prevent someone like Cortés from sailing a fleet equipped at his expense without fearing riots, since Cortés was an upstart, a poor hidalgo in his service who would have starved had not Velázquez given him Indians subject, like Cortés's own life, to Velázquez's right of confiscation, which he could well have done under any pretext whatever. You can imagine, then, how credible Gómara's story is.

115

To illustrate what precedes, let us consider the way Cortés left Cuba. After Cortés was named captain general of the fleet, he and Velázquez did not sleep on the matter but hastened instead to prepare the launching. Velázquez rode his horse every day to the nearby harbor with Cortés and indeed the whole town, to look at the ships and see that preparations went smoothly and rapidly. Once, a jester of Velázquez's company named Francisquillo accompanied them, telling jokes on the way, and at one point he turned to Velázquez and exclaimed, "Ah, Diego!" "What's the matter?" Velázquez asked. "Think of what you're doing, lest we all have to chase after Cortés and hunt him back." Velázquez laughed and turned to Cortés, who as mayor and captain was riding to his right. "Friend, did you hear our fool, Francisquillo?"

Cortés had heard but was pretending to be absorbed in conversation with someone riding next to him, and Velázquez repeated, "We might have to chase after you." Cortés said, "Oh, leave him, he is a fool; you're a fool, Francisquillo. If I catch up with you, I'll take you and punish you."

All this was said in jest and laughter. But the idea of madness and the jester's prophecy grated on Velázquez's soul; perhaps also he remembered the unheeded advice of his friends not to trust Cortés, whom he knew so well, with an enterprise of such importance that so greatly involved his name and fortune. Given his cunning, they said, Cortés was bound to break allegiance and rebel against him, as he had tried once in Barocoa. These and similar persuasions convinced Velázquez to take preventive measures and he determined to release Cortés from his post. But since he used to consult the King's officials, especially Lares, about matters of government and expeditions, secrecy was broken and it was believed that Lares, who had so much at stake with Cortés, informed his friend of Velázquez's intentions; though it is likely that Cortés had guessed the change from Velázquez's countenance, for he was most alert and most versed in mundane wisdom. That same evening, when he knew Velázquez was asleep and the palace empty, Cortés went in the dead silence of night to awaken his closest friends and urge them to embark immediately. With a handful of men he went to the town butcher and left him not an ounce of beef, pork and lamb, although the butcher complained—not very loud, for it might cost him his life—that he would be punished for failing to deliver meat to the city, and Cortés slipped him a gold chain he wore around his neck, as Cortés himself told me. Then he silently joined those whom he had awakened and walked to the ships, where many of those assigned to go with him had already embarked.

At daybreak Velázquez was informed, jumped out of bed and, followed by an astonished crowd, galloped to the harbor. Cortés saw him, manned a small armed vessel with his most trusted people and, holding his mayor's staff in his hand, came within a crossbow shot to the spot where Velázquez stood. Velázquez said: "Well, now, my friend, is this the way to take leave of me?" And Cortés answered, "I beg your pardon, Sir, but these things are

better done than thought about. Do you have any orders?" Velázquez could not think of a reply to this insolent insubordination.
Cortés then turned about and ordered the fleet to make sail as fast
as possible. Thus they left on November 18, 1518, with provisions
yet to be loaded, for the Macaca Harbor (the middle syllable is
long) fifteen leagues away, where the King owned a plantation
and where he stayed eight days while Indian men and women
baked more than 300 measures of cassava bread, a measure weighing 2 *arrobas*, that is, a man's ration for one month. He also took
all he found in meat and other things and said that the King
would pay for it; one can imagine how he treated those who
perchance refused to comply.

Gómara, who worked for Cortés as chaplain and historian, says
that Velázquez suspected Cortés would rebel because he himself
had rebelled against Diego Columbus and because he listened to
Bermúdez and members of his own family when they told him
that Cortés was from Extremadura, thus arrogant, cunning and
fond of worldly distinctions. It is clear they were right in suspecting a rebellion, but the comparison is ignominious. It is true that
Velázquez behaved unscrupulously toward Columbus when he
contrived to receive the government due him as Columbus's
lieutenant, directly from the King's hands as insurance against
Columbus's right of sequestration. But, reprehensible though this
ungratefulness may be, it does not compare with Cortés's rebellion. Cortés was running away with his master's fleet and costly
property, was usurping his power by hanging those who opposed
him—which is an act proper to tyrants—and in the end was to
dishonor Velázquez as well as be the cause of his bankruptcy and
death in bitterness and poverty, as I will make clear later. Surely
then, Cortés's rebellion against Velázquez differed greatly from
that of Velázquez against Columbus.

It seems fitting to question here how the following ship captains
could be excused from being participants in this rebellion: Alonso
Hernández Puerto-Carrero, Francisco de Montejo, Alonso de
Avila, Pedro de Alvarado, Juan Vázquez and Diego de Ordás had
been named ship captains by Velázquez, and it is unlikely that
they were ignorant of Cortés's dealings. If they were not on the
ships, how could they embark by night without taking leave of

Velázquez? If they were already on board, how could they tolerate setting sail and following Cortés when the whole fleet knew how Cortés had managed to join them? I have never been able to ascertain this but it does not seem they could claim ignorance, unless Cortés deceived them by some cunning trick; however, some of them, being from Extremadura also, may be suspected of having taken part in this exercise. . . .

117

After Cortés had repaired his ships [in Cozumel], loading them with abundant food supplies brought him by order of the Indian chief, he assembled horses and men and left the island on friendly terms. The fleet first went to the closest point of Yucatán, called by Hernández and Grijalva Punta de las Mujeres, some ten leagues from the island; then it proceeded to the Cape of Cotoche. One of the ships took water so badly that it fired a distress signal and since there was no harbor in the vicinity, Cortés decided to return to the island. The Indians gave them signs of welcome, the ship was repaired, and as the Spaniards were about to leave that Saturday, a fierce storm rose that forced them to postpone sailing.

On Sunday, the first Sunday in Lent, they celebrated Mass. As they were eating, they saw a canoe crossing the gulf from Yucatán and Cortés sent the daring youth Andrés de Tapia with a handful of men to apprehend it. There were four men in it, naked except for their secret parts, and one had a long beard. Andrés de Tapia jumped on them and they would have run away but for the bearded man who calmed them in their native tongue, then, turning to the Spaniards, asked in Spanish if they were Christians. They answered they were. He fell on his knees and with tears of joy thanked God for having freed him from captivity and for the sight of free Christians. The others joined him in thanksgiving and brought him to Cortés, who was happy to see him; in fact, all rejoiced and were astonished to see him in that state: naked like an Indian and bronzed by the sun, but for his beard he would have looked exactly like a native. He asked if the day was Wednesday but it was Sunday, which means he had reckoned time on his rosary and had made a mistake.

He said he was Jerónimo de Aguilar, of Ecija, and he told his story. Leaving Darién with Valdivia on an errand for Vasco Núñez de Balboa to Hispaniola, his caravel was lost in the shallows and rocks of Las Víboras near Jamaica, as we mentioned in Chapter 42. Some twenty men put a boat to sea with no food or water, and about twelve died of thirst. After fifteen days the current blew them to the coast of Yucatán and they ended up in the territory of an Indian lord who, according to Gómara, sacrificed a few of the men to his idols and ate them while he kept the others for another sacrifice; some of them escaped and arrived in another Indian territory where they were treated humanely. I do not believe this business of sacrificing and eating human flesh; I've never heard of any such practice in Yucatán. Gómara says this because he heard it from Cortés who was the man who fed him, thus it lacks authority and is said to excuse Cortés's evil deeds. Besides, it is typical Spanish talk which Spaniards and those who record their horrible exploits invented to defame these nations universally and excuse the violence, cruelty, plunder and slaughter committed against the Indians every day. That is the reason why Gómara says in his *History* that war and armed men are the true way to eliminate idols, sacrifices and other Indian sins, for, he adds, it makes it easier, quicker and more efficient to bring them of their own accord to the Gospel and baptism. Well, Gómara knows awfully little about the preaching of the Faith and the results of having gone there with armed tyranny!

It worked in such a way that, if God had not chosen to enlighten a few through the preaching of good friars and against all human power and knowledge, all Indians would think, like the majority, that our God is evil, unjust and abominable, since he sent such iniquitous men to afflict and destroy them by means never heard of before. As for how to achieve preaching by peaceful means, see my book in Latin, the last chapters, Chapters 5, 6 and 7 as well as *passim*, entitled *De unico vocationis modo omnium gentium ad veram religionem*. The reader will find out about the state of eternal damnation in which those people live who procured and recommended preaching by means of war, such as Gómara claims. Gómara also adds that after Jerónimo de Aguilar's arrival, Cortés decided to destroy the idols in that village and plant crosses instead. This is one of the nonsensical mistakes of many:

without prior indoctrination over a long period of time, it is mad-ness to destroy idols against the wishes of the idolaters. No one can abandon of his own accord what he believes is his God, what he sucked at his mother's breast, so to speak, and what is authorized by his elders, without first understanding that what is being transmuted into his God is the true God.

Consider: how could the Spaniards indoctrinate Indians in two or three days, or in ten or even in twenty? How could they have uprooted the erroneous opinion of their God and prevented a return to idols as soon as they had left? It is essential first to eradicate idols from the heart of the idolater, that is to say, to eradicate the concept and belief that those idols represent God, by means of constant, diligent and long-lasting indoctrination. It is essential to represent the concept and the truth of the true God to the idolater so that he himself will come to recognize his error and wish to destroy what he edified freely and with his own hands. St. Augustine teaches this in his sermon *De puero centurionis de verbis Domini*. But planting crosses and inducing Indians to worship them is not the worst foolishness committed in these matters. It would appear as a good thing if time were on their side, if they could observe some indication that Indians were learning from it; but, since there was no time or language communication, nor was it the appropriate moment, it appears as a superfluous, pointless thing. Indians think that they are given an idol that represents the Christian God and they can be made to worship a stick. When Christians merely pass through infidel territory—but even if they should stay—the safest and surest rule is to set a good example of virtue so that, as Our Redeemer says, the sight of it will prompt men to praise and glorify the God and Father of Christians: they would see that such believers can only worship a good and true God, as St. Chrysostom says. We spoke at length on the religion, rites and idols of Cozumel in our *Apologetical History.* . . .

119

As for Cortés and his holy company, he left Cozumel with Je-rónimo de Aguilar, very happy at having an interpreter. They hugged the coast of Yucatán in search of the stray ship and found it anchored in a harbor, much to everyone's delight since each had thought the other lost. They said some things worth relating. For instance, they saw a dog barking and pawing the ground as if to call them and when they went ashore, the dog wagged his tail and behaved altogether like a creature of reason, running into the woods to catch rabbits that he brought back and dropped at their feet, just like a thoughtful host. I never found out whether they took the dog or left him there, nor who his owner had been.

The fleet proceeded to the Grijalva river in the province of Tabasco where an Indian chief had dressed Grijalva in gold from head to foot, as we said in Chapter 111. They anchored at the mouth of the river because the entrance is shallow and cross currents are strong and dangerous; I was in great danger there once. Cortés left the ships and sailed up the river in brigs and smaller boats loaded with arms and artillery. Coming parallel to a large settlement, they saw it surrounded by a high and sturdy wooden fence and Indians jumping in their canoes with bows and arrows to prevent them from setting foot on shore. Cortés gave them a peace signal and Aguilar spoke to them in the language of Yucatán but we do not know whether they spoke the same language in Tabasco, probably not. The Indians gestured to them not to leave their boats and Cortés indicated that they needed bread and water, but they merely pointed to the river, signaling there was fresh water there and some returned to town to bring them corn, fruit and chickens. Cortés said it wasn't sufficient for he had many men with him.

When the Indians saw the Spaniards were determined to leave their boats, they asked them to wait until the next day; they would return with more food. Cortés and his company spent the night on a small island in the river; for their part, the Indians, fearing the worst, spent the night making ready to resist and removed their possessions, wives and children to a safe place. Cortés did not sleep either; he gathered all his men and sent some out to see if they could ford the river, which they did, setting up an ambush in the trees as close as possible to the Indian town. At dawn, the Indians brought more food and said no more was available because most of the people had run away, and they bade them farewell, telling them to take what they had brought and go with God or whomever they pleased, since the sight of them scandalized the land.

What Gómara says to justify Cortés's exploit in that town is really delightful: Cortés used Aguilar as an interpreter to communicate to them the fact that he had come for their own good. But, as Gómara himself says in that same Chapter 4, the Indians understood neither the Spaniards nor the interpreter and truly, given the situation, the conversation he reports is ridiculous. He says: "The Indians replied they needed no advice from foreigners whom they did not know, they wanted even less to welcome them to their homes because they looked fierce and bossy"—as if this was an insult, supposing these words were actually spoken—"and if they wanted water, the river was there and they could dig holes in the ground like everybody else."

Cortés answered that "in no way could he desist from entering their town and exploring the land in order to report it to the greatest lord in the world whose envoy he was; therefore, he asked them to receive him graciously because his intentions were good; if not, he would entrust the matter to God, his own hands, and those of his companions." The Indians were saying nothing more than go away; don't bother to play the bully on foreign territory; they wouldn't allow him to shore and warned that if he did not leave, they would kill both him and his friends. Gómara says this in the *History* of his employer, Cortés. What ignorance, what nonsense and what lies! It is clearly a lie of Gómara's fabrication to record such speeches between people who understood nothing of each other's language, as he himself admits. It is clearly ignorance that makes him so justify what Cortés did in that province. The Indians had the right and pre-emptory reasons to kill and expel him from their territory; they were only defending their republic against these new people who were so bold as to insist on their right of entry and report their findings to a lord of the world, even though it displeased the Indians. Cortés brought no miracles, humility or a long-tested holy life to prove his right of entry. As for his saying that he came for their benefit, is there a nation in the world that would not justifiably destroy the speaker of such words?

Gómara's great ignorance makes him invent reasons to justify the tyranny of Cortés and those very reasons condemn and abominate this tyranny very clearly, because all the nations in the world will approve of them as if they were founded on natural law—even though, as I said, they are all false and imprudently forged. The only truth they contain is that the Indians asked to be left in peace because they could be certain that much harm would result from such fierce-looking people, who had come armed to the teeth to insist on entering their towns against the will of the inhabitants. Gómara adds that Cortés fulfilled the royal instructions toward those barbarians: he asked for peace several times before declaring war and entering the territory by force, promising good treatment, freedom and things beneficial to body and soul; and giving them the afternoon until sunset to think about it because he fully intended, with the assistance of his God, to sleep in the town that evening, despite the harm that would result to its inhabitants for refusing his offer of peace and friendship. Gómara writes all these lies; as for the justice of the injunction, or rather, as for the ignorance and insensitivity of the royal council that decreed it, see Chapters 57 and 58. The decimation and desolation of Hispaniola and other islands, as well as of the 4,000 or 5,000 leagues of the continent, is lamentable proof, as the whole world knows, of the kind of good treatment, freedom, peace and congenial co-existence that Cortés and other apostles like him promised the Indians.

The truth of all this violent invasion and tyrannical exploit Cortés carried out in Tabasco, which Gómara tries to justify, is that after receiving the food, and understanding that the Indians were refusing him right of entry, he immediately fired gunshots at the town. Since they had never heard or seen such a thing, the Indians thought fire was falling from Heaven and they fell to the ground, although they courageously fought on with their arrows. The town was taken by force; they were naked after all, and Spanish blades worked immense havoc. The Spaniards ambushed in the trees attacked them from behind; very few Indians escaped death while defending their city. Then the Spaniards were free to ransack the houses, which they found full of corn, chicken and other provisions; as for gold, they found none and this did not please them much, although now they were the undisturbed lords of the town.

120

Cortés dispatched a few captives to the chief of the town with a message of friendship: they should lose their fears and come to him; he would treat them well; he wished to talk to the chief about many things that were to his advantage, and he spoke other such nonsense and made frivolous promises which would provoke the wisest man to hatred, given the damage he had just caused. What guarantees did they offer to compensate for the harm done already and to ensure against further damage? But the chief, his captains and soldiers—or rather guerrillas, since Indians always fight guerrilla wars—aroused the land and decided to attack the Spaniards until not one was left alive.

However, to give themselves time to get ready, they replied with truce messages and asked the Spaniards to leave bad enough alone and not to burn their town, to which Cortés agreed while asking for food. They brought some the next day and apologized for the scarcity by saying everyone had fled. Cortés ordered a search of the woods. One searching party in particular came upon a town and found its people armed, probably awaiting the general rally. The Indians fought with such valor that they wounded many Spaniards with their arrows and pointed wooden lances (some have a point made of sharp fish bone), until they drove them all into a house. The Spaniards fought a good part of the day there, afraid of being burned alive, but the Indian war cry is so loud and frightening that it was heard by the other searching parties, which came to the rescue, freed them and renewed the attack. Although the Spaniards numbered about 200 men, the Indians fought on with great courage.

While this was happening, certain Cuban Indians who had accompanied Cortés ran to him with the news of the encounter. Always alert, Cortés gathered men and artillery and soon arrived on the scene: Spaniards beating retreat, Indians fighting like lions. He fired a few shots and the Indians dispersed, but Cortés did not pursue them because the Spaniards were exhausted and wounded; and in that state of discouragement they went back to the town.

Cortés had the wounded carried to the ships and with more than 400 men, 12 horses and his artillery marched the following day to the same battleground. They found an infinite number of Indians anxious to meet them on the strength of their victory. The land was full of irrigating canals, for they grow peanuts in great quantity there and peanut fields are in constant need of watering and very precious indeed since they use the almond-like nut to make beverages as well as for currency. But they were a great nuisance to the horses and this is why the Indians were able to fight effectively, even though the sight of horses frightened them; they believed man-horse-lance to be one and the same creature. Even though their weapons can only wound and not kill, they put the Spaniards in danger of losing their lives.

Finally, they reached a plain of drier land, and now the horsemen were able to work havoc, spearing innumerable Indians. It is reported that 30,000 people died in that encounter, and such is the way Cortés introduced the Gospel into New Spain. His servant Gómara says that a mounted St. Peter or St. James appeared before them as a reward and wrought destruction among the Indians. But what is really worthy of immortal shame and everlasting scorn is Gómara's statement that Cortés freed some prisoners and sent them to all the chiefs of the land with his regrets for the casualties on both sides and his claim of innocence; he nevertheless forgave their error and gave them two days to apologize for their malice, to effect peace and friendship, and to be appraised of other mysterious things. Should they fail to appear within that term, he warned that he would proceed inland, destroying, burning, razing, killing everyone without sparing a single man, woman or child, armed or unarmed. Those are Gómara's words. You see how Cortés has the world deceived and those who read his false history are to blame for not reflecting that the Indians had not offended us, that Indians are not Moors or Turks who plague and mistreat us; in short, they are to blame for accepting the written word: Cortés killed and Cortés won, he conquered—as they say—many nations, he plundered and stacked gold in Spain and became the Marquis del Valle. Readers are to blame for this, especially the learned among them.

When the poor Indians saw their forces so diminished, they

agreed to avoid total destruction, given the fact that the Spaniards were too strong, used terrible weapons and above all, used that animal that ran so fast and always caught up with them to kill them; and they sent their elders to negotiate peace and safety. Gómara says they came to beg forgiveness, as if they had committed a grave sin; imagine Gómara's insensitivity, or rather, how he scorns truth and justice! Cortés welcomed them, offered them some Castilian trinkets and declared as best he could with sign language that he wanted to see the chief, assuring them he had nothing to fear, in proof of which he freed all his prisoners and had the wounded attended to. It was thought that the chief came with a noble escort to see Cortés and showed signs of grief and apprehension at being deceived. I said he was thought to be the chief because it is customary among Indians to send a person who looks dignified in lieu of the chief. To placate the Spaniards, they brought many chickens—large ones with wattles—bread, fruit, cocoa, gold jewels weighing over 300 castellanos, and fifteen to twenty women to cook and bake corn bread, an arduous task which cannot be done without their assistance. Cortés joyfully accepted these things and showed signs of pleasure, pledging friendship and safety from then on, and since they understood nothing of each other's language, they carried the whole conversation on with gestures.

The Spaniards asked if their land was rich in gold but they indicated that gold came from a great distance. Gómara says here that they smashed their idols as the result of learning of the doctrine of the mysteries of the Cross which Cortés had taught them and that they worshipped the Cross built on their temple. He adds that they swore obedience to the King of Castile represented by Cortés, that they became his allies and that these were the Emperor's first vassals in New Spain. Cortés invents and Gómara lies to flatter Cortés, to sell his tyranny to the King as a great service and to deceive the world further. Indians and Spaniards did not understand one another and, assuming they did, a week is not enough to teach them mysteries of the Faith, the Holy Trinity, the Passion of the Son of God—all of which is part of the mystery of the Cross—and to bring them to destroy their idols. Indians do not leave their idols that easily, having their religion and its cult rooted in their hearts, to be convinced by a handful of mumbled and mispronounced words, especially since Indians hated all Spaniards as their capital enemies for having suffered such irreparable damage and being made to fear extermination. As for their swearing obedience to the King of Spain represented by Cortés, it is a false and evil statement which shows how Cortés waged the first war and how he celebrated his apostolic entry into New Spain. The proof of what he and his holy company accomplished in Tabasco is that the Indians had a change of heart: just a few months earlier, they had welcomed Grijalva so graciously and with such liberality and hospitality as to shower him with gold, as is amply demonstrated in Chapter 109. And this should suffice to convince anyone that Cortés entered those kingdoms like an egregious tyrant, even though it will become more apparent in the course of this history. . . .

122

Montezuma's governor brought Cortés that present [gold and silver worth some 25,000 pesos and an equal amount in exquisite craftsmanship] as well as provisions for the return trip, all the while pressing him to leave, although throughout their stay they were given an abundance of game, fish, bread, fruit and corn, fodder for the horses, and men and women servants. But Cortés had far-reaching ambitions. He told Montezuma's governor that he wished to see Montezuma and he gave him the best of embroidered shirts, a silk tunic, a cap, stockings, necklaces made of colorful glass beads and other such items of his best collection. The governor accepted but showed little pleasure—this was trash for someone of Montezuma's power who had all the riches a pagan could wish for; thus, he reluctantly sent those presents on to Montezuma along with the bad news that Cortés refused to turn back but instead wished to proceed inland.

A week passed and the messengers returned with more presents for Cortés: very fine cloth woven of cotton and feathers, gold and silver jewels, and the message was to insist that Cortés leave as soon as possible, since his welcome had worn thin; moreover, should he persist in not turning back, he was to be left there alone. The governor then said to Cortés "that if he desired more presents, Montezuma would satisfy him as best he could, provided the Spaniards left immediately." Cortés insisted on seeing Montezuma; the governor refused, saying he was obeying orders. Disconcerted, he notified all his Indians to leave during the night; thus, all the provisional camps established and maintained by them to serve the Spaniards were abandoned by morning. Cortés then ordered a boat to sail down the coast to look for a better harbor and a better place to stay and, because he feared an attack by Montezuma's army, he had all but the fighting gear stored in the ships. The boat returned with the news that there was no harbor other than a cove formed by a large rock seven or eight leagues away, and Cortés ordered all ships to anchor there, while he, 400 men and 15 horses went to explore inland; and since their every move was known to the multitude of Indian spies, the people left for the woods with their belongings.

The Spaniards reached a deserted town, well provided with cotton garments and beautiful objects made with feathers, gold and silver. The houses were built of stone and adobe, had straw roofs and were comfortable. Cortés gave orders to leave everything untouched so as not to scandalize the people any further or provoke greater hatred than he had provoked already by refusing to leave the land. They found the same situation and behaved in the same manner in the neighboring villages until the news of such novel conduct spread to the city of Cempoal, some eight leagues from there, for Indians are expert informers and Cortés's moves were known to the whole territory within six hours. The King of Cempoal dispatched sixteen of his ablest men as disguised spies to find out what kind of men the Spaniards were and if perchance they might be those gods, announced to them by their prophets and sorcerers, who would come to them from the East.

They say Cortés understood or guessed—he was a very astute man, which does not excuse his tyranny—that those Indians told him how Montezuma, the King of Mexico, used violence to extort tribute from the King of Cempoal and other subjected tribes. Gómara errs on this point in order to justify Cortés; for instance, he says that Marina or Malinche interpreted for him, but this is intolerable: to carry on such conversations an expert interpreter is needed, not people who communicate with a few phrases like "Gimme bread," "Gimme food," "Take this, gimme that," and otherwise carry on with gestures. He adds that Cortés was pleased to find enmity among the Indians, for it served his purpose well. These are thoughts and desires entertained by tyrants who use such enmity better to subjugate both parties, as he did. Tyrants act with a bad conscience; they lack reason, right and justice, as the Philosopher says in Book V, Chapter 11, of the *Politics*. They take advantage of discords when these exist, or otherwise they create them to divide people and subject them more easily, because they know it is more difficult, sometimes impossible, to subject a people united in conformity, at least it is unlikely that, should they succeed, their tyranny should last. When the Roman captain, Pompey, defeated Tigranus, the King of Armenia, he knew that Jerusalem was divided between two factions headed by the two brothers Aristobulus and Hircanus, and he knew the time was ripe to engage in battle. He entered the city and forced it to submit to Rome, and from then on, unjustly and tyrannically, Judea and the Jews lost their freedom. . . . This is recorded in Josephus, *Jewish Antiquities*, Paulus Orosio, *De Ormesta mundi*, Book VI, Chapter 6, Pedro Comestor, *Historia Escolástica*, Maccabees, Book II, Chapter 7, and other historians.

In this same manner, Cortés rejoiced to find dissension among the kings of that land, and better to deceive the world he said he was helping the one against the other, as if he had heard both parties and as a competent judge would determine which was in the wrong. As if, without this knowledge, he was not committing mortal sin since, clearly, the Cempoal Indians could have lied to him about Montezuma's use of force to have them pay tribute; Montezuma could, after all, have been entitled to it by right. To help one party was to place himself in a position to damn the other party unrightfully; therefore there is no doubt that Cortés sinned, whether he was righting a wrong or not, and was under obligation to make restitution to the aggrieved party. Cortés and his men behaved in this manner in the province of Tlascala, but Cortés really did not care; his only concern was to find means to achieve his goals: to tyrannize and plunder all, great or small, right or wrong—that is, assuming there was a wrong, which is something he could not judge either *de iure* or *de facto*.

Law and reason presume that all kings are lawfully in control of their kingdoms, and Cortés should have assumed as much, regardless of the complaints one party might have had against the other. If it is true that Montezuma had forced the Cempoal Indians into submission, Cortés should have acted legitimately, like Titus Quincius for example, the Roman captain who freed the Corinthians and other Greek peoples oppressed by Philip of Macedonia. Titus conquered Philip and his Macedonians, then he announced to the multitude that, instead of paying tribute to the Romans, the Corinthians, Locrians, Phocians, Eubeians, Acheans, Phthians, Magnesians, Tessalians and Parthians were free men, and the multitude ran toward him to kiss his hands in gratitude shouting, "Titus is today the savior and defender of Greece." The uproar shot into the air like an arrow and the crows who were caught riding the sound wave fell upon them, as Plutarch says in his life of Titus. And if Cortés had imitated him in his dealings with the people of Cempoal, provided of course that they really had been wronged by Montezuma, he could have restored their freedom and constituted himself their savior. But he chose the opposite way and deprived not only the Cempoalese of their honor, their lives and their freedom, but Montezuma also, as Gómara claims so proudly and as the whole world knows. It follows, then, that Cortés deserves the title of pure tyrant, usurper of thrones, murderer of innumerable nations, as every wise person will judge, especially if he is a Christian, and as this *History* in truth will show.

Cortés and company finally arrived in Cempoal, a large city of about 30,000 inhabitants, with great stone buildings surrounded by water and gardens like Eden on earth. At nightfall he dispatched three or four horsemen to inspect the city, and since Indians pave their patio floors and paint them a polished ochre and bronze that glitters in starlight like a shiny silver cup, they mistook it for gold and silver and rushed back to Cortés saying the whole city was made of it. They entered the city; the people came out to receive them and guide them to the royal palace, where the King stepped out accompanied by members of the court and there they stood facing each other unable to communicate a single word. The Spaniards retired to buildings assigned to them and were given the hospitality and care people usually reserve for their fathers. They stayed two weeks there, during which time Gómara says the King complained to Cortés about Montezuma's tyranny, but as I said, this must be taken as a tale of Cortés's own invention and evil designs. It is likely that Cortés himself stirred them against Montezuma by prompting them to stop paying tribute and that they dared not contradict him, frightened as they were by gunshot and horses and the reports of Cortés's exploits in Tabasco. What right did Cortés have to order or to persuade them not to pay tribute to Montezuma? Had he studied the case and was he a competent judge qualified to pass sentence? But would that his desires had stopped there!

123

Encouraged by the prospect of such wealth and the success of his expedition, Cortés decided to secure the state he had usurped by rebelling against Velázquez. He had a few friends when he left Cuba but in the course of his expedition he made many more and used them shamelessly, although greed and ambition kept him from realizing that his conduct was obvious to others. He connived with them to persuade the others to elect him governor of that land after he had publicly resigned from his position as captain of the fleet, thus securing his independence from Velázquez. His plan was the following: as captain he would form a municipal council and a township there which, once constituted, would be empowered to represent the King, and thus to accept Cortés's resignation and elect him in the name of the King. And so he did, confident that they would proceed to his election. He named two mayors, Alonso Puertocarrero from his home town of Medellín, and Francisco de Montejo of Salamanca, both birds of a feather like himself and not worth much, and he filled the posts of aldermen, actuary and so forth.

Consider the kind of authority Cortés used when he, a dissident, conferred power upon officials! Consider, too, the validity and integrity of his tyrannical acts! He named the town Villa Rica de la Vera Cruz and formed its council, then he resigned by saying that he had to explore a coastline and find traces of Juan de Grijalva by order of Diego Velázquez, lieutenant governor of Cuba, and of the Hieronymite fathers who governed Hispaniola, neither of whom had jurisdiction over the new land; thus, he officially resigned his post and asked for an attestation of that fact. The mayors accepted and attested his resignation, then met in council to deliberate his nomination to the post of captain general, head mayor and governor, until the King should be pleased to dispose otherwise. Since they had deliberated the matter beforehand, the council called him and read a longish text that stressed the advantage to God and the kingdom of having a superior to rule these hidalgos in war and in peace. The text also said that they had elected him as the person best qualified to do so; therefore, they begged him to accept the office of judge as well as that of captain general for the conquests they hoped to achieve in that land and for which they invested him with full power in the name of the King of Castile.

This shows the kind of authority and jurisdiction Cortés possessed to do what he did in that country. He accepted the post and offered his services to them; Gómara has no compunction in saying that Cortés accepted readily because at that time he desired nothing else. He might have added that Cortés worked toward and contrived nothing else. Many cursed this absurd election, notably a former servant of Velázquez named Diego de Ordás, Francisco de Morla, and people high and low, like Juan Escudero and other humble men. They accused Cortés of treason against Velázquez and qualified his actions as horrendous and detestable. But Cortés reacted immediately: he had them put in chains in the mainship, and after a few days, the pressure of friends having prevailed, had them released. Some persisted in their belief and planned to steal a brig to cross back to Cuba and notify Velázquez, but a traitor notified Cortés and Cortés apprehended them. He hanged a few (Juan Escudero among them), had others beaten and otherwise punished by insult in such a way that from then on they dared not open their mouths nor make a move, and I think this clearly demonstrates that Cortés behaved like a tyrant. As for the others, they were men of status and they held their tongue until finally they became accustomed to his ways and complied readily. I do not know if they may be excused from having broken allegiance to Velázquez, however; I would think not, to judge from what they did later. Cortés, being a most clever man, decided to secure his position even more since both Velázquez and the King had grounds to hang him. In addition, he would not risk being killed by Indians because of desertion in his ranks. Thus, he arranged to sink his fleet, saving one ship for his envoys to Castile and, to avoid possible plotting against the execution of his plan, he contrived the following.

He met secretly with the ships' crews, first and second mates as well as sailors, whoever was most trustworthy, and, promising them great gifts, asked them to scuttle the ships to make sinking unavoidable, then come to him in groups to announce that the ships were taking water beyond control. They followed his instructions and Cortés showed grief when they made their announcement, for he was practiced in the art of showing the emotions most advantageous to him. He told them to try to save the ships but that if it proved impossible, to strip the ships of usable items before the sea should gulp them down. In the end, people resented this decision and mutiny broke out, but Cortés pacified many a Spaniard with a mind to kill him by offering great hopes of riches. He appointed Alonso Puertocarrero and Francisco de Montejo his envoys to Castile. They were to bring the Emperor the presents of Montezuma and the news of the exploration—the wealth of the land, the efforts of Cortés to subdue the Indians and his hopes of conquering Montezuma, the opulent King of an inland territory. They were also to beseech the Emperor to confirm the appointment of Cortés whom they had elected governor as the person best qualified for the post, who also had invested the totality of his capital in the equipment of the fleet. They were to complain about Diego Velázquez, defame him, not mention his contributions to the fleet, invent cunning arguments and affirm many lies. They even implied that they would not accept another governor, and this insolent letter must have been kept from the Emperor, otherwise Cortés would never have succeeded as he did.

The spared ship sailed from Vera Cruz in July of 1519 and arrived in Seville I believe in October. Benito Martín, now made

Abbot of New Spain, as we said earlier, happened to be in Seville waiting for a ship to Cuba and he knew immediately that Cortés had rebelled against Velázquez. For this reason, the Sevillian officials of trade with the Indies confiscated Cortés's personal gold, amounting to 3,000 pesos for himself and another 3,000 for his father, and they forwarded Montezuma's present to Valladolid so that the Emperor could see it on his way from Barcelona to La Coruña, where he was to embark for Flanders. Benito Martín and the Sevillian officials notified the Bishop of Burgos, Juan de Fonseca, who was making arrangements for the Emperor in La Coruña. The Bishop immediately notified the Emperor by letter, saying that Cortés had rebelled against Velázquez, that his envoys ought to be hanged, that Cortés was a traitor and so on. Meanwhile, Cortés's envoys and the pilot Alaminos went to Cortés's father in Medellín and together they started for Barcelona, traveling like paupers, for the officials had barely left them enough money for the trip. Along the way they learned that the Emperor had left Barcelona and they followed his retinue to La Coruña, which is how I came to know them. . . .

125

In those days things worthy of note were happening on Hispaniola. . . . There lived in San Juan de la Maguana a young scatterbrain named Valenzuela who had inherited a share of Indians ruled by the cacique Enriquillo. As a child Enriquillo had been brought up in the Franciscan monastery of Vera Paz in the province the Indians call Xaraguá (the stress is on the last syllable), formerly ruled by the principal King of five, King Behechio (the penultimate syllable is long) about whom we spoke at length in Books I and II. Enriquillo had learned to read, write and understand our customs. As he was very intelligent, he also spoke our language well and showed the benefits of his learning. His territory was the mountains of the province of Baoruco (penultimate syllable is long) near the southern coast, thirty to seventy leagues south of Santo Domingo.

When he came of age, he married an Indian lady of noble birth, doña Lucía was her name, and they were married as Christians by the Church. Enrique was tall and well built, his face was grave and austere, neither handsome nor ugly, and he served, together with his Indians, the house of Valenzuela, suffering patiently his unjust servitude and daily affronts. Among his few belongings, he had a mare which Valenzuela took away by force. Then, not content with that robbery, Valenzuela decided to desecrate Enrique's marriage by raping his wife, and because the cacique was angry and complained about it, they say he was beaten in fulfillment of the saying: an insulted man is a beaten man. He took his complaint to the lieutenant governor Pedro de Vadillo and was received in the way all Indians are received by representatives of the law: he was threatened by worse treatment if he did not drop his claim. They say he was even thrown in prison and put in solitary confinement. Once free, the poor man determined to come to Santo Domingo and take his case to the Audiencia, the court of appeals, and he came a poor man indeed, tired, hungry and penniless. The tribunal gave him a form letter, charging him to return to Lieutenant Governor Vadillo, which was the way the tribunals and the King's council in Castile always operated: they returned the plaintiff to his own enemies, the offenders.

Back in his town thirty leagues away, Enrique presented his letter, but all the justice he received was worse treatment from Vadillo and Valenzuela, who by this time had heard about it and was threatening to beat him to death. I have no doubt that, given the long-time standing custom of despising Indians (chiefs and subjects alike) and of afflicting them freely without fear of God or the law, Valenzuela slapped him in the face and beat him rather than give him a meal for his troubles. Enriquillo—the diminutive was used generally because those who had known him as a child called him this way—endured the new affront and kept his feelings to himself. But when his master (who had less reason to be his master than Enrique had to be his servant) gave him permission to leave because at a certain time of the year the cacique had to conduct the changeover of mine shifts at the risk of his own skin, Enriquillo, trusting in his right and in his land, determined to leave his enemy's service, to send him no Indians and to defend himself on his own territory. Spaniards call this an act of insurrection when, to tell the truth, it is nothing more than escape from a cruel enemy, in the way cattle run from slaughter.

The appointed time came and went and neither Enrique nor his Indians returned to Valenzuela. Considering Enrique in a state of rebellion, as they called it, for past grievances, Valenzuela set out with eleven men to find him, bring him back by force and mistreat him. When he arrived, he found Enrique and his people armed with steel and fishbone-pointed lances, bows and arrows, stones and whatever weapons they could find. The Indians went out to meet them, led by Enrique, who summoned Valenzuela to retreat because neither he nor any of his Indians meant to return with him. Valenzuela, like all Spaniards, thought of Enrique as a slave and held him in the same contempt as he would a pile of cow-dung, so he began to insult him and, calling him dog and all sorts of injurious names, charged upon his men, who returned the blows so promptly that they killed two or three Spaniards, wounded many and forced the rest to retreat. Enrique refused to pursue them and he allowed them to go, saying, "Be grateful, Valenzuela, that I spare your life; go away and take care never to come again."

Valenzuela and his men hastened back to San Juan de la Maguana with his pride wounded rather than cured. The news of Enrique's insurrection spread over the island. The Audiencia sent an order to subdue him; seventy or eighty Spaniards assembled to go after him and, tired and hungry, found him in the mountains many days later. He came out to meet them, killed a few, wounded others, and the rest agreed to retreat much against their will and their sense of pride. Enriquillo's fame and victories are talked about everywhere; many Indians escape Spanish oppression to join Enriquillo's standard for safety as they would an impregnable rock castle, in the same manner as the oppressed fled to David from the tyranny of Saul in 1 Kings 22. Thus some 300 Indians came from all directions to Enriquillo and acknowledged him their chief, joining Enriquillo's men who, I understand, did not amount to 100. He taught them how to defend themselves from Spanish attacks, for he never allowed his men to go and attack first.

This war against the Spaniards was a just war, and Enriquillo's election a just election, as is made clear by reading the history of the Maccabees in the Scriptures and the history of Pelayo in Spanish writings. Not only was it a legitimate war of self-defense, but by the same token and the same justification, Enriquillo and his Indians could avenge personal affronts, decimation and usurpation of territory by war and punishment. With respect to natural law (I am not speaking of matters of Faith, which adds another right to self-defense), Enrique and the handful of Indians who survived the cruelty and horrible tyranny of Spaniards had every right to pursue the Spaniards, destroy and punish them as their capital enemy, who had destroyed all the great republics the Indians had established on this island. In this they were backed by the authority of natural law, since war is not properly called war but an act of self-defense.

Enrique's right was reinforced, even, by the fact that he was the only Prince left on the island and as such had the power and the right to enforce the law over all the Spaniards. This cannot be denied by saying, as some people ignorant of the fact and of the law are saying, that the Prince of the island was the King of Castile, and that Enrique ought to have taken his case before him. This is said in bad faith and is foolishness besides, because the Indian kings and chiefs never did recognize the superiority of the Castilian King. From the day of discovery to the present, they have been tyrannized *de facto* if not *de iure*; they have been killed in cruel wars and oppressed into a most inhuman servitude, so they were forced to silence, as I have said in Book I and am saying throughout the *History*. Nor was there ever any justice here; it never was used to correct the grievances of Indians, and where there is no justice, the oppressed are entitled to right their own wrongs. This is held as a maxim among jurists, is dictated by natural reason, and is not a derogation of the Castilian King's supreme and universal right over the New World as granted by the Holy See, provided reason guides this right. Everything must be ordered and guided, not by individual whim, but by reason, just as all of God's works are ordered and guided by it. But I have written long treatises on this subject, both in Spanish and Latin.

126

Enriquillo's people inadvertently killed two or three Spaniards coming from the mainland with 15,000 to 20,000 gold pesos. I gather that the killers were a group of independent Indians or a group posted by Enriquillo as sentries. They did commit such crimes which he left unpunished in order to keep the men, but his own orders were restricted to disarming the Spaniards, his principal concern being to obtain swords and lances. They soon became as adept with them as if they had been bullies for a long time, and in their encounters with the Spaniards it was astounding to see how they could fight hand to hand for the major part of the day. They gathered many arms in numerous combats with defeated Spanish patrols, and in addition, Indians stole all sorts of weapons from their masters before joining Enriquillo. His vigilance and care for his safety and that of his men were extraordinary—as if he had been a captain in Italy all his life. He had sentries and spies in all harbors and places most susceptible to Spanish invasion. When informed by his spies of their presence, he and the fifty men he always kept with him removed all women, children, the elderly and the sick to secret places in the mountains ten or twelve leagues away, places that were cultivated and supplied with food, leaving behind his nephew, who was no taller than a yardstick but of great courage, as captain. They fought like lions until Enriquillo came with fresh troops and, choosing his point of attack, weakened and diminished the Spanish force; and the many times Spaniards engaged in battle with him, he was always victorious in routing them.

Once, as they were beating retreat, some seventy-two Spaniards found a cave in the rocks and hid there from pursuing Indians. Enrique stopped his men from starting a fire with the order: "I do not want them burned; disarm them and let them go." They gained many swords that day, and lances and arbalests, even though they had not yet learned to use them. One of those seventy Spaniards took orders in the Dominican monastery of Santo Domingo in fulfillment of a vow he had made if he escaped alive from that hopeless situation. I have this incident from him and it shows Enrique's goodness, because he certainly could have killed all those Spaniards. Besides, his Indians were always under order not to assault a Spaniard except in battle.

If the Spaniards had not yet reached the Indian encampment by the time Enrique and his fifty men returned from the place where the women were kept in safety, his vigilance was such that he always sensed their presence first. His habit was to sleep a while shortly after dark and when he was sufficiently rested he circled his camp on foot while saying the rosary, accompanied by two youths carrying their lances and his sword, I believe even two swords, because that is what he had at the head of his hammock. This way he was among the first, if not always the first, to know if Spanish men were approaching and he could wake his people. For greater safety, he ordered various areas of land to be cultivated, and straw huts built in patches ten or twelve leagues apart over a surface of approximately forty leagues; and in these huts he sheltered women, children and old people, sometimes here and sometimes there, according to his better judgment. The many dogs he needed (to hunt the wild pigs of the region) and the chickens were kept in a village hidden for that purpose and tended by two or three Indians with their wives. This was done so that the barking of the dogs and cackling of the hens would not give them away, and he was careful never to camp near that village. He sent a few Indians at a time for fish, game or other things, but they never could find him where they had left him and neither did they know his exact whereabouts, so that in the event of capture and torture, they could not divulge information leading to his hideaway. But if he sent a larger squad on a mission, this precaution was unnecessary because he felt that the Spaniards could not capture them all, leaving the possibility that someone could warn him.

The fame of Enrique's victories, diligence, courage and war tactics spread more and more over the whole island, especially since, as I said, the Spaniards were beaten every single time. Everyone simultaneously admired and feared him, to the degree that when a recruitment was made, no Spaniard volunteered to go and in fact would not have gone at all if the Audiencia had not issued court orders. This lasted some fourteen years and cost the royal treasury some 100,000 castellanos. A foreign Franciscan monk by the name of fray Remigio offered to meet Enrique and see if words might not be more effective than force. I mentioned this monk before as the person who brought a certain number of Franciscans to this island who were notable both as religious and scholarly men, to preach the Gospel, and I believe he was among those who were involved in Enrique's upbringing. He embarked on a ship that took him where they thought Enrique was hiding. To the Indians the sight of a ship meant the arrival of a Spanish squadron, therefore, they always made sure of the disembarking point by sending out sentries and in this way a group of them arrived where fray Remigio had been rowed to shore. They asked him if the Spaniards had sent him as a spy. He answered no, he had come to ask Enrique to make friends with the Spaniards, to assure him that he would not be harmed, and to persuade him to abandon his hiding place, saying he had been moved to come by sentiments of friendship for Enrique. They replied that he was lying, that the Spaniards had been bad and had lied to them by not keeping their word, that, surely, he meant to deceive them like the rest of the Spaniards, and that they had a mind to kill him. The holy man saw himself in a most distressing situation, but since Enrique had ordered never to kill a Spaniard unless in open battle, they spared his life. However, they stripped him of his robes, tore them into pieces and left him standing in his underwear, while he begged them to inform Enrique that a Franciscan monk had come and would like to see him. Would they please take him to their chief?

They left him there and reported to Enrique. He came to the friar and expressed regret for what had happened, asking him to forgive him and not be angry, although it had been done against his will, which is how Indians console those who suffer hardships. The friar begged Enrique to make peace with the Spaniards and assured him he would be treated well from now on. Enrique answered he would like nothing better, but that he was wise to the ways of Spaniards: they had killed his father and grandfather as well as the lords and people of the Xaraguá kingdom, decimating the whole island. He related the affront he had received from Valenzuela and said he had come to the mountains to avoid the fate of his father and prevent Valenzuela from killing him. He said also that he and his people lived without harming anyone but only defended themselves against the Spaniards who had come to enslave and kill them, and that no Spanish talk could convince them to live a life of servitude with the knowledge that they would perish in the same way as their elders had perished. The friar asked for his robes; Enrique answered that he was sorry, but the Indians had ripped them up and distributed the pieces amongst themselves. Since the ship that had brought him was there plying to windward, they signaled it, and as a boat neared the shore, Enrique kissed the friar's hand and, on the verge of tears, said goodbye. Sailors took in the friar, clothed him with their capes and returned him to his order in the city, where he was given a new habit, not made of silk but of rough cloth, for they were very poor.

127

A few Indians regained courage from the news of Enrique's victories, among them a certain Ciguayo, who must have belonged to the outstanding Ciguayo tribe that used to occupy the mountain territory of Vega Real sloping down to the north sea on the upper coast of this island, which I described at length in Book I. Ciguayo was a valiant man, though naked like all Indians. With a Castilian lance and, I think, also a sword (I do not know the name of the Spaniard he served), he left his oppressor, gathered ten or twelve Indians, and began to assault Spaniards in the mines and plantations where there lived groups of only two or four, killing all those he found and spreading terror over the island. Nobody felt secure even in the towns, living as they did in constant dread of Ciguayo. Finally, the Spaniards formed groups to pursue him and found him many days later. He charged among them like a rabid dog or as if he were bristling with steel from head to foot. After a wild encounter, Ciguayo retreated to a ravine, fighting a Spaniard who sank half his lance into him but even then he went on fighting like a heroic Hector. In the end, losing blood and strength, he was finished off by the Spaniards arriving on the scene; the rest of the Indians, having nothing to do with him, ran away.

After Ciguayo, another strong and valiant Indian rebelled, and his name was Tamayo. He too gathered a squad of Indians and followed the example of Ciguayo, attacking Spaniards outside towns and cities. He caused a lot of damage and his name was terror on the island. He killed many Spanish men, a few women, and whomever else he found alone on the plantations, spared no lives, amassed weapons, lances, swords, and clothing. It is astonishing to think that 300 Spaniards subdued three or four million souls inhabiting this island, three-quarters of them by war and horrible slavery in the mines. Now at the time of these events, there were 3,000 or 4,000 Spaniards here and only two Indians; each with not more than fifteen men, not together but separately one after the other, and they sufficed to inspire such terror that even the people of the towns felt insecure. This is to be attributed to a divine will designed to demonstrate three things: One, that these people were brave and manly enough, despite their nakedness and gentle disposition. Two, that, had they possessed weapons similar to ours, and horses and harquebuses, they would never have allowed themselves to be wiped off the face of the earth. Three, that it is a sign of disapproval of such actions and of punishment to come hereafter for such sins against God and against our fellow men. This seems clear if we read *Judges* 2 and 3, in which it is written that God did not allow total destruction of the people of the Promised Land, so that the survivors would show the Hebrews their errors and their punishment.

Enrique did not know that Ciguayo and Tamayo plagued the island, but opinion had it that Enrique was behind their actions, and for this reason, the Spaniards lived in greater fear and trembling. When Enrique heard the trouble they were causing, he suspected the blame would fall upon him, as it did, and felt sorry. I know this for certain and I will explain why in detail in the following book. Enrique had with him a nephew of Tamayo, called Romero, whom he sent to Tamayo 100 leagues away, in the neighborhood of Puerto Real and Lares de Guahaba (the penultimate syllable is long). His mission was to persuade Tamayo to join forces with Enrique, for he would be safer and Ciguayo's fate would be more likely not to befall him. Enrique would treat him well, making him captain over a certain number of his men, and together they would be stronger and better able to defend themselves. The nephew was very clever and succeeded in persuading Tamayo to come and bring his supply of stolen lances, swords and clothing to Enrique, who gave him a warm welcome. And this is how he kept Tamayo from perpetrating crimes on the island, which shows Enrique's goodness, discretion and prudence. The Spaniards armed almost yearly against Enrique, wasting thousands of castellanos. Once they armed 150 Spaniards or more, headed by a captain they called Bonao but whose real name was Hernando de San Miguel, a hidalgo originally from Ledesma or Salamanca who had been on the island since the days of Christopher Columbus. He had come very young and had grown so tough in wars, he could walk the sierra barefoot. He pursued Enrique for a long time but never found him off guard nor, I believe, did they ever clash head-on.

One day they came so close to each other they could exchange talk but could not come to harm because each was on a sierra peak separated by an abyss about 500 *estados* deep. Such close proximity prompted them to ask for a truce and a safe place for negotiation, which was agreed to on both sides. The Spanish captain asked to speak with Enrique. Enrique appeared on the rock; the captain told him life this way was full of sorrows for both parties and it seemed better to live in peace and harmony. Enrique agreed, for he very much wanted peace; however, the matter did not rest with him but with them. The captain replied that he was empowered by the Audiencia of Santo Domingo representing the King to settle the terms of peace: he and his people would be allowed to live as free men on that part of the island Enrique would choose, and the Spaniards would not disturb them in any way, provided they were left unmolested and their gold were returned. He even showed them the Audiencia provision. Enrique said he would consent to peace and friendship and the return of the gold provided they fulfilled their part of the treaty. The captain and Enrique agreed to meet, each with eight men, on a certain day at a certain place on the shore, and upon that agreement, they parted company.

Enrique began to take measures to keep his word. He sent men to build an enclosure of thick foliage wherein to deposit the gold so that it looked like a King's chamber. For his part, the captain prepared to celebrate peace and not very wisely instructed his crew to steer the ship near the designated place, while he walked along the shore with a drummer and people shouting in rejoicing. Enrique, who was waiting in the foliage with his eight men, saw the ship approaching and the captain walking with many people, drum and noise and all, and felt that the captain had exceeded the terms of the agreement; so, fearing an ambush, he decided not to appear in person and went back to the mountain with his guard. He instructed the eight Indians to excuse his absence by saying he was not feeling well and to deliver the gold, feed them and see that they were pleased in every way.

The captain arrived, asked for Enrique and received that reply. The captain immediately regretted his imprudence (though perhaps without knowing the nature of it), for he was certain, and he was not mistaken, that peace would be sealed right then and fear would disappear from the island. If it did not stop entirely then, at least strife was suspended, until it was stopped altogether later, in the manner I shall describe in the following book. The eight Indians served the captain and his men well as is their custom, and delivered the gold; not a single coin was missing. The captain thanked them, asking them to tell Enrique that he was sorry not to have seen him and that he was ill (he knew very well it was a ruse), and that he trusted in their friendship and mutual respect. The Spaniards embarked and returned to the city; the Indians rejoined their chief. From that day, they left Enrique alone and no harm came to either side until the final peace was made, and this interval lasted a matter of four or five years. . . .

129

The abundance of sugar cane inspired the residents of Hispaniola to engage in another type of business. In Book II I have already mentioned that a certain Aguilón of La Vega was the first to make sugar in the Indies. He extracted the syrup with certain wooden contraptions which, though primitive, made good enough sugar. That was about 1505 or 1506. Later, a surgeon named Vellosa, of Santo Domingo but originally from Berlanga, improved the instruments and made whiter and better sugar, around the year 1516. He was the first to make an almond-flavored sugar paste from it and I saw it, and he applied himself to the business, designing a press drawn by horses to extract the sweet juice of the cane. When the Hieronymite fathers saw the sample Vellosa brought to gain support for his enterprise, they were convinced of the possible profit and arranged to lend him 500 gold pesos from the royal treasury for him to start a sugar mill. I believe they kept lending him money because building mills was expensive. A few residents offered to build horse-drawn presses as well as the more powerful water mills. Today, there are about forty sugar mills in the Indies but sugar is none the less expensive. Before, sugar was made only in Valencia; then seven or eight mills were built in the Canary Islands and the price of an *arroba* went up to a little over a ducat; but now, with sugar mills all over the Indies, an *arroba* costs 2 ducats and the price rises every day.

Before the invention of mills here, a few residents who had acquired money by means of Indian sweat, seeing their Indians die rapidly, asked for a license to import black slaves. Some even promised Clergyman Casas, as I say in Chapter 102, to free their Indians in exchange for a dozen Negroes. At that time the clergyman enjoyed the favor of the King and was in charge of promoting the Indian cause; thus he procured black slaves in exchange for Indian freedom. The council of the Indies determined, on the recommendation of the Sevillian officials, as I said in Chapter 102, to send 4,000 of them to the four Islands of Hispaniola, San Juan, Cuba and Jamaica. A Spaniard on leave from the Indies asked for such license from Governor Bresa, a Flemish gentleman of the King's most private circles. The license was granted and sold for 25,000 ducats to Genoese merchants on the condition—among many others—that no license for black trade would be issued within a period of eight years. The Genoese sold it at the rate of 8 ducats minimum for each Negro. And in this manner, what Casas had achieved to help the Spaniards sustain themselves on the land while freeing Indians turned into a business proposition that was no small obstacle to the securing of Indian freedom. The clergyman soon repented and judged himself guilty of ignorance. He came to realize that black slavery was as unjust as Indian slavery and was no remedy at all, even though he had acted on good faith, and he was not sure that his ignorance and good faith would excuse him in the eyes of God.

There were ten to twelve Negroes on the island who belonged

to the King and had been brought to build the fortress at the mouth of the river, but once that grant expired, others were given and Negroes arrived in great numbers. I believe there are more than 30,000 of them on this island today, and over 100,000 in the Indies. Yet the Indians were not freed nor were their burdens alleviated, and Casas could do nothing for them. The King was absent and the council of the Indies had new members ignorant of the law they were under obligation to know, as I have stated many times throughout the *History*. Sugar mills increased and so did the need for Negroes and profit for the King. At least eighty men were needed to work the water-powered mills and at least forty were needed to work the presses. As a result, the Portuguese, who had long been capturing black slaves in Guinea, for whom we paid good prices, increased the trade by whatever means possible and the Africans themselves, seeing the demand, warred among themselves to sell slaves illicitly to the Portuguese.

Thus, we are guilty of the sins committed by the Africans and the Portuguese, not to mention our own sin of buying the slaves. The monies collected from the sale of licenses and the King's profits were assigned by the Emperor to build the Alcázar of Madrid and Toledo. Before the mills, we used to think that unless he were hanged a Negro would not die. We had never seen any die of illness; like orange trees, they take to this land better than to their native soil. But after they were put in the mills, the work and the cane syrup concoctions they drank caused such deaths and illnesses among them that they escaped their misery by fleeing to the woods and from there cruelly attacked the Spaniards. No small Spanish settlement was safe and this was another plague sent to the island.

It is well to mention still another plague, namely, the infinite number of dogs causing infinite damage on the island. There were great numbers of pigs feeding on sweet roots and delicate fruit and their meat was more savory than the most savory lamb. The hills were full of them but the dogs put an end to hunting parties by destroying the pigs and, not content with that, by destroying the newborn and defenseless calves as well. The damage is great indeed, and does not bode well for the future. Men take these things as bad luck, but we should remember that we found the island full of people whom we erased from the face of the earth, filling it with dogs and beasts whom divine will is perforce turning against us.

130

In order to relate the events of 1518–19 we had left Clergyman Casas in Chapter 105 of this book; he had returned to court after trying to recruit peasants for the settlement of these islands. Now it is time to see what happened after the King's arrival in Barcelona, with court and councils in operation. Father Casas continued negotiations for his peasants at the council of the Indies, which was not officially named so because the Bishop of Burgos convened it at home with members of other councils designated by the King, on what qualifications I do not know. They were: Licentiate Zapata, Hernando de Vega, Don García de Padilla, Pedro Martyr (an Italian we already mentioned, who wrote about the Indies in Latin in his *Decadas*) and Francisco de los Cobos, whose star was beginning to rise. One of the privileges the clergyman requested was that Spanish peasants be given those farms of little value that belonged to the King's estate, thus providing lodging and sustenance as a stimulus while they acquired their own property. However, the clergyman had received word that the Hieronymite fathers had sold the farms thinking it improper that a King should own them.

The clergyman went to the council, declared his awareness of the sale, and demanded a document certifying that farmers would be maintained for one year at the King's expense, otherwise, transporting them to the Indies would be the equivalent of murder. The Bishop of Burgos, who could not help but contradict, replied, "In this way, the King will spend more on those farmers than on a 20,000-man armada." His lordship the Bishop had much more experience with armadas than he had with saying pontifical Masses. The clergyman answered in great anger: "Well, Sir, just because Indians have been killed, does it seem right to you that I should lead these Christians to their deaths too? Well, I won't," meaning "You killed the Indians; do you also want to kill Christians?" He said it curtly but with an obvious intonation; I have no idea how the Bishop, who was no fool, understood it.

Four hundred ducats had been set aside for the peasants, but the clergyman insisted on the certificate valid for one year because, in truth, the peasants would perish without free lodgings and food at the beginning. Since the clergyman would not go and recruit peasants, they thought of appointing someone else, but the clergyman circulated letters to all villages explaining why he could not call them now and warning them against following imposters. It is likely that they would not have left their villages without the clergyman; however, the matter was dropped because such a profitable venture as going to the Indies attracted more than enough people—the King of France would not have dared come within 200 leagues of the coast of Hispaniola, for there were some 200,000 inhabitants on this island alone.

Thus conveniently relieved of the population problem, the clergyman was able to press another point, namely, to have Dominican and Franciscan friars preach in Paria free of Spanish tyranny. Toward the end of Chapter 104 I said that 100 leagues of land had been requested for the Dominicans so that they might preach without being disturbed by Spanish intervention. The Bishop of Burgos had naturally opposed this proposition by saying it would be waste land and bring the King no benefits. The clergyman was astounded to see that the Bishop failed to consider conversion as profitable in itself. Heavy-hearted, he thought about appealing to the Bishop's insensitivity by questioning his sacrilegious zeal to increase the King's treasury and reminding him of his Christian duty to look after the health of so many dying souls. But he knew from experience how the Bishop resented his proposals and rejected every one of them. Therefore, the clergyman secretly spoke with the Flemish members of the King's councils and all those who favored him and had influence with the King, including the new grand chancellor, all of whom were persons outstanding in learning and Christianity. He said he knew a way to bring the King an income from unexpected quarters, without involving a single Spaniard except those he would send with friars in charge of converting Indians and without risking a penny.

The clergyman's reasoning was that he could not carry out his plan without the financial help of the Spanish laity, who would not move a finger unless for material gain, certainly not for the preaching of the Faith or the conversion of souls. Also, once on his land, he had to see that no one would misbehave or steal or aggrieve the Indians, as was the Spanish custom, but instead would effect pacification in such a way that the Indians would not draw back. This was the clergyman's aim and he had to provide material gain to achieve and keep the peace so that the friars could preach the Gospel and bring those people to Christ. The clergyman's maxim was that unless the solution worked for as well as against the Spaniards, the Indians would never be saved; and knowing this for certain from his long experience, he founded the freedom and conversion of Indians on the pure material interests of those who were to help him achieve his goal.

131

This was the substance of the plan: the clergyman would choose from among his Spanish friends on these islands some fifty modest and reasonable persons of good will who would place serving God above greed, yet by lawful means would improve their status. He had limited the group to fifty for two reasons. One, to enter Indian territory peacefully and give rather than take unless it be freely given, 50 men can do the work of 100 or 500 since Indians are naturally gentle people; besides, it is well known that the larger the group, the greater the chances of strife and rivalry. Two, 50 men are more manageable than 100, and more likely to be brought to reason. To finance the plan, 10,000 ducats would suffice, each man contributing 200 ducats toward a year's maintenance, a supply of trinkets with which to win the friendship of Indians and the purchase of two caravels for the trip. In those days 1,000 ducats bought much more than 6,000 today, therefore, the sum of 10,000 was judged amply sufficient. He had decided to clothe the men in white habits embroidered with a red cross resembling that of the Order of Calatrava, except the arms of the cross branched off handsomely at the end, because he wanted to differentiate these men from those Spaniards that the Indians were likely to have seen and experienced as evildoers.

Their mission consisted in impressing upon the Indians the fact that the Spanish King had sent them to apologize for the harm caused by Spaniards acting against the King's will, to spread tokens of good will and to protect them against future injury. The clergyman thought that, should his plan succeed, he would request the Pope and the King to establish a religious brotherhood wearing that habit. So this was how Father Casas intended to pacify the Indians, to erase the horror in which they held Christians, and to preach the Gospel to a people who, worshipping no idols and having no very strong sects other than a few witch doctors practicing superstition, omen and such foolish things, would be brought easily to conversion. This would show the irrationality, iniquity and non-Christianity of the practice now in effect, that is, waging war and subduing people before attempting to preach, as if indeed it was necessary to instill hatred before teaching the Gospel! But they never tried peace; therefore, not one Indian child was baptized and not one adult was converted without first damning thousands of souls to Hell, as Spaniards do, and this condition will prevail until Doomsday if the method remains unchanged. And on the Day of Judgment, the ignorant and the careless will not be spared, let alone those who, through malice, arrogance and ambition, failed to remedy the situation or even made it worse. . . .

138

Clergyman Bartolomé de las Casas kept pressing the grand chancellor and the most distinguished Flemish members of the state council and council of Flanders who supported him against the Bishop and the council of the Indies. He felt the Bishop would block his proposal with more assurance now that the Bishop's council had succeeded in silencing the King's personal clergy; thus he complained to the grand chancellor and his distinguished Flemish friends, who believed in the sound reasoning and Christian spirit of the proposal. Casas did not have personal contact with the King because there was no need of it, but he felt that the King liked him and knew that in conversation the King referred to him by his first name as Micer Bartolomé (the Flemish call clergymen "Micer"). This was the result of the praise the King heard about Casas from men close to him, especially from Monsieur Laxao, who belonged to the King's most intimate circle.

Sure, then, of his backing, the clergyman determined openly to challenge the council of the Indies, especially the Bishop of Burgos who, having more authority, was always contradicting and resisting, though he lost his authority many times through the express interference of the clergyman. He imputed the faulty government of the Indies to the Bishop and his council, and illustrated his case with the example of the destruction of Hispaniola and neighboring islands, including that piece of mainland that Pedrarias was in charge of razing. He alleged also that, while residing in Spain, they had received large allotments of Indians whom their overseers and managers drove to death in order to send them gold, even if that privilege had now been successfully removed by the clergyman, as is explained above. In short, he said all he could say by way of truth against them, as openly and daringly as truth could be spoken by persons of low estate and little authority.

The King was kept informed daily because those who helped the clergyman were people of the King's most intimate circle, and after a few days he decided, on advice from the grand chancellor and his Flemish advisers, that the clergyman himself should name persons from the King's private council to handle his case, acting as judges as it were, between him and the Bishop. M. de Laxao notified the clergyman, who complied with much glee. He named don Juan Manuel, a favorite of the Emperor's father, Philip; and he named Alonso Téllez, the brother of the old Marquis of Villena and the son of Juan Pacheco who had flourished in the days of King Henry IV. These two gentlemen were among the wisest men in the kingdom and were members of the councils of war and state. The third person was a certain Manrique, Marquis of Aguilar de Campo, member of the same councils and the King's chief huntsman. He also named the licenciate Vargas who for a long time had been treasurer of state under the Catholic kings, a very wise and experienced member of the royal council; he named all its Flemish members as well. So then the King ordered meetings of all his councils: war, Inquisition, Flanders, etc., to discuss the case of Micer Bartolomé, so that at some time Cardinal

Adrian, the future Pope and then Grand Spanish Inquisitor, must have been present at those reunions. Thus, thirty to forty members met every time the case was discussed. This was one of the most outstanding events that occurred in Spain: that a poor clergyman with no estate and no outside help other than God's, persecuted and hated by everybody (the Spanish in the Indies spoke of him as one who was bent on destroying them and Castile), should come to have such influence on a King as to have a choice of cabinet members to judge a matter affecting another royal council and to be the cause of so many measures discussed throughout this *History*.

Before going further, it seems well to relate what the clergyman answered to a rebuke made in his absence, by one who had found out about the terms of his negotiation. The Spaniards in the Indies and those here who were influenced by them looked askance on the fact that the clergyman had asked privileges for the fifty men who were to accompany him, and that he had as well offered the King an income. They did not know that the contract aimed at aiding the unfortunate Indians to prevent their disappearance, but those who knew it—and there were many—praised it and saw that it was good.

There was a lawyer from the Inquisition and from the royal council, Aguirre was his name, who had been an executor of Queen Isabella's will, and was fond of the clergyman and what he called the clergyman's "universal cause." When he learned that an income had been promised the King and remuneration asked for the fifty men, he expressed disappointment at this profane way of doing things, finding temporal interests incompatible with evangelical preaching, saying he never suspected this from the clergyman. The clergyman heard it and said: "Sir, if you saw people mistreat Our Lord Christ, laying hands on him, insulting and reviling him, would you not try to have him handed over to you, that you might love him, serve and cherish him, and be unto him all that a true Christian should be?" He answered that of course he would. "What if they refused to give Him to you graciously but instead sold Him to you, would you not buy Him?" He said he would undoubtedly. The clergyman then said, "Well, Sir, that is what I have done. I left Christ in the Indies not once but a thousand times beaten, afflicted, insulted and crucified by those Spaniards who destroy and ravage the Indians. They die untimely deaths, having neither the Faith nor the sacraments. I pleaded with the royal council many times to have the obstacles to their salvation removed, namely, their enslavement to the Spaniards. Where the soil is untouched, I have asked that Spaniards be not allowed where missionaries have begun preaching the Gospels, for Spanish violence and the bad example they set make the Indians curse the name of Christ. They refused, saying a territory occupied by priests would bring no income to the King. I understood they wanted to sell me the Gospels, and, consequently, Christ; and when I saw Him beaten, insulted and crucified, I agreed to buy Him, offering the King benefits and temporal goods, as you have heard." Aguirre was satisfied, and so were those who heard the argument, and from then on the clergyman's reputation improved both for his cleverness and his zeal.

139

After having chosen the above-mentioned distinguished persons, the clergyman solicited the grand chancellor to convene the whole council and discuss his case. Thus the council had many meetings, although only from time to time: the celebration of various Parliaments imposed heavy obligations upon its members, the beginning of the new monarchy delayed all important matters, and the Bishop of Burgos, insulted by the clergyman's choice of so many council members, excused himself from attending as many meetings as he could, alleging bad health and all sorts of reasons. As soon as the grand chancellor and the Flemish members of the council realized this, they tricked him. They did not mention the order of business and he, thinking they would discuss war—a frequent topic then—or matters of state, would decide to come. But when he heard the proposals on Indian affairs, especially that of Micer Bartolomé, he knew that he had been deceived and was enraged; and as he was not a patient man, he showed it. He was all bitterness and gall, seeing himself surrounded by so many personages and knowing that none of the forty odd counselors there would approve his point of view—certainly none of those appointed by the clergyman, and having on his side only three or four obscure persons who called themselves members of the Indian council. Since the clergyman's supporters saw the King every day, although the council was not in session, if the Bishop was present also, someone would purposely mention the Indian question in order to provoke the Bishop to make a statement which they could argue before the King. But the Bishop was a wise man; he kept silent and only stayed long enough to take decorous leave of the King.

In those days he was so annoyed from such harassment that he never went to the palace without his brother, Antonio de Fonseca, who, as we said earlier, was a most illustrious man, wise, prudent, grave and gentlemanly, and as chief treasurer of Castile enjoyed such confidence and esteem with the Catholic King that Queen Isabella authorized his being addressed as Lordship, although he had no title. The Bishop enjoyed the King's confidence as well and had enough authority and the wisdom not to waste an ounce of it; but since few were with him and many against him, he brought his brother for support. The above persons met for many sessions about the clergyman's proposal, which was by nature both particular and universal, dealing as it did with the freedom of Indians and the safeguarding of the Indies. The Bishop and his allies resisted whenever possible the granting of land exemptions, alleging most trivial and frivolous reasons. The clergyman, who attended some of these meetings, clarified doubts as they arose about facts and lawful rights and followed the Gospel of Christ because most of them had little or no theology, except the Bishop of Badajoz, a certain de la Mota born in Burgos, a theologian and royal chaplain who sided with the clergyman and had come from Flanders with the King's private council.

Finally, the grand chancellor ruled for the majority that the clergyman's petition be granted and that he be given assistance to carry out his missionary work, bringing knowledge of their Creator to the people of the new countries. They began to draw up the terms of the agreement and the clergyman thought that his pains at court had come to an end, when the Bishop, angry and offended, and intending no rest for himself or the clergyman, convoked all the Spanish lawmen in charge of Indian affairs who were in Barcelona at the time and asked them to oppose the agreement and thus reject the clergyman and achieve his own goals. He arranged this in the following manner. Gonzalo Hernández de Oviedo had just returned from the Indies after serving the King as inspector of the gold mints—a post the Bishop had obtained for him—as we said earlier while speaking of Pedrarias. Oviedo was skilled in the art of persuasion and thrived on speeches. He was one of the Indians' greatest foes, as we shall see later, blinder to the truth of things than any other man, because of greater greed or ambition—qualities that have destroyed the Indies. The Bishop used him by sending him to the grand chancellor with a servant of the chancellor's house whom he had asked to "tell the grand chancellor that this gentleman is in the King's service and having just returned from the Indies, he can give him information about those countries." He sent Oviedo as a fresh witness to prevent the chancellor from believing the clergyman's stories, to warn him of the injury done to the King's treasury—a fact which many Spaniards now in court would readily support—and to offer to serve the King by bringing more income and more advantages than the clergyman could bring.

In short, he said all he could to convince the chancellor that he was wrong in supporting the clergyman and to dissuade him from drawing up an agreement in his favor. But the chancellor was unmoved: he had understood the Bishop's passion and seen the malice of the clergyman's opponent. He even seemed to like the clergyman more after he heard Oviedo suggest that the Spaniards were offering more income to the King from that same territory which the clergyman claimed. The Bishop asked two or three more persons, among them the solicitor of Hispaniola, Licentiate Serrano, to establish a claim against the clergyman and distribute that territory among themselves. One asked for 100 leagues in return for 60,000 ducats for the King as against the clergyman's 30,000 within the same time limit. The other two followed suit; I believe there were only three. The proposal was made before the council of the Indies since their bread was buttered there. The grand chancellor and the King were notified; the contract was tabled. The King ordered a special meeting of all the councils that had

already granted the land to the clergyman; everyone was astonished to see the craftiness and perseverance, or rather, obstinacy, of
the Bishop, for they had recognized him to be at the source of all
this.

They discussed the matter and called the clergyman, who again
exposed the tyranny committed in the new lands because of the
Bishop's bad government. In order to justify his land grant and the
control of such lands by a handful of selected Spaniards—only
those few whose business it was to convert would be allowed to
go—he had to stress the scandalous behavior, the cruelties and
slaughter committed in the Indies and which, together with the
encomienda system, continued to be the major hindrance to the
propagation of the Faith. The Bishop and his council suffered
terrible torments on hearing this. The clergyman was called to a
special meeting. He saw himself in the midst of a most learned
and illustrious group among enemies and friends. His enemies,
that is, the Bishop's council, feeling that the clergyman had more
allies than they did (having only themselves) kept to moderate
views and, listening, hardly spoke. His friends, on the other hand,
who comprised the majority of all other councils, put many tough
questions before him. Either they were eager to know and be
satisfied that the clergyman's arguments—which they always supported—were sound and just or they wanted to prick him so that
he would expose the Bishop's and the council's faulty government
in the Indies.

You should have seen how the clergyman answered and satisfied
everyone, always standing up for himself, defending the Indians,
denouncing the injustice and irreparable damage done to them
which were obstacles to their salvation. The Bishop and his friends
maintained such a silence that they did not answer the accusations
directed against them; and the Bishop's brother, Antonio de
Fonseca, finally spoke for all and said, "Señor padre, you cannot
say that the gentlemen of the council have killed all the Indians
since you have taken from them those they used to have." The
clergyman answered freely and on the spot: "Sir, your Lordships
haven't killed all the Indians, only an infinite number of those you
used to own, but slaughter is being carried on by Spanish individuals with your Lordships' assistance." Antonio de Fonseca was

dumbfounded and the rest of the assembly looked at one another with astonishment; some of them smiled as if in mockery. Under the sting of the affront the Bishop stood up as red as fire—though green and dark-complexioned by nature—and very upset, said: "A member of the royal council is well off indeed if he, being on the council, ever must plead a cause with Casas." Clergyman Casas answered promptly and with his usual freedom: "Sir, Casas is better off yet if, after a perilous journey of 2,000 leagues, he comes to warn the King and his council against going straight to Hell for the tyranny and destruction of the Indies and, instead of being shown gratitude; he must plead a cause with the council."

Well, if the reply to Antonio de Fonseca had surprised and pleased the assembly, this surprised and pleased them even more, for it brought the Bishop to a high point of anguish, inner turmoil and confusion, next to which the previous provocations were as nothing. And this in itself was nothing compared to what was in store for him, because the Bishop persevered in trying to crush the clergyman who, it seemed, was possessed by God's fighting spirit, knowing his cause to be truth, justice and the preservation of the greater part of mankind. When the chancellor saw the embarrassment of the Bishop and his friends, he asked the clergyman to leave the room and all those who had remained unprejudiced voted in favor of the clergyman. That evening, the clergyman went to see the chancellor who told him, among other things, that "His Lordship the Bishop is furious; I hope to God this business ends well," which seemed to indicate that he, being a modest and kind man, had found the Bishop's words out of place and had appreciated the clergyman's words that had left the Bishop humiliated, though by no means humble. . . .

142

Gonzalo Hernández de Oviedo and those who had thought to share the land assigned to the clergyman were humiliated also, notably Oviedo who, being the Bishop's man, had expected a larger profit. Later, he wrote something about this struggle in his *History*, keeping to the truth when unavoidable, and otherwise silencing most of the rest or mixing it with lies much to his purpose in his disparagement of the Indians, as he always did, for he was their capital enemy and did not understand the clergyman's intentions as he should have, had he been a true Christian. He naturally carried his errors and insensitivity over to his *General and Natural History*. God knows how wrong he was to impute desire for power as the basis of the clergyman's motives (in Chapter 5 of the last book, Part I). He also says, as if in mockery, that the people stipulated in the clergyman's petition could not be soldiers, warriors or troublemakers but rather must be peace-loving and gentle people. The clergyman will not deny this but he will deny what Oviedo invents about his wanting his farmers to be knighted in the Order of the Golden Spur. He wanted farmers indeed, but he wanted them as settlers, which proves how little Oviedo understood of his plans. To ridicule them he calls them Brown Knights, to distinguish them from some future Knights of the Golden Spur.

Oviedo concedes that the clergyman's petition was granted because Laxao's influence weighed more than the wishes of the council and other high-ranking officers on leave from the Indies who had tried to disabuse the King. But my account of this struggle tells the truth and no one dared disabuse the King; they dealt only with the Bishop as the person most irritated and displeased by the clergyman's petition. I shall refer to Oviedo's account later, from which a priest by the name of Gómara, chaplain to the Marquis del Valle, took all the lies he tells about Casas, adding all sorts of other things that never happened at all.

Twice now I have mentioned that Oviedo was the Indians' major enemy and, though I said something of it in Chapter 23, I think the time has come to expose the impudent errors he wrote, since he knew nothing of his subject. In this way, the Christian and pious readers will be forewarned of Oviedo's lack of scruples and will not believe the ugliness of his arguments or his contradictions. Above all, Oviedo generalizes from an absolute position, attributing infamous and terrible customs to all the nations of the continent, making all Indians incapable of receiving Faith, doctrine and virtue. He equates them with brute beasts without exception, as if the Son of God had not died also for them and divine Providence had abhorred them to such a degree as to exclude every single one of them from predestined glory. Whenever he writes about Indians, his *History* is nothing but blasphemy and annihilation, as if his aim and pleasure were to spread defamation of the Indians throughout the world—since his book is so popular—persuading the reader unjustly to hate all Indians, denying them a human condition to justify the horrendous crimes Oviedo himself committed together with his consorts. He admits that during Pedrarias's destructive government in the region they called Castilla del Oro, he participated in the cruel tyranny there from 1514 to this year of 1519, but he sells this to the King as distinguished service. In the sixth column of his prologue to the *Natural History*, he says:

Don Ferdinand, the Catholic King and grandfather of Your Majesty, sent me to the continent to inspect the minting of gold. I performed this duty when it was called for, just as I fought in the conquest and pacification of some of these regions, serving God and Your Majesties as captain in those rough beginnings when towns and cities were being founded and which now belong to Christians who still maintain the divine cult for the glory of the Spanish Crown.

Verbatim. So then, here is Oviedo turned conquistador and his service to God and Their Majesties I think are well explained in the preceding chapters. Our Spaniards have destroyed the Indians in two ways, as the *History* shows: disastrous wars which they call conquests and distribution of land and Indians which they present under the veneer of the name *encomienda*. Oviedo took part in both without feeling ashamed—rather he glories and takes pride in saying he owned Indians and threw them into the mines, like the other tyrants. In Chapter 8, speaking of how gold was extracted, he uses the words, "I have had my Indians and slaves dig gold for me in the province of Castilla del Oro. . . ."

Surely, he did not inherit those slaves from his father, nor did he take them in battle against Berber Moors; they were not Negro slaves either, since at that time no Negro had been brought to the Indies, as I have already mentioned. He is referring to Indians who were being captured every day contrary to every right. He also called "his" those Indians that fell to his lot in addition to other booty when they raided villages and subjugated the people with violence, in the way I have described earlier; and for this he, Pedrarias, who misgoverned the land, officers of the King, and the Bishop were all responsible, as I have shown in Chapter 64. The alert and Christian reader will judge if Oviedo may be trusted as a faithful and true witness *omni exceptione maior,* in any of his contradictions and consequently, how worthy of credit his statements against the Indians are. It is amazing how his arrogant prologue tries to persuade the Emperor and all other readers that he does not deviate an inch from the truth and how he repudiates the fables other historians wrote safely at home in Spain about the events they did not witness, as if he himself had seen the things he describes. He wrote from Santo Domingo; it might as well have been Seville since he witnessed only the events in which he participated, namely, the tyranny and destruction of that region in the five years he was there.

It must be conceded that his testimony is credible when he speaks of his own fatal deeds and those he helped perform, but he tells only what serves to defame the Indians and justify Spanish cruelties, ambition and greed. Except for things that pertain to the Darién region, he wrote what sailors and criminals told him and what was bound to please him, things like, "We conquered, subjected those dogs fighting to keep their land; we made slaves; we distributed the land and exploited the mines." But if they said, "We killed this many thousand; we threw this many to the dogs, we butchered that village, men, women, children and elderly; we stuffed their straw houses with as many people of all sexes and ages as we could find and burned them alive," you may be sure that we find little of this in Oviedo's *History.* However, if they told him Indians worshipped idols and sacrificed ten human beings, Oviedo blows it up to 10,000, and he imputes to them abominations which they could not have known about except by direct participation, and of this kind of thing the *History* is full. And Oviedo finds these stories true, as he affirms in his book, while wishing that God preserve him from the danger of the proverb: A mouth that lies, kills the soul.

143

What I think of Oviedo's writing and all his chatter is that he is correct whenever he describes the trees and plants of this region. He saw them and so can anyone who wants to see them. As for what happened in the days of Christopher Columbus, he is wrong. When he came to this island, only some fifty Indians and a handful of Spaniards remained, among whom was the sailor Hernán Pérez, whom Oviedo believed as gospel truth; though a good man, Pérez was unreliable. Whether he heard it from Pérez or invented it himself, what he says about Indians is false, especially the stories of their unnatural vices, as we knew from our own investigation a long time before Oviedo even thought of coming to the Indies.

Thus we can say Oviedo lied, although unconsciously, blinded as he was not to find sinful the mass slaughters he helped commit and which are still committed today. Blinded too, by the presumption and arrogance to believe himself a scholar when he could not even read Latin—despite the fact that he includes a few Latin quotes in his book, which he had translated for him by priests who happened to pass through Santo Domingo—an attitude that led him to believe liars and tell lies without knowing it. In Part I, Book II, Chapter 6, this blindness makes him say that in 1525 and 1532, the council of the Indies asked him to declare under oath what he thought of the Indian people. He accordingly answered that they were guilty of all sorts of crimes and abominations, were ungrateful, had little memory and less intelligence, and whatever good they possessed disappeared after adolescence. He adds that, had he been on his deathbed when they took the oath from him, he would have made identical statements, and I believe it, given his insensitivity.

With what kind of conscience can he swear his descriptions are true, when he hardly saw fifty Indians on this island? He admits they did not number 500, which is true, since of the natives less than 50 survived, and he could not have seen any from other tribes guilty of sodomy and other abominable vices. Speaking of the reason they were destroyed, he says:

The mines being rich and man's greed insatiable, some worked their Indians excessively, others failed to feed them properly. Indians are born lazy, idle, melancholy and cowardly, vile and ill-natured, liars, with a short memory and no perseverance. As a pastime many took poison in order to avoid work, others hanged themselves, and others died in the epidemic of smallpox that spread over the whole island. Thus, in a short time, they were all gone.

In Book VI, Chapter 9, Oviedo speaks of the Scythian and Indian cannibals:

God allowed them to perish for a reason and I have no doubt that He will wipe them all out very soon for the multitude of their sins. They are an incorrigible people; no amount of punishment, reward, or admonition produces results. By nature they lack piety and shame, having the worst kind of desires and acting in the worst ways. God may want to change them, but they have no thought of it themselves. If they did in childhood, they may very well be saved, provided they had baptism, but after adolescence few of them want to take the trouble to become Christians even when baptized. And since they have no memory, they forget whatever is taught them almost immediately.

In the preface to Book V he says,

Forty-three years have passed since Columbus and the first Christians were here; therefore, these people should know something about such a vital issue as the salvation of their souls, especially because religious men have been here to remind them of it. But Indians stubbornly refuse to understand the Catholic Faith and to think they will ever be Christianized is to beat a dead horse. So, they only wear Christianity on their sleeves, or rather, on their heads because they have no clothes. They have no heads either for that matter, not like other people. They are so thick-skulled that Christians hold as a basic principle never to hit them on the head in battle to avoid breaking their swords. As their skull is thick, so is their intelligence bestial and ill-disposed, as will be shown later by their rites, ceremonies and customs.

These are Oviedo's words. Supposing it were true, what more could he say to defame the New World (where an infinite number of peoples live) and deceive the Old World where the *History* circulates? To slander one single person with a truth which can hurt him greatly is a grave mortal sin that puts the slanderer under obligation to make amends to the person injured. What, then, is Oviedo's sin, and what amends must he make, having defamed with such horrendous sins such a multitude of people, an infinite number of towns, provinces and regions teaming with human beings he never saw or heard of? For his defamatory work has caused Christendom to hate all Indians, and men from Spain and other nations to come and kill Indians as they would fleas, men who, for this reason, invented cruelties they would not use on wild tigers, bears and lions, nor in fact would these beasts torture other beasts, even when famished, as they tortured these defenseless and naked people.

Oviedo's amends should be greater still because he lies regarding many nations and fabricates the ugly things he says about many others, flaunting his inventions freely and daringly, making them apply universally to all when in truth idolatry alone could apply to all of them in various shapes and degrees, since they have had no one to bring the knowledge of the true God to them. On this point, Oviedo ought to consider the state of his own ancestors, as well as that of everyone who lived before the Son of God lifted the world out of the shadows of ignorance and enlightened it with the evangelical word. Since he boasted of being a great historian and knew Pliny—whom he read in Italian, not Latin—neither would it have hurt him to consider that Indians were not the first cannibals to sacrifice lives to idols (as he says above in Chapter 9 of Book VI) and practice abominations derived from idolatry. They were not less human for it, being able men of good memory, capable of change, loved by God and worthy of hearing evangelical preaching. The Apostles and other holy preachers of the primitive Church and their successors were not repelled, nor did they despair, as Señor Oviedo does, of their conversion and salvation.

144

It is well to comment on each defect Oviedo attributes to the Indians, many of which are his own invention, since because of them he seems to be so certain that every one of the Indians must be excluded from conversion and salvation. He says they were sodomites, and in Chapter 23 I have stated the truth: this defamation is vile, false and ill-intentioned. He says they are ungrateful, but let any idiot be the judge! For what blindness struck the good Oviedo that he should transfer his own terrible ungratefulness— his and that of the people who destroyed Indians and their lands—onto the hurt and much-wronged Indians without whose humanity, benevolence and assistance against starvation and infinite dangers, they would have perished a million times. Look at the kind of gratefulness and reward they showed the Indians, killing and obliterating millions of souls on this and other islands and 18,000 leagues of the continent. Look at the benefits they received, and Oviedo dares call them ungrateful when he admits, much to the obscuring of this point, that the Hieronymite fathers had been informed of the deaths and other injuries suffered by Indians allotted to lords and prelates residing in Spain.

The fathers knew how the managers and overseers treated the Indians, desiring the gold for themselves that was costing Indian lives and misery, and they knew how the most important people here received favors from those lords and prelates, the aim of everyone being to acquire, send and receive gold, which is why Indians were mistreated and worked excessively. They died at such a rate that out of a group of 200 to 300 all were consumed in no time, it becoming necessary to replace them from Indians already assigned to married couples and other Spaniards here. In this way the settlers' Indians diminished, while those given to noblemen increased in number; but they all died of the same maltreatment, and that is why they were extinguished. Oviedo admits this. In the preceding pages he had spoken of "those same noblemen who lived in Spain prospering from the illicit sweat of Indians," just as in Book III, Chapter 6, he says, "For my part I do not absolve those Christians who were made rich from the work of Indians if they mistreated them or neglected their salvation," and again, a few lines above, "Let each one examine his own conscience and see that he treats Indians as he would his neighbors, although in this respect little remains to be done on Hispaniola, San Juan, Cuba and Jamaica since the Indians are being extinguished."

You see how Oviedo admits, though reluctantly, the abominable conduct of the Spaniards and their "gratitude" toward the Indians. And he dares accuse Indians of ungratefulness! Let this example show how true all his affirmations are. He adds that he does not find the Indians guiltless because God punished them for their vices and sacrifices to the devil, etc.; but he seems to be unaware that those who inflicted such destruction will suffer many more torments in Hell, being Christians whose duty it was to bring the knowledge of God through their good example and therefore rid the idolaters of the sins of idolatry. This was the case of our ancestors who, idolaters and sinners as they may have been, received judgment and punishment from God, not from cruel executioners and derelicts. Oviedo claims that Indians are born idle, full of vice and unfit for work. I have already dealt with their vices and I wish to God that, except for matters of Faith, the Spaniards had not sinned before God more abominably than the Indians have, and did not deserve more eternal fire than they do. As for their work habits, I agree, because they are as delicate as a Prince's children, because of a benign climate, the pleasantness of the land, and other natural causes I described in Chapter 4 of *De unico vocationis modo onmium gentium ad veram religionem*.

In addition, they lived unprotected by clothing, ate frugally and of less substantial foods than ours. However, it sufficed and did not prevent them from living and multiplying at such an incredible rate as to have founded the large settlements we encountered when we came, and to have had an abundance of the necessities of life with very little work. They used their leisure—which was considerable since their souls did not burn with greed for wealth and estates—in honest recreation such as certain strenuous ball games, dances and songs that were recitations of their historical past. They had sacrificial and other religious rites only in those places where idols were worshipped; otherwise they gave no or very little sign of idolatry, as I said in my *Apologetical History* written in Spanish. They also made very beautiful objects with their hands when they were not occupied with agricultural, fishing or domestic chores. The wars they occasionally engaged in with one another were frontier wars that seemed like a child's game and were easily stopped.

So, they were not as idle as Oviedo thinks when he heaps vice upon vice on them, which in truth were not thought of as "vices" by the Indians but virtues answering to a life view much closer to natural reason than that of the Spanish after they came to these parts, if we except matters pertaining to the Christian Faith. And for this Oviedo ought to praise them, instead of spreading slander and defamation. He adds that Indians are of a melancholy temperament, turning into a vice something that is natural to them. But many are sanguine and happy people, as can be seen from the qualities of the land and the effects of their fondness for celebrations, songs and dances. He reports that they are base and cowardly. Men are not base because they are humble, peaceful and gentle as these people were, but rather because they are dishonest and sinful, and in this God knows we beat them all. They had some customs that seemed wrong and shameful to us Christians, such as urinating in a sitting position, breaking wind in public, and other similar things which the Christian Faith easily would have remedied.

However, what you will not find is a man hearing from another that he sleeps with his wife or another woman, nor one engaging in dishonest relations, as you will find among our Christian men here. Their cowardice is not an absolute vice but a natural thing that stems from benignity and good breeding that intends no harm. Cowardice is a vice when a person, moved by the fear of death or other danger, turns away from a virtuous act that is demanded of him, as, for example, the case of a man who sees his republic suffer slavery or death, whose fear of death makes him act against virtue or keeps him from helping and resisting and, if necessary, from giving his life to defend his country. In this case, surely, many Indians resisted and fought with enormous courage considering their nakedness and lack of weapons, as well as the variety and strength of Spanish arms, especially horses. Seeing themselves tyrannized and oppressed, dying every day from unjust labor and open war with Spaniards who disemboweled them with swords, trampled them with horses and speared them from horseback (one horseman alone could kill 10,000 men in an hour's time), they fought so courageously whenever they could that they equaled lions and the most valiant heroes of the past.

Oviedo should be asked, since he glories so much in his captainship, robbing and enslaving men whom he killed in the mines, how Francisco Becerra fared, and Joan de Tavira, Vasco Núñez and many. others killed by Indians in battle. In the wars the Spanish waged against them on this island, naked Indians performed prodigious deeds as proof of their courage, and I related some of these in Book II above. One sign of courage is to dare to die, which presupposes one of the natural causes that make men brave, that is, an abundance of blood. Nature, knowing itself, trusts itself the more when this principal life-sustaining humor abounds, and Indians are notoriously red-blooded, which is a sign they naturally have less fear of death, and, consequently, that they are naturally brave. They have amply demonstrated their courage but their misfortune consisted in lacking weapons and horses. Had they possessed these to defend themselves against such crude enemies, they would not have died in such numbers, their victors would have had no reason to boast, and Oviedo would not have chattered so much. I have described the courage of these people, as well as its natural causes, in the *Apologetical History* and in Chapter 4 of *De unico vocationis modo* mentioned above.

145

Oviedo declares that all Indians are inclined toward evil: he must have studied little philosophy and have even less experience. He did not know even one of the many Indian languages from which he could have drawn such a conclusion. He judges rashly what he could have known only by divine revelation or by conjecture from many conversations with all the people of this land over a long period of time—and even then it would be impossible to affirm anything with any certainty. He says they have little memory and, as usual, he errs and contradicts himself. Indians have such a long memory that they remember events from a remote past as if those events were written down. I shall use the same Oviedo to support my statement when he says, Book V, Chapter 1, that Indian songs were history or a relation of past events, wars as well as peace, the continuation of which ensures against their being forgotten.

Instead of having books, these songs remain in their minds and in this manner they recite the genealogies of their chiefs and lords, deeds and temporal misfortunes, especially victories won in battle, etc. Those are his words. So then, their memory is not short, as Oviedo states. It is obvious also that the amount of Christian doctrine they learn by heart in one day is greater than ten intelligent men would learn in twenty. The reason for this is natural, as I proved in Spanish in my *Apologetical History* and in Latin in *De unico vocationis modo:* all these people *a toto genere*, that is, exceptions are extremely rare, are endowed with inner and outer senses not only good but excellent and far superior to those of many other nations. It follows that they have intelligence, which is something Gonzalo Hernández Oviedo lacked utterly, for he never dealt with Indians nor cared for them except to command and use them as beasts with the same obtuseness as any other Spaniard. He adds that they are liars. I wish to God he and the Indians had not lied because the Indians lied when the Spaniards provoked them, and I do not believe that an Indian would lie to his chief or to another Indian any more than he would kill himself. The lies they still tell today (where Indians are still alive) are caused by the vexations, the horrible servitude and the cruel tyranny they suffer. They cannot escape anguish, pain, and ill-treatment unless they lie and deceive, pleasing and placating the constant furor of the Spaniards. A propos of this, since they know by experience that the Spaniards are liars who neither tell the truth nor keep their word, they have refrains and sayings that are worth considering. Not once but many times a Spaniard would ask an Indian if he was a Christian and the Indian would reply: "Yes, Sir, I am a bit Christian because I have learned to lie a bit; another day I will lie big, and I will be big Christian." We could quote many sayings like this one that perplexed the Spaniards, whose bad examples have so miserably stained our Christian religion in the simple hearts of these people.

Oviedo says Indians lack constancy because they do not persevere and, when possible, escape this infernal life where they are perishing, and neither do they persevere in the virtuous path of the Christian religion. Well, Oviedo can say nothing important or trifling, for he was not worthy of seeing and understanding and he cannot moderate the erroneous insults he accumulates on the

Indian people. He points a poisoned arrow at himself when he says that in order not to work and as a pastime many killed themselves. It is true that many killed themselves but it is self-evident that it was no pastime. As I said, his heart shot a poisoned arrow against himself, for he shows himself to be a horrendous, cruel, intolerable and abominable tyrant to force a gentle and patient people, who endured more torments than any other mortals, to choose to kill themselves as the lesser of two evils. To prove this, it would be good if Oviedo could answer that he heard it said they killed themselves as a pastime before the Spaniards arrived here and began their oppression. The inhumanity our brothers practiced was to destroy a vast expanse of land using methods novel and unheard of. Indians, on the other hand, had no knowledge of the true God, but they believed the dead went to another life where the soul eats and drinks, enjoys the pleasures of dance, song, and ample rest. Why should we marvel then, if they aspired to the enjoyment of the other life and rushed to it, if in this one they suffered constant death? Besides, we know only of a few cases of suicide by hanging or taking poison here and in Cuba.

Oviedo says that God must have a reason to permit them to be destroyed, intending to wipe them out for their sins, and that Indians do not respond to punishment, reward or admonition. On the matter of permission, I say God keep us from prerogatives, as a holy man used to say, as well as from being instrumental in another's perdition. God always punishes evil with a greater evil, according to the phrase *Vindicabo me de inimicis meis cum inimicis meis.* And woe unto those whom God takes as a scourge, for after the chastening, He is likely to throw the scourge into the fire, as St. Augustine said. But Oviedo, being on the scourging side, was not aware that God could destroy them justly only for original sin. They may be in a state of sin but we are not free to despise them for it, nor to rob and kill them. Woe unto us indeed if as robbers and killers and dispensers of bad examples (instead of the good examples we are to show them to attract them to Christ), we should corrupt them and prevent their salvation. However divine justice may punish and torture them in this life, however it may seem to have forsaken them by delivering them into our insatiable greed, no Christian will doubt that God's

chosen few will indeed include those Indians whom He has predestined to enjoy divine vision in the eternal life. Just by chance
(or even without chance), it may be that once God has exterminated these people through our cruel hands, He will spill His
anger over us all for our violence and our tyranny, inspiring other
nations to do unto us what we have done unto them, destroying us
as we destroyed them, and it may be that more of those whom we
held in such contempt will sit at the right hand of God than there
will be of us, and this consideration ought to keep us in fear night
and day.

146

According to Oviedo, the Indian people are lost because they do
not respond to punishment, coaxing or good advice; they have no
pity or shame; their desires as well as their deeds are of the worst
kind. Oviedo's obtuseness of mind is truly astonishing. He describes their perversity with a conviction meant as a display of
truth, examining it inside and out as he would a gem of his own,
when in reality he dealt with Indians for only five years, only in
Darién, and only to rob, murder and enslave them. He put them
to work in the mines and other enterprises where they died of
exhaustion, hunger and cruel afflictions. Even there he did not see
them, having put them in charge of a butcher they called a mine
operator, or a rancher, and otherwise, a *calpisque*, which was a race
of the most infamous and cruel men ever to be seen, and Oviedo
paid no more attention to his Indians than if they were ants or
bedbugs. How, then, could Oviedo have known if Indians in
general were inclined to evil? If he replies he heard it from people
who knew Indians, the same applies to them, all false witnesses
caring only to plunder, enslave and annihilate.

Oviedo should make himself clear on the nature of punishment,
cajolery and good advice. Does he refer to Indian indoctrination
and moral improvement or to the fact that they fled from the
infernal conditions of the mines where death was awaiting them?
When they fled, they often were pursued and brought back to be
skinned alive with lashes and other tortures, and for this Oviedo

says they are incorrigible and do not respond to punishment. Sometimes they coaxed them with mild words, asking them to be good, by which it was meant they should stay in the mines and not think of escape. But because they fled their infernal life, Oviedo says they did not respond to kindness and good advice. And that is the way it was: punishment, coaxing and torments which ended by destroying them and are still destroying those alive today; and on top of this, Oviedo pays for his share of such large-scale destruction by defaming them forever, it being impossible to cause them greater harm since they have thrown them into the pits of Hell.

Oviedo would not say such things if he had seen the fruit of evangelical preaching in those Indians saved from the Spanish knife. But he vomits the infamous poison from the guts of his soul, and instead of heeding his malicious fantasy he would have done well to heed the reports from trustworthy people from New Spain and Peru, where capable priests achieved priceless results in matters of conversion. Another invention of his insensitivity is that Indians refuse Christianization after adolescence, paying no attention and forgetting what is taught them. In the five years he lived in Darién and the twenty or thirty years he lived on this island, where, as I have said, when he came the Indians had practically been exterminated, did he see the preaching of the Faith? How could the poor, overworked and persecuted Indians have desired the Faith if they never heard of it? . . .

In the 43 years since the Christians first arrived, they could not have known more about their salvation than they would have in 200 years under this regime of murder and destruction. He says missionaries were at hand, but that is false. When missionaries came here, most of the Indians had already been destroyed or else the Spaniards oppressed them so cruelly there was no room in their minds for preaching nor in the Indians' for hearing, busy as they were thinking of escape to the woods to remedy their starvation on roots and herbs, and flee a life where death lurked every day. Oviedo calls them pitiless. Let God and any halfwitted man judge the acts we inflicted upon them pitilessly and cruelly; and on Judgment Day, who will be condemned as the more pitiless, we Christians or the Indian infidels? . . .

It seems superfluous to continue answering Oviedo's comments since he says such varied things and contradicts himself so often as to discredit his infamous statements about all of the Indian peoples. For example, in Book II, Chapter 13, he notes that Indians are different everywhere but that they are gentle and pacific, except for a few war-minded chiefs; and in Book III, Chapter 2, he says the contrary: Indians of this island live in constant peace. In Book II, Chapters 6 and 12, he recounts the fact that Christopher Columbus lost his thirty-eight men for having mistaken Indians for a tame and gentle people ("seeing such domesticated-looking people, the admiral thought it safe to leave a few Christians there"), from which it appears that, had the thirty-eight Spaniards not wronged the Indians and stayed together instead of scattering inland, they would not have been killed, as I said, relating the incident in Book I, Chapter 86.

147

So then, Oviedo presented a false picture of the Indian people to the world, and we have discussed his reasons. Let us now return to our history and to what was happening in Barcelona in 1519. For one thing, Bartolomé de las Casas won a terrible fight, for God and the Truth were on his side. The first Bishop of Darién, fray Juan Cabedo, had decided to visit the court, I know not for what reason, though I conjecture from his words that he certainly had not come to stop the cruelties that tyrannized his flock. He came by way of Cuba, where he heard many complaints against Casas, the clergyman who worked to free Indians by taking them away from the Spaniards and who for this was criticized as an enemy of the Spanish hidalgos and as an enemy of Spain. It seems that Cabedo's actions at court were inspired by Casas's reputation both in Darién and Cuba. It was presumed that Diego Valázquez had bribed him, hoping that Cabedo's influence as a Bishop and a most august preacher would win him the support of the new Emperor, Charles V. Cortés had rebelled and was conquering both in Darién and Cuba. It was presumed that Diego Velázquez hoped to be nominated to an important post there, as he would certainly have been, had not Cortés stolen the show before him.

As I said, the Emperor was holding court in Barcelona, but the plague there had caused him to set up quarters three leagues away in Molín del Rey, with his councils and grandees settled about one league from his palace in forts and other buildings. The Bishop accommodated himself as best he could in one of those places and occasionally dined with the Bishop of Badajoz—they had been royal chaplains together—who had found lodgings in a turreted castle one-quarter league from the Emperor's site. One day the Bishop appeared in the palace and Clergyman Casas saw him then for the first time. They were in the royal dining areas; the clergyman asked who this dignified brother was; they told him he was a Bishop in the Indies. The clergyman went up to him:

"I come to greet you, Sir, as I too am involved in the Indies."

The Bishop asked Juan de Samano, who later became secretary of the Indies, "Who is this priest?"

"He is Señor Casas, Sir."

The Bishop exclaimed with great arrogance: "Oh, Señor Casas, I've got a real sermon for you here."

Casas, unafraid, answered in a huff: "I've been dying to hear it, Sir. And I've got two sermons myself worth all the gold you brought back from the Indies, if you care to hear them."

"Your cause is a lost cause," the Bishop said.

Samano said: "All these gentlemen here are satisfied with Señor Casas, Sir." (By "gentlemen" he referred to the members of the councils.)

"It is possible to be dishonest and commit mortal sin with the best intentions in the world," the Bishop said, adding a word very much out of place for a Bishop.

The clergyman meant to answer *Iuxta stultitiam* but the King's door opened and the Bishop of Badajoz entered the room and left with fray Juan Cabedo. The clergyman felt that fray Juan Cabedo could endanger his own interests, and because the Bishop of Badajoz had much influence on the King and had favored the clergyman up till then, he decided to go to the castle, and he found the two bishops finishing their meal. Also present were Diego Columbus, the second admiral of the Indies, and don Juan de Zúñiga, the brother of Count de Miranda who was to become Prince Philip's tutor. The Bishop of Badajoz and Admiral Columbus were playing chess to pass the time before returning to the palace. The clergyman came in while everyone was watching the game and someone mentioned that wheat had been grown in Hispaniola. The Bishop Juan Cabedo answered that this was impossible, and the clergyman, who always carried a few grains of island wheat in his pocket, turned to him and said sweetly: "My word, Sir, I've seen very good wheat on Hispaniola. I could even show you a sample."

The Bishop turned red with indignation. "And how do you know? Or is this like your other business, you, who seem to know so much!"

The clergyman answered modestly: "Is my business evil, Sir, or unjust by any chance?"

"What do you know of these things, anyway? You don't have the learning to be carrying on any business at all."

The clergyman tried not to anger the Bishop but he answered a little more freely: "My learning isn't so little, Sir, and to show you what I know of my business, I'll tell you that you have sinned a thousand times by doing nothing about the freedom of Indians, that you eat and drink the blood of your own flock, and that if you don't give back everything you acquired in the Indies, you are no better than Judas as far as salvation is concerned."

The Bishop saw that he could not answer seriously, so he laughed at the clergyman, who continued: "You're laughing, Sir, when you ought to bewail your misfortune and that of your flock."

"Oh yes," said the Bishop, "I keep tears right here in my pocket."

"Real tears are a gift of God, Sir, and you ought to pray to Him for tears of blood."

The Bishop of Badajoz kept silent and went on playing as if amused by that conversation. The clergyman took this as a good sign and continued to confound Juan Cabedo, although he would have stopped at one word from Badajoz, because he did not wish to alienate him.

Finally, the Bishop of Badajoz put an end to it all by saying, "Enough, enough," while the admiral and don Juan de Zúñiga spoke to defend the clergyman. The admiral gave his opinion of the clergyman's good intentions as well as on the clergyman's

business, for he knew him personally; don Juan de Zúñiga spoke of
what he had heard about the clergyman from the members of his
entourage. And so, after a while, the clergyman calmed down and
returned to his lodgings. . . .

166

In Book II we mentioned how the Spaniards deceived the King
in order to bring the Lucayo Indians to Hispaniola to replace the
dying natives. Once the permission was granted, Spaniards engaged in nothing else but the capture of Lucayos by hook or by
crook, depopulating the thirty or forty islands unjustly and by evil
ways, and completing their extermination by working them in the
pearl fisheries. Then, seeing how the Spaniards in Cuba tracked
down Indians and depopulated the Guanajo Islands to the west, as
we said in Chapter 91, the Spaniards in Hispaniola devised ways to
track down Indians in islands to the east, using the same methods
as for the capture of Lucayos: a group of three or four men invested some 7,000 gold pesos, bought one or two ships and
gathered provisions and a company of some sixty ruffians on salary
or a promise to share the loot.

They added an inspector who was as much of a thief as they but
was less fearful of God and seemed to have been given a soul for
no purpose at all. His job was to oversee the operation, that is to
say, to make sure proper warrants were given and instructions
carried out properly. Part of these instructions consisted in reading
the injunction that brought to the knowledge of the Indians the
fact that God exists, that He is represented on earth by the Pope,
that the Pope gave this land to the kings of Castile whose vassals
they were, that they should come and swear allegiance, otherwise
war would be declared upon them, and that they would be enslaved, etc. What greater scorn to the Faith is there, and what
greater injustice? How could the ill-inspired learned men who
governed this land not be ashamed and embarrassed to read this,
men who were obliged to know that it was contrary to natural,
divine and human law? This injunction (let the reader pause here
and refer back to Chapters 57 and 58) was sometimes supervised

by an idiot of a priest only to justify better the tyranny. Seeing evil all around him, he sometimes disclosed part of it, either because he actually could not see the whole as evil since the Royal Audiencia had authorized it and thus he participated in the loathsome act; or because, pleased to see the number of prisoners, he received a share of slaves or a good salary.

Their port of embarkation was Santo Domingo; their method was the following: they would arrive at a pre-arranged spot and read the injunction on board the ship with the same result as if they had read it within hearing distance of the inhabitants since they read it in our jargon and the Indians understood not a word of it. The inspector then testified to the fulfillment of the royal decree at such and such a place. The Indians would come in their canoes to offer food and the Spaniards would give them trinkets in return and to reassure them would set foot on land, but at nightfall they would attack the town and, rallying to the cry of St. James, capture as many Indians as they could, killing a few in order to inspire terror. They would load the ships with prisoners and repeat their act elsewhere until the ships were full. They always had to throw a good many bodies overboard, for many died of lack of food and drink, of the heat below deck and of anguish at finding themselves in such a bind, as we said in Chapters 43–45 of the second part of this *History*, referring to the Lucayos. They would dock in Santo Domingo and disembark their sad unhappy group, naked and thin to the point of death, pushing them ashore like cattle. Once there, the starving Indians would try to find roots and herbs to eat because, as the Indians were common property, no one would take it upon himself to feed and clothe them until the lots were drawn; the ship's cassava had barely kept them alive.

Since certain people were always ready to publicize the most notorious cruelties committed on those raids, which the hearers knew as well as the doers, they would try to deceive the world by naming someone at random, someone who perhaps had taken part in the action, to investigate the method used in the capture. Oh, God Almighty, how could You suffer patiently and for so long that nothing evil and unjust was ever found out about the fact that a people peacefully inhabiting its own land was attacked and sacked and enslaved! And if it should happen sometimes that the capture was condemned on grounds more shamefully ugly than others, the Indians were not released or returned to their land. It was argued that since they were here, they could at least profit from Christianization (as if anyone cared about it); they said Indians would die on the return voyage and gave other similar pretexts to keep them. Seeing them on the sandy riverbank sitting or prostrate from starvation for three days on end in the sun and the rain, waiting for the lots to be drawn, their hearts heavy with sadness and fear, was one of the most heart-breaking sights—for hearts not made of stone. As for the drawing of lots, when a father was separated from his son, a husband from his wife, a mother from her daughter and a wife from her husband, a new torment was added that doubled their misery, and they cried out their grief with tears and lamented their unhappiness, perhaps cursing their fate. What we committed in the Indies stands out among the most unpardonable offenses ever committed against God and mankind, and this trade as one of the most unjust, evil and cruel among them.

I want to talk about another kind of raid on the mainland, some forty-five leagues south of Cumaná, that dispensed with the bother of warrants and injunctions. This happened in a province, a large town on the coast of a cape that curves into the sea and forms a harbor, a cape they called Codera. The lord of the town was named Higoroto, a first name as well as a noble patronymic, and this lord, although an infidel, was very virtuous, and his people lovingly imitated him in peace and hospitality. They treated the Spaniards with love and welcomed them to their homes like brothers, so that Spanish fugitives, running away from justice in another province or sometimes from the rough treatment of Indians they had attempted to raid, arriving there exhausted and in rags, were received by Higoroto who graciously provided food, shelter and all they needed for recovery.

When the Spaniards were ready to leave, he provided them with a canoe and ample provisions of food and Indians, for the trip to the small island of Cubagua where the Spaniards had their settlements, and thus he rescued some of our men from death who otherwise would not even have been heard from again. In short, Higoroto and his people were of such quality, and he helped the Spaniards in such a way that all Spaniards called Higoroto's town the inn of refuge and consolation. Then it occurred to some wicked man to show gratitude for such benevolence by means of an exploit. To avoid returning empty—in all likelihood, his ship had not been able to raid the coast—he docked there. The Indians and their lord welcomed him and they fêted him and his crew as was their custom. The Spaniards returned to the ship and invited many Indians, men and women, children and adults, who as usual climbed on board with confidence. But when they had embarked, they made sail for the island of San Juan and sold them as slaves. I was in San Juan at that time and I saw this and knew what they had done to show Spanish gratitude to Higoroto and his people. The town had been completely destroyed, because the Indians who had not been captured dispersed in the mountains and valleys to avoid such dangers; and in the end they all perished from the tyrannical evil wrought by the Spaniards, who went to settle and decimate Venezuela, as I will show in the following book. All these bad Christians regretted the evil brought to the town of Higoroto by this great sinner, not so much for the ugliness of the act itself since all of them performed similar ones constantly, but rather for having lost that safe and good hospitality which Higoroto dispensed to all indiscriminately.

167

Who can enumerate the insults and adequately describe the ugliness and gravity of these raids that brought so many slaves to Hispaniola and San Juan and killed so many in the mines and other types of work? I would put the number at two million as is shown by the desolation of the mainland coast that used to swarm with people. Surely, it is worthy of consideration how divine justice revealed itself: all the people who participated in those raids and staked money on them ended in poverty; and, after death, their estates no matter how large were consumed in a short time by diverse means. We knew someone on this island who left an estate valued at 300,000 or 400,000 castellanos. Some six years after his death, mismanagement had almost imperceptibly devalued it to less than 50,000, and it went steadily down so that his heirs were unable to enjoy it if they were lucky enough to come before it was all gone; and such cases abound.

As for the ceremonious injunction ordered by those who ruled and called themselves learned jurists (they were hired for that office and not on account of their good looks; therefore, it is not permissible that they should be ignorant of such inhuman and gross injustice), I want to relate what happened to me once, when treating the subject with the president of these jurists. I was telling him, with ample support of authoritative examples to persuade him, that those raids were unjust, loathsome, and worthy of eternal damnation; that the injunction scorned truth and justice as well as our Christian religion and the charity of Christ who had suffered so much for the salvation of these souls; and that it was unfair to set time limitations for their conversion since Christ had not limited the world except to give it the totality of time from the beginning to the Day of Judgment, as he gave every individual the limits of his own life within which to convert and use his own free will. I said it was unfair that men shortened this divine privilege in such a way as to squabble over the time limit, some requiring three days between the time of the injunction and their conversion, while others proposed fifteen days. He answered me: "Yes, fifteen days is little time; it would be well to give them two months in which to decide." I felt like screaming when I heard such profound and massive insensitivity. What greater ignorance and blindness could there be in a person who professed to be learned and governed so much land and so many people! He did not even recognize that the injunction was unjust, absurd, lawfully void, and that, supposing it just and lawful, still, it being written in the Spanish language coerced the Indians into obedience since they could not understand it—to understand it would have required not two months but fourteen or twenty even. How could he think that Indians would believe a mere statement unsubstantiated by proof, read by men held to be infamous and cruel evildoers, purporting that God in Heaven had given the government of the world to a man called the Pope who in turn had given all the kingdoms of the Indies to the Castilian kings, and that should they fail within two months to swear obedience to the Castilian King, it was lawful to declare war upon them? How could the president of that Audiencia even believe that Indians were under the obligation to obey the kings of Castile, when they had their own rulers even before being brought to the knowledge of God, their Creator and Redeemer? But this ignorance and blindness had its origin in the royal council, which was responsible for ordering the terms of the injunction. Would to God that today, in the year 1561, the council might be rid of it! And with this imprecation, and the glory and honor of God, we bring this third book to an end. *Deo gratias.*

Selected Bibliography

BATAILLON, MARCEL. *Etudes sur Bartolomé de Las Casas*. Paris, 1967.

CASTRO, AMÉRICO. *Fray Bartolomé de las Casas*. Paris, 1965.

GIMÉNEZ FERNÁNDEZ, MANUEL. *Bartolomé de las Casas*, Vol. I. Seville, 1953– .

GUILLÉN, CLAUDIO. "Un padrón de conversos sevillanos (1510)," *Bulletin Hispanique*, LXV (1963), 49–98.

HANKE, LEWIS. *The Spanish Struggle for Justice in the Conquest of America*. Philadelphia: University of Pennsylvania Press, 1949.

———. "Bartolomé de las Casas: estudio preliminar," in *Historia de las Indias*, ed. Millares Carlo. 3 vols. Mexico, 1951. I, ix–lxxxvi.

KLEIN, HERBERT S. *Slavery in the Americas*. Chicago: University of Chicago Press, 1967.

MENÉNDEZ PIDAL, RAMÓN. *El Padre Las Casas: su doble personalidad*. Madrid, 1963.

SIMPSON, LESLEY BYRD. *The Encomienda in New Spain*. Berkeley, Calif.: University of California Press, 1950.

WAGNER, HENRY R. *The Life and Writings of Bartolomé de las Casas*. Albuquerque, N. Mex.: University of New Mexico Press, 1967.

ZAVALA, SILVIO A. *New Viewpoints on the Spanish Colonization of America*. Philadelphia: University of Pennsylvania Press, 1943.

———. "Las conquistas de Canarias y América. Estudio comparativo," *Estudios Indianos* (Mexico, 1948), 9–94.

293

Index